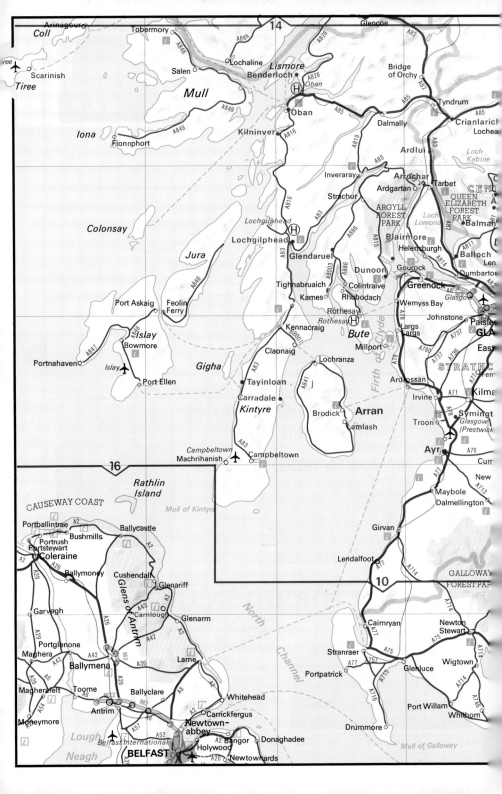

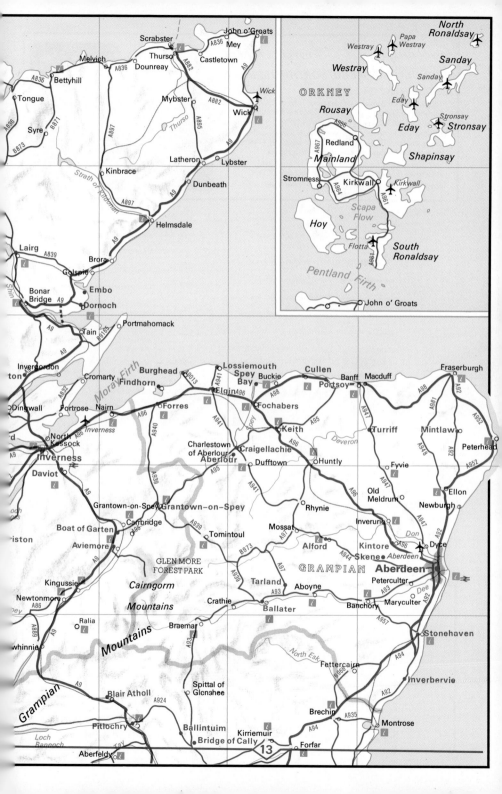

Collingwood Arms Hotel

CORNHILL-ON-TWEED, NORTHUMBERLAND

Tel: Coldstream 2424/2556   **TD12 4UH**

The Collingwood Arms is a well appointed hotel on the A697 road to Scotland. The hotel offers comfortable rooms together with good fresh produce to complement a menu at reasonable prices.

An ideal stop for touring the Border country with its castles, stately homes and breathtaking scenery. The coast being only 13 miles away has many fine beaches, coves and quaint fishing harbours.

Special rates apply for weekend or winter breaks. Laundry facilities available for fishermen or golfers. Children and pets welcome.

Members of the English, Scottish and Borders Tourist Boards.

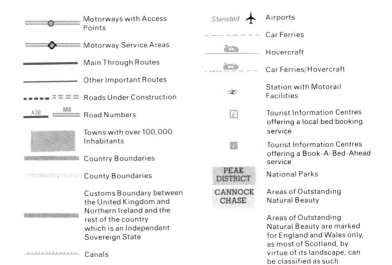

Motorways with Access Points	*Stansted* ✈ Airports
Motorway Service Areas	––––––– Car Ferries
Main Through Routes	Hovercraft
Other Important Routes	Car Ferries/Hovercraft
Roads Under Construction	Station with Motorail Facilities
A38 M6 Road Numbers	ⓘ Tourist Information Centres offering a local bed booking service
Towns with over 100,000 Inhabitants	ⓘ Tourist Information Centres offering a Book-A-Bed-Ahead service
Country Boundaries	
County Boundaries	PEAK DISTRICT National Parks
Customs Boundary between the United Kingdom and Northern Ireland and the rest of the country which is an Independent Sovereign State	CANNOCK CHASE Areas of Outstanding Natural Beauty
	Areas of Outstanding Natural Beauty are marked for England and Wales only, as most of Scotland, by virtue of its landscape, can be classified as such
Canals	

Scale   1:1,175,000

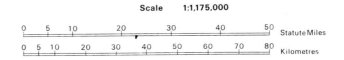

0   5   10   20   30   40   50   Statute Miles

0 5 10   20   30   40   50   60   70   80   Kilometres

STAY WHERE YOU SEE THE SIGN OF A REAL SCOTTISH WELCOME

We've made sure there's a comfortable welcome waiting at hundreds of places to stay in Scotland.

Now there's no need to puzzle over which hotel, guest house, B & B or self-catering accommodation best suits you.

We've introduced a new easy to understand classification and grading scheme so you can find at a glance *exactly* what you're looking for.

WHAT DOES CLASSIFICATION MEAN?

The *classifications,* from 'Listed' to five crowns, are awarded according to the *range* of facilities available. In hotels, guest houses and B & Bs, a 'Listed' classification guarantees, for example, that your bed conforms to a minimum size, that hot and cold water is available at all reasonable times, that breakfast is provided and that there is adequate heating according to the season.

In self-catering accommodation, one crown means that you have a minimum size of unit, at least one twin or double bedroom, dining and cooking facilities suitable for the number of occupants, and a refridgerator.

Naturally, more crowns mean more facilities. A five crown establishment will provide many extras for your holiday comfort. To name just two, in five crown hotels *all* rooms have 'en suite' bathrooms, and five crown self-catering units provide the labour-saving fittings of home, including a dishwasher.

All classifications have been checked by our fully-trained team of independent officers.

CLASSIFICATION AND GRADING OF ACCOMMODATION IN SCOTLAND

WHAT ABOUT GRADING?

While classification is all about facilities, *grading* is solely concerned with their *quality*. The grades awarded — 'Approved', 'Commended' or 'Highly Commended' — are based upon an independent assessment of a wide variety of items, ranging from the appearance of the buildings and tidiness of the gardens, to the quality of the furnishings, fittings and floor coverings. Cleanliness is an absolute requirement — and, of course, our officers know the value of a warm and welcoming smile.

Like classification, grading is carried out by the Scottish Tourist Board's expert team.
You can find excellent quality in all kinds of places to stay in Scotland, irrespective of the range of facilities offered: for example, a 'Listed' B & B, with the minimum of facilities, but offering excellent quality, would be awarded a 'Highly Commended' grade while a five crown self-catering property would be graded as 'Approved' if the quality of its extensive facilities was assessed as average.

SO HOW DOES THE NEW SCHEME HELP YOU PLAN YOUR HOLIDAY?

Quite simply, it offers a guarantee of both the range of facilities and their quality. Many of the establishments listed in this brochure have been inspected and this is highlighted in their entries. When you choose accommodation that has been classified, or classified and graded, you have the reassurance that what is being offered has been independently checked.

Equally, if you're on a touring holiday, and booking accommodation as you go, the new scheme can help you. All places to stay which have been inspected bear a distinctive blue oval sign by their entrance showing the classification and grade awarded. And if you call in at a Tourist Information Centre you can ask for a list of local establishments that have joined the scheme, which will include those which are shown in this brochure as *awaiting inspection* at time of going to press.

Whatever kind of accommodation you're looking for, you can be sure the new classification and grading scheme will help you find it.

Please note that where self-catering establishments offer a number of units of differing classifications and grades, their entry in this brochure is shown as 'Up to' the highest award held. You should ascertain the specific classification and grade of an individual unit at time of booking.

Please also note that establishments are visited annually and therefore classifications and grades may therefore change from year to year.

CONTENTS

Gazetteer – Rivers, Lochs & Sea Angling

Pastime Publications Ltd gratefully acknowledge the assistance of The Scottish Tourist Board, Area Tourist Boards, and others in compiling this guide.

First published by The Scottish Tourist Board 1970
Typesetting by Newtext Composition Ltd.
Printed & Bound in the U.K.

Worldwide distribution by
The British Tourist Authority
BTA

INDEX

Also see colour adverts.

Sea angling is a very popular pastime in Shetland as these youngsters at Lerwick Harbour show.

TEN OF THE BEST

BY BRUCE SANDISON

Bruce Sandison introduces ten of his favourite trout lochs and describes how to fish them.

I am often asked which are my favourite trout lochs and I always find it almost impossible to be precise. What is right for me may not be right for others. We all seek different things and all have different views about what makes a day's fishing memorable.

Some of my best days out have been days when I returned fishless; occasionally, the results of my efforts may only produce one, specimen fish; on others, a good basket of small, perfectly shaped, pink fleshed breakfast-sized trout; but they have all been memorable.

Nor does everyone relish a long, windy walk to a remote mountain lochan; many wish to step straight from the car and into a boat; indeed, some anglers dislike bank fishing, preferring the comfort and ease of a decent boat from which to launch their attack.

But as far as Clan Sandison is concerned, we make it a rule that if we have decided to go fishing, then we go, regardless of the weather. Long experience has taught us that a storm in the morning does not necessarily mean a storm all day; although sometimes it does.

Often, in high winds, when it is impossible to launch a boat, great results may be had from the bank; indeed, most of my trout fishing is from the bank and some of my best fish have been taken in shallow water, very close to the shore.

I enjoy all these differing aspects of trout fishing and I have tried to compile a list that will suit varying tastes; from the expert, intent on one for the glass case, to the angler introducing his children to the gentle art for the first time.

I have also included brief details of what to do if you are blessed with a family who do not share your enjoyment in trout fishing; and suggest how they might amuse themselves whilst you get on with man's proper function - the removal of trout from their natural habitat.

However, as we say in Scotland: You won't catch fish unless your flies are in the water. The lochs described are excellent. The fish are most certainly there. All you have to do to catch them, is put your flies in the water - and cross the right fingers and say the right prayers!

You will find details, names, addresses and telephone numbers of the locations described in "the main body of the kirk" of this guide. Best of luck when you arrive - and Tight Lines in all your efforts.

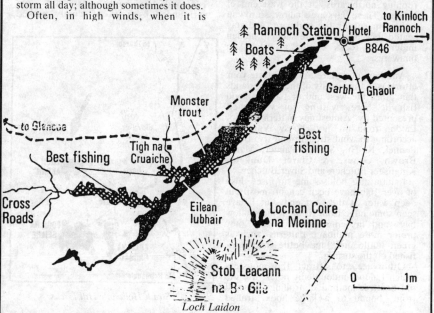

LOCH LAIDON on Rannoch Moor is an ideal place for beginners; and Moor of Rannoch Hotel have excellent boats for hire along with reliable outboard engines. The outboard is essential, because Laidon is a long loch, fingering more than six miles westwards across the moor towards Glencoe.

The drive out to Rannoch Station, where the road ends, is tortuous but magnificent; passing Loch Tummel and Loch Rannoch, along 'The Road to the Isles'. One of Scotland's most famous mountains guards the way: Schiehallion, a graceful, conical peak to the south of Rannoch and when you arrive at Laidon, getting afloat is easy. It is possible to drive the car almost to the waters edge and mooring bay.

Baskets of up to forty trout are the rule, rather than the exception; removing large numbers of small trout, in this instance, is good fishery management: There is more food left for the rest. Consequently they grow to greater size.

Laidon is a deep loch and best results are obtained by keeping close to the shore, no more than about ten yards out. A good rule, anywhere in Scotland. If you can't see the bottom, then you are probably fishing too far out.

It is true to say that you may catch fish anywhere along the margins; but my favourite fishing area is in the long bays running northwards, at the west end of Laidon. These bays are shallow, so row in rather than using the outboard; and stay seated, because there are sudden, hidden underwater rocks waiting to catch you unawares.

Another good place to concentrate your efforts is in the vicinity of the small islands that grace the west end of Laidon; good fish lie here, waiting for your well presented fly. Almost any pattern will do. Laidon trout are not choosy. Vary size according to wind strength and try: Black Pennel, Ke-He, Soldier Palmer, March Brown, Grouse & Claret, Dunkeld, Kingfisher Butcher, and Silver Butcher.

Laidon also holds some surprises. Fish of over 10lb have been caught, mostly in deep water at the west end; but I have seen some huge trout rising in the shallow bays and my information is that they prefer more mundane patterns, such as green bottle and blue bottle imitations, fished on the surface.

Otherwise, to attract the monsters which Laidon undoubtedly holds, use the old Scottish method of trolling: A small trout, bound to a large hook, a trolled behind a slowly moving boat at a depth of some 30ft. Boring work but it may just fill the glass case all we anglers picture above our mantelpiece.

If the family enjoy walking, then a good track wends along the north shore of the loch from Moor of Rannoch, passing delightful, sandy bays where, supervised, children might picnic and splash.

More organised pursuits may be found back at Kinloch Rannoch, where there are facilities for water sports: Sail-boarding, dinghy sailing, artificial ski-slope and an indoor swimming pool, centred around the Kinloch Rannoch Hotel which also has really first class self-catering units, many complete with their own sauna. The ideal way to end a hard day and ease tired muscles.

Loch Laidon and Rannoch Moor is one of Scotland's special places; a vast wilderness of mountain and moorland, abounding with outstanding wildlife. Best of all for the angler, is the outstanding quality of trout fishing. The memory of happy days on Laidon has cheered many a long, dark, fishless, winter's night.

AKRAN, CAORACH & SEILGE
Much of Strath Halladale in North Sutherland has been devastated in recent years by tax-avoidance forestry. Lochs such as Sletill and Leir, which my wife and I fished for many years, are now surrounded by rows of closely packed

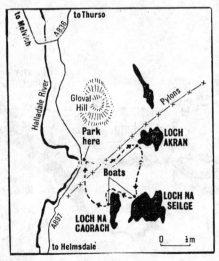

Strath Halladale Hill Lochs

foreign conifers. For us, they have been destroyed, and we no longer fish them.

However, at the north end of the Strath, there are three lochs, as yet untouched by the tree-farmers, and they are excellent, providing a wide variety of sport in splendid surroundings: Akran, Caorach and Seilge. Reaching them involves a brisk walk, but nothing that any semi-fit angler can't manage easily.

Each loch has a good boat, and bank fishing also produces good results. Akran is the place to take beginners. Absolutely packed with brightly marked, wild brown trout which average 6oz in weight. A fishless day on Akran is almost unknown and trout rise with dash and spirit to most patterns of fly.

There is an ideal picnic spot, on the west shore, near to the boat mooring bay; sandy, sheltered by high heather banks, where non-fishing members may laze away a long summer day whilst you fish.

Trout may be caught anywhere in the loch, but my favourite drift is down the south shore, about fifteen yards out, drifting past the rocky headland and into the pan-handle bay. I can't remember ever fishing this drift without taking at least a brace of fish, even in the harshest of fishing conditions.

Caorach lies to the south of Akran, and is about the same size, but longer and narrower in shape. I always prefer to fish Caorach from the bank and have had some really splendid sport with fish which average 8oz/12oz in weight, and the odd trout of up to 2lb. Part of the delight of fishing Caorach is that you never know when the big ones will rise. Each offer must be treated with the greatest respect.

As you approach the loch, following the fence line down to the shore, look quarter right to the far bank. The loch begins to narrow here and this is the most productive spot - either from bank or boat. The bay beyond that can also fish well, but the north end tends to hold smaller fish and is very shallow. Concentrate at the south end.

Seilge is the best of these three lochs, regarding size of fish, although it can also be the most dour. Follow the north shore line round Caorach, carefully crossing the marshy ground near the oulet burn, and you will see a broken line of fence posts marching eastwards across the moor. They lead to Seilge, a few hundred yards hike.

Seilge is a classic Scottish hill loch: Good marl bottom, high ph and plenty of food for trout. The boat is sound, although somewhat heavy to row in a strong wind, but it drifts well and in my experience, Seilge fishes better from the boat, rather than from the bank.

The most productive drift is down the east shore, between the small island and the bank, about eight yards out. Excellent fish lie here and trout of 2lb are often taken. The average weight of fish is more modest but as an example, on our last outing in September 1989, during the course of the wild day, we caught 12 fish and kept 4 weighing 5lb 8oz, the heaviest being a fine trout of 1lb 12oz.

Since honesty is always the best policy, I have to confess, that all these fish were caught by my fishing partner, although I was using exactly the same patterns of flies - and I haven't spoken to my wife since.

Flies to use on Seilge should include: Black Pennel, Greenwell's Glory, and Silver Butcher. Most of the standard pattern Scottish loch flies will produce results on the other Strath Halladale waters described.

For non-fishing members of your party, there is a first class riding centre in Strath Halladale, offering full day and half day treks. There are outstanding beaches at Melvich and further westwards towards Bettyhill. Also easily within reach is one of Scotland's most delightful link's golf courses, at Reay; eighteen holes of sheer delight with an excellent, friendly nineteenth hole at the end of the round.

To visit the far north and not fish these Strath Halladale hill lochs would be a crime. My fishing life would be sadly diminished if they ever fell to the tree-farmers. Get there if you can and experience all that is best of Scottish hill loch fishing.

LOCH STILLIGARRY Few places in Europe can match South Uist for the quality of its brown trout fishing and the beauty of its surroundings. The machair lochs are quite simply the best. Last season produced nearly 800 trout averaging 1lb 1oz in weight, with a heaviest fish weighing 4lb 8oz, taken from Grogarry Loch.

South Uist is an island of contrasts, guarded in the east by a line of hills and mountains, crowned by Hecla and Beinn Mhor, home of golden eagle. At their feet lie bleak, heather and peat moorlands, leading to a superbly fertile western coastal plain, rich in lime; a spring-time wild flower paradise.

And a trout anglers paradise as well. Lochs such as Groggary, Stilligarry, West Ollay and Bornish hold superb fish and apart from these premier machair waters, there are dozens more which hold the promise of fine trout fishing, and from August onwards, outstanding sport with salmon and sea-trout.

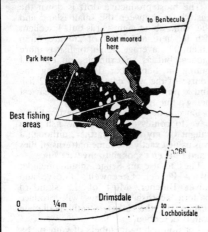

Loch Stilligarry

My favourite machair water is Stilligarry. Shallow and weedy with a mad scattering of tiny islands, points and rocky outcrops where good fish lie. Trout of over 3lb are taken most seasons and the average weight of Stilligarry fish is in the order of 1lb.

They are beautiful fish, perfectly shaped, pink fleshed and they fight like the devil. These trout display all the characteristics which make machair trout so highly prized: Deep-bodied, golden, with bright red spots.

But Stilligarry also holds a stock of wild fish which are almost like sea-trout in appearance, silvery, which when hooked leap spectacularly and run like mad, sending the reel screaming and nerves tingling.

Because of weed, as the season advances, Stilligarry becomes difficult to fish; then, best results come from boat fishing. In spring and early summer, however, bank fishing can be just as rewarding and I have had my best sport on Stilligarry whilst bank fishing.

I remember one gorgeous fish in particular, caught on 2nd April a few years ago. It was a cold day, with a bitter east wind blowing down from Hecla, and I had begun to despair of catching anything when the fish took and set off like a rocket for the middle of the loch. After a nerve-wracking struggle, I eventually managed to coax him onto the bank. He weighed just under 3lb, but had fought with the ferocity of a 10lb spring salmon.

The best fishing areas on Stilligarry are in the vicinity of the islands, of which there are ten, and in the narrow bay where the boat is moored. My favourite Stilligarry flies are: Charlie Maclean, Loch Ordie, Black Pennel, Ke-He, Invicta and Silver Butcher.

South Uist offers a vast choice of activities for non-fishers, although it must be said that they will have to like the outdoor life; bird watching opportunities abound, throughout the island and in two excellent nature reserves: Loch Druidibeg at the north end of South Uist and the Balranald reserve on North Uist.

There are ancient monuments, brochs, duns and wheel-houses, hill walking and climbing; and South Uist is joined to its neighbours, Benbecula and North Uist, so all the islands may be explored. Best of all, are the amazing beaches which run down the west coast. Shining white, deserted sands, where you may walk all day without meeting another soul.

For a more adventurous day out, it is possible to visit the island of Eriskay, past the place where the SS Politician foundered during the last war, made famous by Compton Mackenzie in his book, Whisky Galore; to where Bonnie Prince Charlie first set foot on his native soil in 1745, at the sandy bay which still bears his name. The start of his doomed attempt to recapture the crown of Britain.

The only way to properly appreciate all that South Uist has to offer, to both anglers and visitors alike, is to go there and see for yourself. I shall be returning, again, next June. And, God willing, for many a June to come.

LOCH WATTEN This Caithness water is one of the best trout lochs in Scotland, easily accessible and readily available to members of the public. A number of riparian owners offer boats for hire, although some are of a very poor standard and it is always best to look first, before leaping afloat.

However, once you are afloat, you will find high quality sport with beautiful wild brown trout that are distinctively silver in appearance and average 10oz in weight. There are larger fish; 1989 produced an excellent specimen weighing 4lb 8oz, caught by local angler Douglas Woodall, and most seasons produce trout of over 3lb.

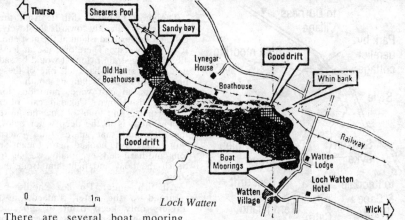

Loch Watten

There are several boat mooring locations and visitors would be advised to consider wind direction before deciding where to start out from. Watten can often be very windy in one area, but relatively sheltered in another. The correct starting point may save a long, wet, bumpy ride either up or down the loch seeking such shelter.

Because it is exposed, an outboard motor is almost essential when fishing Watten. A few are available for hire and information may be obtained from boat owners or the Loch Watten Hotel. A drouge is also vital, to hold the boat steady whilst drifting.

Watten is some three miles long by up to half a mile wide and the average depth is in the order of 7ft. The water has a high ph, 7.7, and is lime rich, providing top-quality feeding for its pink-fleshed residents.

Most areas of the loch will produce results, although bank fishing is not as good as fishing from a boat. Locals all have their favourite hot-spots; some swear by Shearer's Pool, at the north end of the loch: A wide, shallow, weedy bay, where some really excellent fish have been taken.

There is also an area known as 'The Golden Triangle', at the north end, reputed to be the best fishing grounds on Watten: Roughly between the red boathouse at Oldhall, on the west shore, and Sandy Point and Lynegar Boathouse on the east shore.

Others concentrate their efforts in the middle of the loch, enjoying long drifts and catching at least their fair share. My own favourite drift is along the Whin Bank, between the only island in Loch Watten and the shore, in Lynegar Bay, at the Watten Lodge end.

One thing is certain, no matter where you drift on this delightful water, there is always the chance of fish; and this makes Watten particularly attractive to anglers who are new to Caithness, or who have only limited time to spare. Cast with confidence, the loch is full of trout.

And, twice in recent years, salmon. Two fish have been caught and this indicates, I think, that there are probably more about than is realised. Watten is joined by a narrow burn to Wick River, and after heavy rain there is no reason why salmon should not enter the loch. Be prepared.

My trout cast for Watten, in the early months of the season, would be: Ke-He, on the 'bob', March Brown in the middle, and Silver Butcher on the 'tail'; from July onwards, I would perhaps change to: Black Zulu on the 'bob', Greenwell's Glory in the middle, and Silver Invicta on the 'tail'. I also cross my fingers, quite a lot.

Apart from Watten, there are several other excellent trout lochs and if you have to find something for the family to do whilst you explore them, then Caithness has plenty to offer. There are good beaches for the bucket and spade brigade at Reiss and Dunnet, a links golf course, also at Reiss; pony trekking from Latheronwheel and dramatic cliff-top castles and ancient monuments to be explored.

As far as Watten is concerned, I have to declare an interest: It is my local loch. In fact, as I write, from my window, I can see several boats in action and conditions look perfect: gentle, south west breeze, ruffling the surface; so guess where I shall be heading, just as soon as I finish this piece!

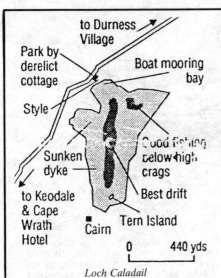

to Durness Village
Park by derelict cottage
Boat mooring bay
Style
Sunken dyke
Good fishing below high crags
Best drift
to Keodale & Cape Wrath Hotel
Cairn
Tern Island
0   440 yds

Loch Caladail

CALADAIL This is one of the 'famous four', the limestone lochs of Durness in North West Sutherland: Caladail, Borralie, Croispol and Lanlish. All, I hasten to add, expert waters, where only the finest techniques will do.

The water is gin-clear and it is possible to make out, in detail, the marks on stones on the bottom, twenty feet down. The slightest casting error sends fish scurrying for safety, making strong men weep with despair.

Nevertheless, Scotland without these magnificent trout lochs would be like an angler without a rod. The quality of the fish is supreme, certainly matching the South Uist machair lochs and surpassing them with regards to size of fish.

Lanlish used to regularly produce wild brown trout of well over 10lb in weight. Even recently, I have seen fish taken that weighed over 8lb. Not cannibal trout, ferox, but splendidly proportioned, magnificent fish.

Last June (1989) my wife, son and I had a morning on Caladail when everthing was perfect; one of those rare days all anglers dream about. Fish rose regularly and during the course of an unforgettable three hours, we caught eight trout, three of which we kept weighing in total, 7lb.

Access to Caladail is easy; a short walk over springy, wild flower strewn turf, to the boat mooring bay. To preserve the quality of the water, outboard motors are strictly forbidden, so be prepared for some hard rowing on windy days - or pack a strong, young son.

The most favoured drift is from the mooring bay, directly towards the lovely, gull and flower-clad island at the east end. It can be weedy. Therefore, use at least 4lb breaking strain nylon. It would be sad if it broke and perhaps left one of these fine fish with a cast trailing its mouth.

Even in an east wind, notorious for keeping fish down, Caladail can offer great sport, and one of my favourite fishing areas is in the deep water below the high buff that guards the western shore. One fish, hooked here, fought so long and hard that, eventually, we had to beach the boat and fight him from the shore.

All fish under 1lb 8oz should be returned to the water. Indeed, most anglers only keep trout of 2lb and upwards, and often, only specimen fish of more than 4lb, of which several are taken each season.

In high winds, traditional patterns of Scottish loch flies will produce results: Black Pennel, Loch Ordie, Ke-He, Soldier Palmer, Woodcock & Hare-lug, March Brown and Butchers. When the wind drops, men are separated from boys; only small sedges and nymphs, dry fly and fine casting technique will tempt the fish. Wonderful sport.

Whilst you are cursing on Caladail, the family will find plenty to do nearby. Trips out to Cape Wrath Lighthouse on the remote Parph Peninsula; visits to the famous Smoo Caves or bird sanctuary on Handa Island; glorious beaches and a fine craft village at Balnakeil - a painless way to empty a purse.

If I had to choose only one loch from the ten listed here, then it would most probably be Caladail. The trout are splendid and the scenery is magnificent. Fishing this loch is a constant delight - and a constant challenge.

LOCH NA H-OIDHCHE The Loch of the Night, is a remote hill loch lying at an altitude of almost 1,500 ft, some three hours walk south from the Gairloch/ Dingwall Road in Wester Ross.

It's a long narrow loch, probing deep into one of Scotland's most dramatic landscapes, lined southwards by mighty Liathach (3,456 ft), the Grey One. On either side, mountains guard the shore: Baosbheinn, the Wizards Mountain, and Beinn an Eoin, the Mountain of the Birds.

Ruadh-stac Mor rises majestically from a barren landscape, scattered with tiny, sparkling blue lochans, full of hard-fighting little fish. Eagle rule the wide skies; golden plover and curlew pipe plaintively from mossy tussocks; and their call echoes amongst grey corries, home of wildcat and stag.

Few places in Scotland offer the angler fishing amidst a more beautiful landscape; and few Scottish lochs can offer such fine sport as Loch na h-Oidhche. But you must be in the right place at the right time, and this can be difficult.

Because of its high altitude, the loch rarely shows of its best until late June, and even early July, depending upon how harsh the winter has been. The water is deep and it takes a long time to warm up sufficiently to stir the trout into action.

But when conditions are right, then sport will be fast and furious, for these fish fight hard and give a splendid account of themselves. They are not large, averaging about 10oz/12oz, and the remarkable thing about Loch na h-Oidhche is that trout are very similar, almost as though they had been individually selected, by hand.

Both boat and bank fishing bring results, but often, because of high winds, it is only possible to fish from the bank. The loch acts as a sort of wind tunnel which frequently makes launching the boat an act of sheer madness.

Better to stay safely on Terra Firma, and creep up on them from the bank. The bottom shelves very quickly, and it is easy to get your flies to where the fish lie: just where the shallow falls away into the deep.

A number of burns and streams cascade down from the surrounding hills, and this is the place to concentrate your efforts, from boat or bank. In reasonable weather, from the boat, try the north and south ends, always in the shallower water, and watch out for action.

As the name indicates, the best time to fish Loch na h-Oidhche is either early in the morning or late evening. What to do whilst you are waiting? Easy, walk a little further south from the end of the loch and you will find three other lochs, all of which fish best during the day - and one of them has trout of up to 3lb in weight.

If you have non-fishers with you, force them to come along; even if they can't stand fishing, they will be entranced and captivated by the cathedral-like beauty of the surroundings; and, who knows, they might even be tempted to have a cast themselves.

LOCH MEADIE A perfect beginner's loch, close to the narrow road that twists from Altnaharra to Loch Hope in Sutherland. Fishing is controlled by Altnaharra Hotel, where Paul Panchaud can generally find a boat for visitors.

From the road, Meadie looks a modest affair. In fact, beyond the wide, island scattered south bay, the loch narrows into a long finger, almost touching Ben Loyal, the Queen of Scottish mountains, six miles to the north.

This is traditional Highland water, absolutely full of small fish where everything hooked should be taken; in order to try and reduce the trout population and increase the average weight of fish. Easier said than done, because it is hard to kill these beautiful little trout.

My wife, Ann, fishing there during 1988, had some 50 such fish during the course of a single day - and returned them all. Having said which, fishing Meadie the

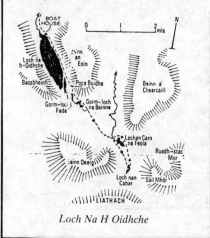

Loch Na H Oidhche

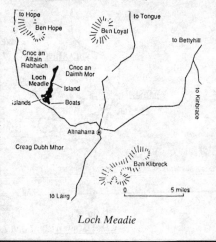

Loch Meadie

following day, I caught but three, so was not faced with real dilemma of the catch and kill policy.

The south bay, particularly round the islands, is the most popular fishing area; but in reality, there are far greater delights further north; not least of which is the small island guarding the entrance to the narrows. Like many similar islands in our northern lochs, these scraps preserve an ancient habitat, rich in the type of plant life that used to cover much of the Highlands in days past: Alder, willow, birch, dwarf oak, crowberry, blaeberry and a mass of wildflowers of great variety.

If for no other reason, the chance of a solitary hour on one of these charming islands is reason enough for launching the boat on Meadie. But remember, these places are part of our sadly diminishing natural heritage and must be cared for and respected. Look. Don't touch.

Beyond this island on Meadie, there is a narrow channel, weed fringed on either side, and I defy anyone not to catch trout here. Drift after drift brings fish dashing to the flies and if ever you wanted to hook someone on the delights of fly fishing, then this is the place to take them.

If not, send them on a trail through Scottish history in Strathnaver, a great,

living museum. The old church at Farr, near Bettyhill is a good starting point, since it will explain much of what is to be seen.

From there, wander down the Strath back to Altnaharra; past burial chambers five thousands years old; note the line of brochs, zig-zagging southwards; the sad monument to Donald Macleod, who wrote so movingly about the Strathnaver Clearances of the 19th century; the remains of the village of Grumore, by Loch Naver, where Patrick Sellar began the brutal work of evicting 2,000 defenceless people from their homes in April 1814.

Meet and compare notes in the Altnaharra Hotel, surrounded by specimen-fish-filled glass cases: A few that did not get away. Loch Meadie casts a magic spell on all who visit her. The fish may not be large, but her charm and beauty most certainly is.

LOCH LEVEN It is impossible to talk about trout fishing in Scotland without mention of Loch Leven, arguably the most famous trout loch in the world. Stock from Loch Leven have found their way all over the planet and, to me at least, Loch Leven is synonymous with all that is best in Scottish trout fishing.

Tinged, however, I must say, with nostalgia; because Loch Leven is but a

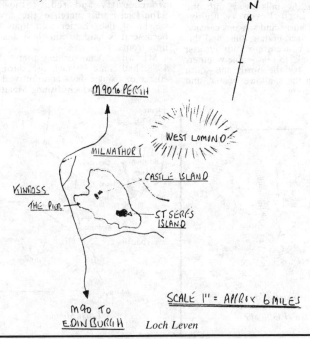

Loch Leven

poor shadow of its former self. I first fished Loch Leven in its glory days, during the 1950's, when any suggestion of stocking the loch would have been greeted with cries of derision.

Unfortunately, due to changing circumstance, and probably because of increasingly chemical-intensive agricultural methods on farms surrounding the loch, since the 1950's catches declined to disastrous levels; until, in recent years, artificial stocking had to be introduced to try and help the loch recover.

Native stock are used and results are encouraging, although fish still tend to prefer bottom feeding, rather than rising to surface flies. This has encouraged the use of English reservoir techniques and non-Scottish exotic patterns of fly such as: Baby Doll, Whisky Fly, Ace of Spades and others.

These lures, rather than flies, are fished below the surface, being stripped back towards the boat at various speeds, whilst waiting for a trout to grab. Many do, and fish of over 4lb are now caught regularly.

In spite of this change in circumstances, from time to time, trout do rise naturally to surface flies. Then, it is like the old days, when the famous Loch Leven 'yellow bellies' lazily head-and-tail over a small Dunkeld double, and scream off into the distance, leaping furiously along the way.

Fishing on Loch Leven is highly organised and divided into two sessions: Day and evening. Nor is it inexpensive. But compared to prices south of the border, it still represents excellent value for money. Information about best drifts can be obtained at The Pier, before setting off.

Regardless of my personal opinion about the raking-the-bottom bunch, I still class Loch Leven as one of Scotland's outstanding trout fisheries. Indeed, in my mind, it remains the sparkling jewel in Scotland's angling crown.

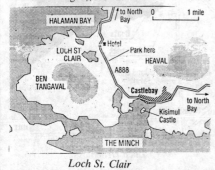

Loch St. Clair

LOCH ST. CLAIR If you are looking for a holiday venue that is primarily centred on the family, then the island of Barra in the Outer Hebrides is one of the most perfect in all Scotland.

Getting there can be a bit of a fright, given the sometimes stormy passage from Oban to Castlebay, but the people are friendly, the beaches utterly beautiful and the whole island is accessible and welcoming.

Of course, you don't have to risk your tummy on the Minch; there is an excellent air service from Glasgow to Barra, tides permitting: The airfield, on the famous cockle strand, is the only airfield in the world to be covered twice a day by the tide.

There are five trout lochs on Barra, where you may escape whilst the others explore; and by far and away the best of these is Loch St. Clair, a few miles from Castlebay, along the only road that circles the island.

St. Clair is one of the most exciting lochs that I have ever fished and I unhesitatingly recommend it to you. It is not large, but there is more than enough water to make for an interesting week's sport; and the fish are really superb, averaging in the order of 2lb. Not easy to catch, though - where are good trout easy to catch - but well worth the effort involved trying.

The loch is close to the road. A short walk down a grass field soon brings you to the south end, where there is a dramatic ruined, miniature castle on a small, man-made island. The water is deep here, and fishing from the bank, it is good policy to keep well back, below the skyline, for fear of scaring the trout.

Working down the west shore, there are a number of inlet burns and shallow bays, where it is possible to wade with reasonable safety. Good fish lie within range, all down this shore, but as you progress northwards the water deepens again, forcing you back on to the bank.

The east side of the loch is also shallow and offers good opportunities for bank fishing, depending upon wind direction. Wind direction is rarely steady, because of the surrounding hills; and a perfectly good cast towards a rising fish in one direction, might easily end up round your ears when the wind suddenly shifts.

The water is clear in the shallows, taking on a darker, peaty stain as it deepens; and this is mirrored in the colour of the fish. They are almost burnished gold when first landed, with large, bright red spots, beautifully marked in the classic Highland manner. They fight magnificently. The fish I caught on my last visit would gladden the heart of any angler, anywhere in the world and provide splendid sport. A boat is also sometimes available for visitors.

If you should tire of the delights of Loch St. Clair, have a day off and take the family over to the neighbouring island of Vatersay. On a warm Hebridean summer day, I know of nowhere else in Britain that can offer such wonderful peace and seclusion on such shining sands.

LOCH HEILEN Threaten me with never being able to fish Loch Heilen again and I will do anything you choose. But heaven knows why, because this is one of the dourest, most difficult waters I have ever fallen in love with. Days pass without either sight or sound of fish. At times, even I, who know a lot better, would swear that there wasn't a trout in the place. And yet, I keep going back for more.

Heilen, in Caithness, is a few miles drive from my front door and it contains some super fish: Trout of over 8lb have been caught in recent years; and I have had fish of 4lb 8oz, 3lb 8oz and 2lb 10oz. Anything under 2lb should always be returned to the water.

The loch covers an area of some 160 acres and lies at the centre of a site of special scientific interest. Surrounding fields are rich in wild flowers, including grass of parnasus, purple and spotted orchid and that most elusive of all Scottish flowers, exclusive to the far north, primula Scotica.

During winter months Heilen provides home and haven for huge flocks of grey-lag geese from Scandinavia and Icelandic whooper swans; throughout the year, wildfowl adorn its surface with occasional visits from both black-throated and red-throated divers.

The loch is very shallow, having an average depth of only three feet and consequently, bank fishing can be as productive as fishing from a boat. However, because Heilen is very exposed, high winds often churn up the bottom turning the water into the colour and consistency of pea soup, making it pointless to fish.

But when conditions are right, and fish rise, there is nowhere else on planet Earth that I would rather be. The trout are amongst the hardest fighting and most beautiful that I have ever seen and one fish from Heilen is worth a dozen from anywhere else.

It's just catching them that is the problem; and the place to try, is across from the boat mooring bay, on the east shore, near to where an old fence enters the water. There are one or two deep holes here that can sometimes produce a fish.

From there, drift diagonally across the loch, aiming if possible for the old boat house on the far bank. All the way, there is the chance of a fish; generally when you are admiring the sunset, or sorting out a fankle.

The best time to launch your attack on Loch Heilen, is in May and June; thereafter, although you might still catch fish, the loch becomes progressively more weedy. Very much a case of searching for clear water or a rising fish.

As to which flies to use, I can only suggest those which have been successful for me; a sadly brief list for fifteen years fishing: Loch Ordie, fished almost as a dap, during a hard wind; size 16 Greenwell's Glory, late on a May evening; Silver Butcher, below the surface on a hot summer day; Silver Invicta, size 14, whilst looking the other way.

If you are the sort of angler that likes a real challenge, then Heilen is the place for you. If, however, you should be sufficiently expert, or lucky, to catch a Heilen trout on your first visit, please, do me a favour don't tell me.

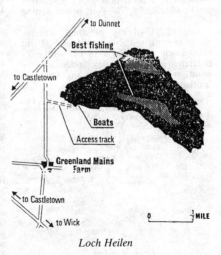

Loch Heilen

SIX RECIPES

BY LEWIS-ANN GARNER

This is a lovely supper dish, simple to make and easily adaptable to feeding varying numbers of guests. The main reason I like it is because it makes good use of the smaller salmon that my husband seems to prefer to catch. The recipe below is for eight.

Salmon Kedgeree
1 salmon, poached and skinned
1lb basmati rice, cooked and cooled
4oz sultanas
2 pears, diced but not skinned
6oz button mushrooms, chopped
1 dessertspoon each of freshly chopped parsley, dill and thyme
1 clove of garlic
Butter for frying
Salt and black pepper
Paprika and parsley to garnish

Rub garlic clove over the insides of a large frying pan. Melt butter in it and gently fry the mushrooms. Add the sultanas, herbs and the pears, taking care not to break up the pear pieces.
In a large mixing bowl flake the salmon and carefully mix in the rice. Add this to the frying pan with salt and pepper to taste. Cover and heat through thoroughly adding a little water if it seems dry.

Transfer to a heated serving dish and sprinkle with a little paprika and garnish with sprigs of parsley. Serve immediately.

The following recipe is one I use as a starter at special occasions. You could substitute your own favourite fruit in place of the one that I have used. To serve four people.

Salmon and Passion Fruit
Allow 4-6oz of smoked salmon per person
2 kiwi fruit, thinly sliced
1 green crisp hearted lettuce
1 lemon
Parsley to garnish
Bunch of chives, snipped finely
8 slices of cucumber
2 tomatoes

Slice the smoked salmon thinly and divide equally between four plates. Peel and slice the kiwi fruit and interlay between the slices of salmon. Make a salad of the remaining ingredients and arrange around the salmon on each plate. Garnish with parsley sprigs and serve each with a wedge of lemon.

My father once in a weaker moment gave me two sea-trout, a fish I never seem to have any luck catching. These sea-trout had come from the Outer Hebrides one of his favourite hunting grounds. During the long winter months they made a lovely change from the freezer full of brown trout we seem to end each season with. I usually allow one sea-trout for two people.

Vermouth Sea-trout
2 Sea-trout, cleaned, gutted, topped and tailed
2oz butter, melted
1lb tomatoes
1 tablespoon tomato puree
4 fl oz Vermouth
2 teaspoons lemon juice
1 dessertspoon chopped dill
Salt and pepper
Lemon-thyme sprigs to garnish, and lemon wedges to serve

Plunge the tomatoes in boiling water for a few seconds and then peel them. Put these with the puree into a blender and liquidise. Set to one side. Rub the sea-trout with salt and pepper and fry in the melted butter in a thick based pan. Add more butter if necessary. Transfer to a warmed shallow casserole. Put the liquidised tomatoes into the pan and cook until reduced to about half the original quantity. Stir in the Vermouth and lemon juice. Bring quickly to the boil stirring all the time. Add the chopped dill and pour over the sea-trout. Cover and cook at 180°C for about 45-50 minutes. Serve with lemon wedges and garnished with sprigs of lemon thyme.

This recipe is one I use for a quick and easy dish at buffets and parties. I prepare it the day before and refrigerate covered until it is needed. If you use smoked sea-trout it will give the dish extra flavour. To serve twelve at a party and six as a starter.

Sea-trout Pate with Chervil

2lbs poached filleted flaked sea-trout
8oz ricotta cheese
8fl oz sour cream
2 tablespoons lemon juice
2 tablespoons chopped chervil
Salt and freshly ground black pepper
Chervil to garnish

Put the flaked sea-trout in a blender with the cheese and cream. Blend until smooth. If you don't have a blender then mash the ingredients by hand and put them through a sieve. Stir in the finely chopped chervil, lemon juice and seasoning. Pack into a souffle dish, cover and chill. If using as a starter then put into individual souffle dishes. Garnish with chervil just before serving. Dill or parsley may be used in place of the chervil but do taste as you add to make sure the flavour of the sea-trout is not masked.

The brown trout of the Don are what I used in this recipe. Quality fish of a good reliable size are guaranteed, providing you can catch them . . . It only seems fair to point out that my husband caught one of them, myself the remainder in this instance. To serve four.

Brown Trout stuffed with Spinnach and Almonds

4 x 1lb trout
12oz spinnach
4oz flaked almonds
3oz dried brown bread crumbs
1tsp freshly chopped fennel
1tsp freshly chopped parsley
2 eggs beaten
Salt and pepper
Butter for frying

Clean and gut the trout, leaving the head and tail on. Dry on absorbant kitchen paper.

Par boil the spinnach, drain and chop finely, stir in the bread crumbs, herbs and salt and pepper.

Melt a little butter in a frying pan and fry the almonds until golden brown. Stir this into the stuffing mixture. Gently mix in the beaten egg.

Stuff each trout and wrap each one individually in foil. Place in a shallow oven-proof casserole and bake at 180°C for 30-40 minutes. Serve immediately.

If you like herbs then this recipe is a must. The herbs I have used are just some of my own choice, you can mix up your own favourite combinations. To serve four.

Trout with Honey and Herbs

4 brown trout
4 tablespoons clear heather honey
1 tablespoon chopped marjoram
1 tablespoon chopped thyme
1 dessertspoon chopped parsley
1 dessertspoon chopped chives
1 dessertspoon chopped loveage
2 tablespoons lemon juice
Salt and pepper

Gut and clean the trout, leaving the heads and tails on. Dry on absorbant kitchen paper. Rub the insides of the trout with salt and pepper. Warm the honey and brush this over the skin of the trout but not the head and tail. Combine the herbs with the lemon juice and sprinkle over the trout but not the head and tail. Using skewer prick the skin of the trout all over and then leave to marinate for a couple of hours. Wrap each trout individually in foil and bake in a pre-heated oven at 180°C for about 50 minutes. Check during cooking that it is not drying out. If it is then add a little water. Serve at once.

FOLLOW THE COUNTRY CODE

SET A GOOD EXAMPLE
AND TRY TO FIT IN WITH THE
LIFE AND WORK OF THE COUNTRYSIDE

GAME ANGLING CLUBS

CLUB	SECRETARY	CLUB	SECRETARY
Aberfeldy Angling Club	R.M. Stewart, Police House, No. 1 Kenmore Street, Aberfeldy, Perthshire.	Earlston Angling Association	P. Hessett, 2 Arnot Place, Earlston. Tel: 577.
Airdrie Angling Club	Roy Burgess, 21 Elswick Drive, Caldercruix.	Eckford Angling Association	R.B. Anderson, W.S., Royal Bank Buildings, Jedburgh, Roxburghshire. Tel: 3202.
Annan & District Angling Club	J. Glen, 110 High Street, Annan, Dumfriesshire.	Elgin & District Angling Association	Mr. F. Rhind, "Birchview", Wester Whitewreath, Longmorn, Elgin, Morayshire.
Badenoch Angling Association	Mrs. J. Waller, 39 Burnside Avenue, Aviemore, Argyllshire.		
Berwick & District Angling Association	D. Cowan, 3 Church Street, Berwick. Tel: (0289) 330145.	Esk & Liddle Fisheries Association	R.J.B. Hill, Solicitor, Bank of Scotland Buildings, Langholm, Dumfriesshire.
Blairgowrie, Rattray & District Angling Association	W. Matthew, 4 Mitchell Square, Blairgowrie, Perthshire. Tel: (0250) 3679.	Esk Valley Angling Improvement Association	Kevin Burns, 53 Fernieside Crescent, Edinburgh.
Brechin Angling Club	D.E. Smith, 3 Friendly Park, Brechin, Angus.	Eye Water Angling Club	W.S. Gillie, 2 Tod's Court, Eyemouth, Berwickshire.
Castle Douglas & District Angling Association	Ian Bendall, Tommy's Sports Shop, Castle Douglas, Kirkcudbrightshire. Tel: (0556) 2851.	Ford & Etal Estates Fishing Club	Mr. W.M. Bell, Heatherslaw, Cornhill on Tweed. Tel: Crookham 221.
Chatton Angling Association	A. Jarvis, 7 New Road, Alnwick.	Fyvie Angling Association	G.A. Joss, Clydesdale Bank plc, Fyvie, Turriff.
Coldstream & District Angling Association	Mr. E.M. Patterson, 27 Leet Street, Coldstream, Berwickshire. Tel: 2719.	Gordon Fishing Club	Mrs. M. Forsyth, 47 Main Street, Gordon. Tel: 359.
Cramond Angling Club	R. Whyte, 23 Brunswick Street, Edinburgh.	Greenlaw Angling Club	J. Purves, 9 Wester Row, Greenlaw.
Dalbeattie Angling Association	N. Parker, 30 High Street, Dalbeattie. Tel: (0556) 610448.	Hawick Angling Club	R. Sutherland, 2 Twirlees Terrace, Hawick. Tel: 75150.
Devon Angling Association	R. Breingan, 33 Redwell Place, Alloa.	Inverness Angling Club	G.M. Smith, 50 Nevis Park, Inverness.
Dreghorn Angling Club	Dr. D.D. Muir, 6 Pladda Avenue, Broomlands, Irvine.	Irvine & District Angling Club	A. Sim, 51 Rubie Crescent, Irvine.
Dumfries & Galloway Angling Association	R. Marcucci, 64 Georgetown Road, Dumfries DG1 4DF. Tel: (0387) 62868.	Jedforest Angling Club	J.T. Renilson, 4 Canongate, Jedburgh, Roxburghshire.
		Kelso Angling Association	Mr. Hutchison, 53 Abbotseat, Kelso, Roxburghshire. Tel: 23440.
Dunkeld & Birnam Angling Association	J. Doig, 42 Willowbank, Dunkeld, Perthshire PH8 0JU. Tel: 612.	Kemnay Angling Club	A. Calder, 22 Kendal Road, Kemnay.
		Killin, Breadalbane Angling Club	Douglas Allan, 12 Ballechroisk, Killin. Tel: (05672) 362.
Dunoon & District Angling Club	D.& D.A.C., 7 Blair Lane, Stewart Street, Dunoon. Tel: Dunoon 5732.	Kilmaurs Angling Club	J. Watson, 7 Four Acres Drive, Kilmaurs.

CLUB	SECRETARY	CLUB	SECRETARY
Kintyre Fish Protection & Angling Club	F.W. Neate, Kilmory Place, High St, Campbeltown.	Peebleshire Salmon Fishing Association	Blackwood & Smith W.S., 39 High Street, Peebles.
Kyles of Bute Angling Club	R. Newton, Viewfield Cottage, Tighnabruaich, Argyll.	Perth & District Anglers' Association	G. Nichols, 30 Wallace Crescent, Perth.
Ladykirk & Norham Angling Association	Mr. R.G. Wharton, 8 St. Cuthbert's Square, Norham. Tel: (0289) 82467.	Pitlochry Angling Club	R. Harriman, Sunnyknowe, Nursing Home Brae, Pitlochry. Tel: (0796) 2484.
Lairg Angling Club	J.M. Ross, St. Murie, Church Hill Road, Lairg, Sutherland IV27 4BL. Tel: Lairg 2010.	Rannoch & District Angling Club	J. Brown, Esq., The Square, Kinloch Rannoch, Tayside. Tel: Kinloch Rannoch 268.
Larbert & Stenhousemuir Angling Club	A. Paterson, 6 Wheatlands Avenue, Bonnybridge, Stirlingshire.	River Almond Angling Association	H. Meikle, 23 Glen Terrace, Deans, Livingston.
Lauderdale Angling Association	D.M. Milligan, 1 Newbyth Stables, East Linton, East Lothian.	St. Andrews Angling Club	Secretary, 54 Nicholas Street, St. Andrews.
Lochgilphead & District Angling Club	H. McArthur, The Tackle Shop, Lochnell Street, Lochgilphead.	St. Marys Loch Angling Club	Mr. J. Miller, 8/5 Craighouse Gardens, Edinburgh. Tel: 031-447 0024.
Loch Keose Angling Association	c/o Tourist Information Centre, Stornoway, Lewis.	Stanley & District Angling Club	D.J. Jeffrey, Airntully, Stanley. Tel: Stanley 463.
Loch Lomond Angling Improvement Association	R.A. Clements, C.A., 224 Ingram Street, Glasgow.	Selkirk & District Angling Association	Mr. A. Murray, 40 Raeburn Meadows, Selkirk. Tel: 21534.
Loch Rannoch Conservation Association	Mrs. Steffen, Coilmore Cottage, Kinloch Rannoch.	Stormont Angling Club	The Factor, Scone Estates Office, Scone Palace. Perth.
Melrose & District Angling Association	I.P. Graham, Dunfermline House, Buccleuch Street, Melrose. Tel: 2148.	Stranraer & District Angling Association	Ted Ainsworth, c/o Creach More Golf Club, Stranraer.
Morebattle Angling Club	Mr. H. Fox, Orchard Cottage, Morebattle.	Strathmore Angling Improvement Association	Mrs. A. Henderson, 364 Blackness Road, Dundee. Tel: Dundee 68062.
Murthly & Glendelvine Trout Angling Club	Chairman, P.M. Castle-Smith, The Boat of Murthly, By Dunkeld, Perthshire.	Turriff Angling Association	I.Masson, 14 Mains Street, Turriff.
New Galloway Angling Association	N. Birch, Galloway View, Balmaclellan, Castle Douglas. Tel: New Galloway 404.	Upper Annandale Angling Association	J. Black, 1 Rosehill, Grange Road, Moffat. Tel: Moffat 20104.
North Uist Angling Club	Factor, North Uist Estate, Estate Office, Lochmaddy, North Uist.	Upper Nithsdale Angling Club	W. Forsyth, Solicitor, 100 High Street, Sanquhar, Dumfriesshire. Tel: Sanquhar 50241.
Peebleshire Trout Fishing Association	D.G. Fyfe, 39 High Street, Peebles. Tel: 20131.	Whiteadder Angling Association	Mr. J. Boyd, St. Leonard's, Polwarth, Greenlaw. Tel: Duns 82377.

SEE MAPS ON PAGES 2-5

SCOTTISH GAME FISHING INTO THE NINETIES

BY BILL CURRIE

The Dee in May

It is not a foolish remark to say that to see forward clearly you must look backwards. I do not, of course, mean that we should look back on the salmon and sea trout fishing we have enjoyed in the past decade and assume that, since these years have now passed, all the good times have gone with them. Writing at the turn of the eighties into the nineties, I am conscious of very important changes having taken place in the past decade and of several important effects they are having on

Scottish game fishing which will, I believe, improve our fishing greatly.

Let me begin with a very positive advance which we are beginning to reap the benefits of and which will build up our salmon and sea trout fishings in the nineties. I refer to the reduction in coastal and estuary netting of salmon and sea trout. The Salmon Conservation Trust bought off nets on the Dee, the Don, from the coastal waters off Buchan and

Aberdeenshire and from the river netting stations on the Tweed and elsewhere. One of the immediate effects being noticed is that catches of grilse and sea trout on the east coast rivers are increasing. This is summer holiday sport, and it augurs well for visitors to Scotland in the nineties. Any increase in the river stock of fish should lead to a building up of catchable fish in the angling waters affected.

Even where estuary and coastal nets are still operated, there has been an important change. The coming of salmon farming has emphasised the uneconomic nature of many netting stations. The price of salmon on the fishmonger's slab has remained low. Given lower returns anyway, severe competition from farmed fish has made vulnerable netting stations shorten their season or withdraw their operations completely. Further on some rivers, the proprietors of the rod fishings have made financial arrangements to keep the nets off in early spring, to enhance the rod fishings for these highly desirable early salmon. The Tweed again is an example of this, but other arrangements exist on the Spey, the Helmsdale, the Thurso and other waters.

There has been a realisation throughout the country that the value of a salmon in freshwater, fished for by a visitor is worth many times the fishmonger's value for that fish if it is netted out commercially. I was at one local conference in 1989 where a calculation was made showing that salmon caught by rods in freshwater could be up to 70 times more valuable than those netted out in the estuary. These figures may seem exceptionally high, but when hotels, employment, transport and fishing costs are all taken into account, the added value of a salmon which is rod caught soon mounts up. This concept of the salmon as locally valuable is one of the considerable achievements of the eighties and it will mark the conservation and development of salmon fishing in the nineties.

But the angling fraternity must also take on board new ideas of conservation and good management. There has been a growing tide of discussion in the press about various kinds of restraint as a contribution to conservation and development of our rod fisheries. For example, the Secretary of State, under the new Salmon Act (1986) has made an order preventing the use of prawns and shrimps on the Dee. A similar regulation has been in force on the Tweed for some time. Many rivers have voluntarily adopted a fly only approach, at least in times of low water or in summer fishing, but some rivers are wholly fished by fly. This is a form of restraint, but in my own experience, adds to the fun of fishing, especially in summer and autumn. It also stresses that fishing is done for sport, and not for sheer numbers of fish taken. I would personally like to see a ban on the sale of rod caught fish, and it would not surprise me if this comes in the nineties. It could come as a bargaining point where nets are willing to restrict their operations further if rods fish only for sport. That would seem to me to be a fair point and would be agreed by most anglers in Scotland.

Ten years ago I would not have been as optimistic about the future of Scottish game fishing as I am today. Stocks were, at that time, showing serious decline in many waters. There was rampant interceptory netting and long lining at sea. We had poor legislation. The eighties brought us a new Act with many good features in it; it brought an international flavour to the husbanding of Atlantic salmon with the establishment of NASCO (North Atlantic Salmon Conservation Organisation) which is a powerful body operating at government level (based in Edinburgh). The eighties gradually brought in quotas for high seas fishing and produced an awakening of local fisheries development bodies which work closely with tourist initiatives and with local clubs. In brief, we have set the scene in the eighties for better organisation and better stocks for the nineties and that can only be good news to those who read Scotland for Fishing, whether they are local anglers in Scotland or visitors to our country.

As far as trout fishing is concerned, the eighties brought a decline in wild trout stocks, but the establishment of protection orders on major rivers like the Tay has had a beneficial effect. In Highland lochs, especially the smaller hill waters, Scotland has an enviable resource of trout which can be the basis of holiday family fishing of the best kind. The environment of our trout lochs, - the hills, the moorland setting, the naturalness and unspoiled nature of the land - is something to be treasured and there are many signs that trout fishing in the Highlands, having been the poor relation of the family, is now being revalued and improved. I can tell you, after a life of game fishing, that walking up to a Highland trout loch with friends for a day's fishing is the finest way to get to know the Scottish landscape and the most delightful way of spending a summer day. My hope is that the nineties will continue to prove this and that our wild trout stocks and access to them will grow.

TROUT FLY DRESSING

BY ALAN SPENCE

Long dreich nights stretch ahead. Through drab November, festive December to the real winter of the early months of another year. For over six months, with the exception of a few waters stocked with rainbows, the trout angler is gone from loch and river side. Only the fortunate anglers who indulge also in fly dressing retain contact with their sport through grim mid-winter.

Pictorial, piscatorial mental images spin the thread for the tapestry linking winter hearth and summer water. Recollections of balmy spring days; casting a team of flies from a drifting boat, the eye straining last light of the mid-summer evening rise on a river pool. Anticipation of next season's delights, through the craft of fly dressing helps carry the addicted over the close season.

Striving with steel, silk, a touch of fur and feather, the fly dresser, with these relatively crude materials, endeavours to copy the delicate translucent body and wings of natural aquatic and terrestrial insects.

In the past the art of "busking" a feather and fur creation was the only method by which the trout angler was able to furnish his horse hair or gut casting line with a suitable artificial offering. In a leather and parchment wallet he would carry a selection of hooks, silk, fur and feather to perform the task on the spot to match the natural fly of the moment.

The art of fly dressing gradually fell from favour among anglers in the early years of this century to be replaced by flies dressed and sold by tackle dealers throughout the country.

There were always enthusiasts who preferred the home tied version to those offered by tackle dealers, but until two decades ago they were very much in the minority. Now many anglers have returned to the craft of tying or dressing their own flies, hopefully to imitate the appropriate insect on which the trout are choosing to dine in proper time and season.

Tying and fishing with artificial flies is an art reaching back at least 600 years into the past. In one way the early anglers and fly dressers were more fortunate than those today in that they had an unlimited supply of natural materials.

Much of the plumage used in some patterns came originally from birds which have now long enjoyed the protection of the law, in most instances suitable substitutes have been found from other sources, or by dyeing readily available feathers.

What is mainly missed today are the capes, or neck feathers containing the hackles feathers of domestic poultry and game cocks. Once every farm yard even every country cottage had it own flock of hens, providing eggs and birds for the pot. To the fly dresser it was the bird for the pot which was of most interest.

Mature cockerels over two years old had superb stiff neck feathers, ideal for the stiff shiny hackles required to tie dry flies. Birds culled for the table in mid-winter when the plumage was at its best provided the best hackles for both sheen and bouyancy.

Badger; white or cream with a black centre, furnace, grizzle, blue dun the permutation of capes from free range breeding were endless. All replaced by the broiler chicken and battery hen, today's equivalent of the domestic hen offers little to the fly dresser.

An expanding business has grown up importing hackles, or capes from India and China where the farming methods still support the fowl bearing multi hued feathers beloved by fly dressers. Specialists breed birds genetically selected for the quality of hackles in the cock bird capes at a price of around, £50 per cape. In fact the supply of fly dressing materials is a growth industry right across the board.

Suppliers scour the world for sources of suitable natural materials plain and exotic, while manufacturers vie to provide the thinnest yet strongest tying silk or the sharpest hooks.

Almost every issue of the angling press carries reviews on the newest and most glittering synthetic materials to tempt both fly tyer and trout. Many of them are extremely effective, especially when applied to waters where rainbow trout are stocked.

Yet the old traditional materials retain their adherents. A pinch of fur from a hare's ear, a sparse silk body with a few turns of partridge hackle can today be as deceitful to the native brown trout as any of the modern materials.

Traditional flies for river and loch have always been different in appearance. River flies are usually drab, for example the Greenwells Glory first tied to imitate the Dark Olive on the Tweed has a dull yellow silk body with a few turns of gold wire, a furnace hackle, black in the centre with chestnut brown edges and slips of starling flight feathers for wings.

The Greenwells Glory is one of the few trout flies which non-anglers can name and it remains as effective today as when James Wright of Sprouston first tied it for Canon Greenwell in the late 1800s.

Now look at a typical loch fly such as the Peter Ross, black and gold barred golden pheasant tippet feathers form the tail. The body gives way from silver tinsel and wire to crimson seal's fur, the hackle is black, while the wing a bold black and white barred feather from the flank of the teal.

Like the Greenwells Glory the Peter Ross and its ilk, once termed fancy patterns, remains a deadly lure to trout. While the tag 'fancy' was applied to many loch trout flies, it is now accepted that the silvers, and brilliant body materials in fact represent what is occurring in the natural insect as it emerges or hatches through the surface film.

On lochs the main food for the trout is some species of the chironomid or non-biting midge species. Starting life as an egg laid by the adult midge which hatches into a larvae, the blood worm in fact is a variety of colours but mainly bright red.

Before hatching, the larvae transposes into a pupae which makes its way to the surface ready to change from aquatic creature to air borne insect. It is at this moment that modern photography has shown that a rush of blood to the opening wings as the pupael shuck splits gives for a few seconds a flash of bright colour.

Fly tying can be learned by young and old alike. The triumph when the first hackle is bound down, the first pair of near perfect wings tied in place is only matched by the thrill of the first trout caught on a self tied fly.

Instruction in fly dressing takes place throughout Scotland under the guidance of angling clubs or as evening classes run by education authorities. Beginners who may have thought they were possessed of five thumbs will find to their delight that after a couple of lessons they can turn out a simple fly perfectly acceptable to the eye and more importantly to trout also.

John Marshall demonstrates fly dressing at "Borders Country Fair".

SMALL FLIES FOR FUSSY TROUT

BY ALAN SPENCE

Changing flies at dusk can be a problem without magnifying glasses.

Trout while existing on a varied aquatic diet can be at times extremely fussy feeders, feeding on only one of several insects on or in the water at a given time, or even taking that insect at a specific stage in its life cycle. Often despite the presence of large and meaty mouthfuls on river or loch, the trout will select instead some minute insect, difficult to see by the angler and difficult to imitate with an artificial fly.

On rivers the tiny caneis or fisherman's curse may be targeted instead of succulent tempting olives. Lochs in turn find trout zeroed in on minuscule midge pupae when large sedges abound.

Having experienced the situation on both river and loch, two seasons ago it seemed time that something was done to rectify the situation. Nights of frustration with the water aboil with feeding trout, and scant return in the creel at evenings end do not reflect the popular image of the calm patient angler.

Basis for the campaign were Captain Hamilton down eyed dry fly hooks made by Partridge of Redditch in sizes 18 and 20. Being somewhat doubtful of personal ability to busk fur on feather on minuscule slivers of steel, for a start, only one packet of each size was purchased.

Some success was attained with these tiny dry flies on stillwaters, but it was on rivers that they really proved their worth in the time and effort required in their construction. Dry fly is today an accepted method on all Scottish waters, providing some of the most exciting sport casting to a specific visible fish.

Most summer evenings my arrival at the riverside is hours before any natural fly hatch or proper rise can be expected to take place. Here and there however the surface of a long slow running pool is dimpled as an opportunist trout takes an unidentified fly. Previously on odd occasions these fish had succumbed to size 16 hackled flies such as a Tups Indispensable or the Badger series.

More often than not the size 16s, which looked enormous on the calm surface in daylight, were ignored or the trout simply swirled at them before turning aside without sampling.

A pleasant surprise in dressing the down eyed Captain Hamilton dry fly hooks was that for some reason they were easier to tie and finish off than the standard up eyed dry fly hook.

Size 18 and 20 dry flies require a small hackle to give the fly a balanced appearance. It was an equally pleasant surprise to find that among the cheap bargain dozen capes purchased from an importer there were sufficient of these hackles to tie dozens of small flies.

The Tups has always been a favourite with the built in buoyancy of the fur thorax helping to keep such a mini imitation afloat. With practice it was even possible to get two hackles on the Tups, a dyed blue dun and a golden honey dun tied back to back.

The value of a small fly was demonstrated on one occasion when three steadily rising trout refused a size 18 artificial. A change to size 20 brought all three, or at least three which rose in the same lies to the net.

Yet again there have been occasions when the bulky thorax of even the size 20 Tups has appeared out of place, a view shared by trout which treated the offering with the utmost contempt.

A change to a more slim line artificial such as a Badger and Yellow or a small Greenwell Spider were the undoing of some such pernickety trout.

The trap of changing to larger artificial flies as the light fades is easily entered. Often in the poor light it is a time consuming job changing to larger, then back to the small flies. The larger pattern which might remain visible to the angler for an extra half hour is ignored. Better sticking to the small pattern which has proven successful, guessing its position and striking when a fish rises in the vicinity.

Entirely a better way to spend the last half hour of a June evening than watching a splendidly cocked winged size 14 dry fly sailing past unmolested.

The hooking power of these small hooks, something of which there were originally some doubts, is excellent. Perfectly shaped to fit around the jaw bone of the pound trout which are the average on my club water.

Other tackle must be scaled down accordingly, 3lb breaking strain points and a light rated rod around 5-6 A.F.T.M. is the ideal. The Turle knot is better than the tacked half blood knot as it adds no extra length to the silhouette of the fly.

Changing down to size 18 and 20 flies may not solve all the problems in dry fly fishing but it certainly helps deceive trout picking at small natural insects. The following dressings have so far brought the best results yet there is no reason why any favourite dry fly should not be tied in smaller sizes.

Tups Indispensable
Hook. Partridge 18 & 20 Captain Hamilton down eyed.
Silk. Multistrand Primrose.
Tail. Four fibres of light dun hackle.
Body. One turn of yellow floss silk.
Thorax. 50/50 Natural sheep's wool well mixed with scarlet seal's fur.
Hackle (s) Light golden dun, optional with dyed blue dun.

Badger and Yellow
Hook. As above.
Silk. Light Yellow or primrose multistrand.
Tail. Four fibres badger cock.
Body. Unwaxed tieing silk or yellow floss silk.
Hackle. Badger cock.

Mini Greenwell
Hook. As above.
Silk. Light Yellow or primrose multistrand.
Tail. Four fibres furnace hackle.
Body. Waxed silk.
Hackle. Furnace.

The last dressing can be varied by the amount of wax applied to the tieing silk, darker or lighter hackles can be used giving a further variation.

What are most useful for both dressing and tying these small flies are a pair of specialised fly tyers spectacles, or a pair of high magnification 'off the shelf' reading glasses now available without prescription.

Tups Indispensable size 18 – the fur and wool thorax makes this a very buoyant fly.

CLOSE SEASON

The following are the statutory close season dates for trout and salmon fishing in Scotland.

TROUT

The close season for trout in Scotland is from 7 October to 14 March, both days inclusive, but many clubs extend this close season still further to allow the fish to reach better condition.

Fresh trout may not be sold between the end of August and the beginning of April, and not at any time if less than eight inches long.

SALMON

Net Fishing	Rod Fishing	River District
1 Sept-15 Feb	1 Nov-15 Feb	Add
27 Aug-10 Feb	1 Nov-10 Feb	Ailort
27 Aug-10 Feb	1 Nov-10 Feb	Aline
27 Aug-10 Feb	1 Nov-10 Feb	Alness
27 Aug-10 Feb	1 Nov-10 Feb	Applecross
27 Aug-10 Feb	1 Nov-10 Feb	Arnisdale (Loch Hourn)
27 Aug-10 Feb	16 Oct-10 Feb	Awe
27 Aug-10 Feb	1 Nov-10 Feb	Ayr
27 Aug-10 Feb	1 Nov-10 Feb	Baa & Goladoir
27 Aug-10 Feb	1 Nov-10 Feb	Badachro & Kerry (Gairloch)
27 Aug-10 Feb	1 Nov-10 Feb	Balgay & Shieldaig
27 Aug-10 Feb	16 Oct-10 Feb	Beauly
27 Aug-10 Feb	1 Nov-10 Feb	Berriedale
10 Sept-24 Feb	1 Nov-24 Feb	Bervie
27 Aug-10 Feb	1 Nov-10 Feb	Bladenoch
27 Aug-10 Feb	1 Nov-10 Feb	Broom
27 Aug-10 Feb	16 Oct-31 Jan	Brora
10 Sept-24 Feb	1 Nov-24 Feb	Carradale
27 Aug-10 Feb	1 Nov-10 Feb	Carron (W. Ross)
10 Sept-24 Feb	1 Nov-24 Feb	Clayburn (Isle of Harris (East))
27 Aug-10 Feb	1 Nov-10 Feb	Clyde & Leven
27 Aug-10 Feb	1 Oct-25 Jan	Conon
14 Sept-28 Feb	15 Oct-28 Feb	Cree
27 Aug-10 Feb	17 Oct-10 Feb	Creed or Stornoway and Laxay (Isle of Lewis)
27 Aug-10 Feb	1 Nov-10 Feb	Creran (Loch Creran)
27 Aug-10 Feb	1 Nov-10 Feb	Croe & Shiel
27 Aug-10 Feb	1 Oct-31 Jan	Dee (Aberdeenshire)
27 Aug-10 Feb	1 Nov-10 Feb	Dee (Kirkcudbrightshire)
27 Aug-10 Feb	1 Nov-10 Feb	Deveron
27 Aug-10 Feb	1 Nov-10 Feb	Don
27 Aug-10 Feb	1 Nov-10 Feb	Doon
1 Sept-15 Feb	16 Oct-15 Feb	Drummachloy or Glenmore (Isle of Bute)
27 Aug-10 Feb	16 Oct-10 Feb	Dunbeath
21 Aug- 4 Feb	1 Nov-31 Jan	Earn
1 Sept-15 Feb	1 Nov-15 Feb	Echaig
1 Sept-15 Feb	1 Nov-15 Feb	Esk, North
1 Sept-15 Feb	1 Nov-15 Feb	Esk, South
27 Aug-10 Feb	1 Nov-10 Feb	Ewe
		(Isle of Harris (West))
27 Aug-10 Feb	6 Oct-10 Feb	Findhorn
10 Sept-24 Feb	1 Nov-24 Feb	Fleet (Kirkcudbright)
10 Sept-24 Feb	1 Nov-24 Feb	Fleet (Sutherland)
27 Aug-10 Feb	1 Nov-10 Feb	Forss
27 Aug-10 Feb	1 Nov-31 Jan	Forth
1 Sept-15 Feb	1 Nov-15 Feb	Fyne, Shira & Aray (Loch Fyne)
10 Sept-24 Feb	1 Nov-24 Feb	Girvan
27 Aug-10 Feb	1 Nov-10 Feb	Glenelg
27 Aug-10 Feb	1 Nov-10 Feb	Gour
27 Aug-10 Feb	1 Nov-10 Feb	Greiss, Laxdale or Thunga
27 Aug-10 Feb	1 Nov-10 Feb	Grudie or Dionard
27 Aug-10 Feb	1 Nov-10 Feb	Gruinard and Little Gruinard
27 Aug-10 Feb	1 Oct-11 Jan	Halladale, Strathy, Naver & Borgie
27 Aug-10 Feb	1 Oct-10 Jan	Helmsdale
27 Aug-10 Feb	1 Oct-11 Jan	Hope and Polla or Strathbeg
10 Sept-24 Feb	1 Nov-24 Feb	Howmore
27 Aug-10 Feb	1 Nov-10 Feb	Inchard
10 Sept-24 Feb	1 Nov-24 Feb	Inner (on Jura)
27 Aug-10 Feb	1 Nov-10 Feb	Inver
10 Sept-24 Feb	1 Nov-24 Feb	Iora (on Arran)
10 Sept-24 Feb	1 Nov-24 Feb	Irvine & Garnock
27 Aug-10 Feb	1 Nov-10 Feb	Kannaird
27 Aug-10 Feb	1 Nov-10 Feb	Kilchoan
27 Aug-10 Feb	1 Nov-10 Feb	Kinloch (Kyle of Tongue)
27 Aug-10 Feb	1 Nov-10 Feb	Kirkaig
27 Aug-10 Feb	1 Nov-10 Feb	Kishorn
27 Aug-10 Feb	1 Oct-10 Jan	Kyle of Sutherland
10 Sept-24 Feb	1 Nov-24 Feb	Laggan & Sorn (Isle of Islay)
27 Aug-10 Feb	1 Nov-10 Feb	Laxford

Net Fishing	Rod Fishing	River District	Net Fishing	Rod Fishing	River District
27 Aug-10 Feb	1 Nov-10 Feb	Little Loch Broom	27 Aug-10 Feb	1 Nov-10 Feb	Pennygowan or
27 Aug-10 Feb	1 Nov-10 Feb	Loch Duich			Glenforsa & Aros
27 Aug-10 Feb	1 Nov-10 Feb	Loch Luing			
27 Aug-10 Feb	17 Oct-10 Feb	Loch Roag	27 Aug-10 Feb	1 Nov-10 Feb	Resort
27 Aug-10 Feb	1 Nov-10 Feb	Lochy	1 Sept-15 Feb	1 Nov-15 Feb	Ruel
27 Aug-10 Feb	16 Oct-10 Feb	Lossie			
10 Sept-24 Feb	1 Nov-24 Feb	Luce	27 Aug-10 Feb	1 Nov-10 Feb	Sanda
27 Aug-10 Feb	1 Nov-10 Feb	Lussa	27 Aug-10 Feb	1 Nov-10 Feb	Scaddle
		(Isle of Mull)	10 Sept-24 Feb	1 Nov-24 Feb	Shetland Isles
			27 Aug-10 Feb	1 Nov-10 Feb	Shiel
27 Aug-10 Feb	1 Nov-10 Feb	Moidart	27 Aug-10 Feb	1 Nov-10 Feb	Sligachan
27 Aug-10 Feb	1 Nov-10 Feb	Morar	27 Aug-10 Feb	1 Nov-10 Feb	Snizort
20 Sept-24 Feb	1 Nov-24 Feb	Mullangaren,	27 Aug-10 Feb	1 Oct-10 Feb	Spey
		Horasary and	10 Sept-24 Feb	1 Nov-24 Feb	Stinchar
		Lochnaciste	27 Aug-10 Feb	1 Nov-10 Feb	Sunart
		(Isle of North Uist)			(except Earn)
			21 Aug- 4 Feb	16 Oct-14 Jan	Tay
27 Aug-10 Feb	1 Oct-10 Feb	Nairn	27 Aug-10 Feb	6 Oct-10 Jan	Thurso
27 Aug-10 Feb	1 Nov-10 Feb	Nell, Feochan	27 Aug-10 Feb	1 Nov-10 Feb	Torridon
		and Euchar	15 Sept-14 Feb	1 Dec-31 Jan	Tweed
27 Aug-10 Feb	16 Oct-14 Jan	Ness			
10 Sept-24 Feb	1 Dec-24 Feb	Nith	10 Sept-24 Feb	1 Nov- 9 Feb	Ugie
			27 Aug-10 Feb	1 Nov-10 Feb	Ullapool
10 Sept-24 Feb	1 Nov-24 Feb	Orkney Isles	10 Sept-24 Feb	1 Dec-24 Feb	Urr
27 Aug-10 Feb	1 Nov-10 Feb	Ormsary (Loch			
		Killisport), Loch	27 Aug-10 Feb	1 Nov-10 Feb	Wick
		Head & Stornoway			
			10 Sept-24 Feb	1 Nov-10 Feb	Ythan

There is no close season for coarse fishing.

THE FORTH FISHERY CONSERVATION TRUST

The Trust was formed in August 1987, with the aim of improving all the fisheries within the Forth catchment area which extends from Fifeness to Balquidder in the north, and Loch Katrine to Torness in the south. The initial aim was to purchase a boat to assist the Forth District Salmon Fishery Board stop illegal netting of salmon on the Estuary.

Within twelve weeks two 18ft high speed launches were acquired for use by the new Superintendent Water Bailiff, Ian Baird, and the impact on the illegal netting operations has been dramatic. The River Teith and its tributaries experienced a good run of spring salmon and sea trout are running through almost unhindered.

The Trust has also stimulated discussions on salmon poaching and fish conservation at the hghest legal and government levels and will continue that dialogue.

Although a number of enthusiastic clubs have worked hard to open up fisheries, to restock and protect them, the Forth catchment area remains a virtually untapped fishery. These could be developed to provide leisure, tourism and employment for the region.

There are three major tasks the Trust wishes to undertake.

1. To increase efforts to eliminate all illegal fishing both on the estuary and throughout the whole river system.
2. To identify ownership of all stretches of water and fisheries in the area so that more effective supervision may be introduced.
3. To review the existing population and habitat of all fish species and assess the potential for increasing their numbers throughout the area.

This information will help all clubs, landowners and local inhabitants to make the best possible use of available resources and improve the quality of salmon, sea trout and coarse fishing throughout the Forth catchment area.

SCOTTISH FRESHWATER FISH RECORDS

Bream   5 lb 15 oz. 12 dr = 2.714 kg. Castle Loch, Dumfriesshire. H. Wood, 1973.

Carp   21 lb 14 oz. = 9.800 kg, Private water, Mike Heath. 1988.

Dace   1 lb 3 oz. 8 dr. = 0.55 kg. River Tweed, Coldstream, G. Keech, 1979.

Eel   5 lb 8 oz. = 2.495 kg, Loch Ochiltree, T. May, 1987.

Goldfish   1 lb 9 oz. = 0.709 kg, Forth & Clyde Canal, B. Stevenson, 1978.

Grayling   2 lb 14 oz. 2 dr. = 0.709 kg, Lyne Water, R. Brown, 1987.

Perch   4 lb 0 oz. 4 dr. = 1.82 kg, Loch Lubnaig, J. Stevenson, 1984.

Pike   47 lb 11 oz. = 21.631 kg, Loch Lomond, Tom Morgan, 1947.

Roach   2 lb 11 oz. = 1.219 kg, Private Water, Paul Russel, 1987.

Tench   4 lb 14 oz. = 2.211 kg, Spectacle Loch, B. Gilbert, 1983.

No records exist for the following species. Claims can be made over the qualifying weights:

Barbel	1 lb.	**Gudgeon**	4 oz.
Bleak	2 oz.	**Rudd**	2 lb.
Cat Fish	1 lb.	**Ruffe**	4 oz.
Chub	2 lb.	**Silver Bream**	8 oz.
Crucian Carp	2 lb.	**Zander**	1 lb.
Golden Orfe	2 lb.		

How to claim a record:

1. No claims will be considered for coarse fish which have been killed.

2. The claim should be made on a form available from the Development Secretary of the SFCA. The Development Committee must be satisfied by the evidence that the fish was correctly identified and weighed, and was captured by fair angling.

3. New claims will be considered subject to the following minimum requirements:
a) Photographs of the fish must be available.
b) The scales must be certified as being accurate.
c) Witnesses will assist the claim and if possible these should be experienced anglers.

SCOTTISH FEDERATION FOR COARSE ANGLING

The Federation was formed in 1975 to promote and encourage the sport of Coarse Angling in Scotland. It is recognised by the Scottish Sports Council as being the governing body for Coarse Angling throughout Scotland.

Objects and Functions
To obtain waters for coarse angling.
To assist with fisheries management.
To assist with stocking of waters.
To promote and develop coarse angling in Scotland.
To promote and organise competitions and league matches.
To provide team representation at the World Championships (CIPS-FIPS-ED).
To organise international events for Scottish anglers.

Members
At present, seven clubs are affiliated to the Federation. Individual membership of the Federation is available although it is preferred that individuals join clubs affiliated to the Federation. The annual subscription for Club Membership of the SFCA is £25 with a joining fee of £12.50.
Individual membership is offered at £3.00.

Coaching and Courses
Some SFCA member clubs hold 'in class' coaching sessions for novice anglers, while others operate 'on the bank' instruction thus providing knowledge under varying conditions.

Committee Structure
The affairs of the Federation are at present conducted by a Management Committee comprising the Chairman, Hon. Secretary, Hon. Treasurer and Club representatives.
A development and a Match Angling Committee also exist to deal with specific projects.

Office Bearers
Chairman
Jim Cairnie, 54 Watling Street, Uddingston, Nr. Glasgow.
Tel: Uddingston 817764.

Secretary
Jim Brown, 13 Boghead Road, Kirkintilloch, Nr. Glasgow.
Tel: 041-776 6741.

Treasurer
Tony Ball, 92 Westergreens Avenue, Kirkintilloch, Nr. Glasgow.
Tel: 041 775 2964.

Development Committee Chairman
Fraser Simpson, 3 Newrose Avenue, Bellshill, Lanarkshire.
Tel: (0698) 748603.

Development Committee Secretary
Mark Hutchison, 84 Rockburn Crescent, Bellshill, Lanarkshire.
Tel: (0698) 746260.

Match Committee Chairman (Team Manager)
Alistair Keir, Tigh Na Fluers, M11 O Gryfe Road, Bridge of Weir, Renfrewshire.
Tel: Bridge of Weir 612580.

Match Committee Secretary
Dave Brampton.

Press Officer
D. Carnell, 6 Kathleen Park, Helensburgh.
Tel: (0463) 78725.

Central Match Angling Club:
C. Palmer, 64 Dawson Place, Bo'ness.
Tel: Bo'ness 823953.

Edinburgh Angling Club:
Ron Woods, 23 Terragles, Penicuik.
Tel: (0968) 74792.

Forth and Clyde Coarse Angling Club:
P. Morrisey, 18 Daiglen. Tillicoultry, Clacks.
Tel: 0259 50757.

Glasgow Match Angling Club:
F. Hetherington, 4 Rosebery Place, Eliburn, Livingston.

Glasgow & West of Scotland Regional Association of the Pike Anglers Club of Great Britain:
Ralston MacPherson, 17 Barhill Court, Kirkintilloch.

Kirkintilloch Angling Club:
J. Brown, 13 Boghead Road, Kirkintilloch, Nr. Glasgow.
Tel: 041-776 6741.

Linlithgow Angling Club:
E. Gilbert, 12 Claredon Road, Linlithgow.
Tel: Linlithgow 845115.

Milton Angling Club:
D. Morrison, 112 Scaraway Street, Milton, Glasgow.

Motherwell Angling Club:
W. Williamson, 24 Lindum Crescent, Motherwell.

Strathclyde Angling Club:
John Rae, 86 Graham Street, Wishaw.
Tel: Wishaw 359655.

Competition
Summer and Winter Club
Leagues are held each year.
Overall results provide the
Scottish Team and
Individual champions.
Scottish National Junior
Open Championship.

All Scotland championship -
Scottish residents only.

Scottish Federation Open.

Scottish Federation Cup -
Federation members only.

Home International Series.
International friendlies
against other countries.

Participation in the World
Championships.

Scottish Pole Angling
Championship.
Member clubs also arrange
club match programmes
throughout spring, summer
and autumn.

Specimen Group
A newly formed and active
element of the Federation.
Objectives include:
Providing an efficiently
managed fishery befitting
the Federation membership.
Continually updating the
'Available Waters Register'
for the benefits of all
Scottish coarse anglers and
visitors.

THE S.F.C.A. COARSE ANGLER'S COUNTRY CODE

1. Never throw away hooks, line or shot.
   Take them home and get rid of them properly.

2. Plastic bags can kill.
   Take away all rubbish from your spot,
   even if it was there before.

3. Know the fishery rules and return all coarse fish,
   including pike and eels, unharmed.

4. Help protect wildlife, plants and trees.
   Fish well away from birds' nesting places.

5. Place your keepnet to hold your fish properly.
   Stake it out if you can.

6. Use barbless hooks when you can.
   Take care when casting.

7. Park cars away from entrances.
   Keep to paths and close all gates.

8. Carbon rods conduct electricity.
   Keep well away from overhead power lines.

9. Don't light fires.
   Report any sign of pollution.

10. Keep dogs under control.
    Don't disturb the peace of the countryside.

DEFEND YOUR SPORT
JOIN THE SCOTTISH FEDERATION FOR COARSE ANGLING

IN PURSUIT OF THE HUMBLE COD

BY ALAN SPENCE

Big headed and pot bellied, the cod or codling can hardly be described as the most attractive of fish. Even the close family cousins, pollack and coalfish are sleek and streamlined in comparison to the portly shape of the family head.

Codling, the term refers to cod below 10lbs in weight and are to be found all around the coasts of Scotland at some time of the year. Mainly a fish of deep water, being less common in sandy estuaries than in the open sea, where they seem to prefer depths of water in excess of thirty feet.

Humble as the cod may be it forms the foundation for much of the sea angling sport around Scotland from Tweed to the Solway. Prolific breeders, cod lay their eggs by the thousand, although like all fish bred in the wild only a small proportion of these are destined for maturity.

It comes as no surprise to find that the codling has an appetite matching its mouth and belly, nor is it fussy upon what it dines. Just about everything which swims above or crawls upon the seabed forms part of its diet at some time of the year.

This may range from the shore crab in its soft state found among the kelp beds in summer, to shoals of small fish of every species throughout the year. In between there may be a variety of molluscs, small squid and octopus and sundry marine worms.

By its shape the cod is ill equipped as a streamlined fighting fish when hooked, being more capable of a marked dogged resistance rather than long line smoking runs. Like many instances in sea angling however the tackle required is to overcome the circumstances of capture rather than subdue the fish itself.

Take for example shore angling along the coast from Berwickshire northwards. Here the favourite haunt of the inshore codling is among the hardest roughest ground. Places which consist of long reefs or scaurs, drying at low tide but where the codling forage as the flood tide surges inshore.

Over scaurs at times long cast is necessary to place the bait where the codling are feeding. A sinker snagging situation if ever there was one, requiring a six or eight ounce lead to achieve casting distance. To fish in these circumstances with lines of below 25lbs breaking strain leads to inevitable tackle losses, not that heavy lines guarantee its avoidance.

To cast heavy leads a powerful rod is required, far in excess of that needed to subdue the average codling expected. From some rock stances deep water may be encountered close inshore, where long casting is unnecessary to reach feeding grounds. This deep water among rocks usually has a sea bed foul or rugged in the extreme where again heavy tackle is needed to break out the gear. Most angling for codling over deep water inshore takes place with a paternoster rig, that is the hook is set up on a short snood at a distance above the lead. There is an alternative method where a light rod and a minimum amount of lead can be employed, giving the codling an opportunity to give a much better account of itself.

Sliding float gear is perhaps mainly associated with pike fishing but is easily adapted to suit deep water around rocky sea gullies. Rather than launch into a long winded explanation on rigging the sliding float the sketch shows how this rig is set up.

Inshore in summer the codling assumes a different colour than when found offshore in deep water. This can be anything from a dirty muddy brown right through to golden kelp colour or even red when the bottom has weed of this colour. Summer codling feed extensively upon soft crabs, making it no surprise therefore to find that this is one of the best baits available for summer fishing.

Indeed so highly do some anglers rate the soft crab as a codling bait that in north east England many enthusiasts collect these during the summer months to freeze down for winter use. Other baits from the shore which the codling may sample are lug and ragworm plus mussel, hermit crab and razor fish.

While from the shore line the greater skills are required to capture codling, for every one caught from rock edge and beach ten will be taken by boat anglers. Afloat a similar problem to the shore angler faces the boatman. Again it is circumstantial where the bait must be presented on or near the sea bed in depths of water up to or indeed over twenty fathoms (120ft) with a tide strength of up to three knots.

It is futile to fish for a near bottom dweller with the bait presented in mid-water. Therefore weight to get the bait to the feeding fish is required. Sometimes in deep water and strong tides a surprising

Some anglers have a definite touch, even when dealing with the hungry pot bellied codling.

amount of weight is necessary - a pound of lead is not too much in some circumstances. That is extreme however as in most instances between six and twelve ounces will suffice.

When fishing on a charter boat it pays to keep the end rig simple, due to the possibility of mutual entanglement with fellow passengers' gear. Two or three hook paternoster with the hooks on six to nine inch snoods attached to simply blood loops is bad to beat. Useful also for changing rigs and undoing tangles are link swivels.

By fitting link swivels at the join between main line and trace and again as a lead link it makes it possible to detach these instantly, a major contributor to bonhomie and fraternity onboard a crowded charter boat.

What of baits afloat? Like its brother among the inshore kelp beds the deep water codling is not fussy. It will in fact just about eat anything, yet there are some days when it appears to have a fixation on a particular bait.

Marine worms and mussel are favourites among natural baits, the soft crab is less favoured in deep water, yet it can have its days in inshore grounds. What does enter the scene afloat are artificial baits in various forms.

Movement, in the absence of scent from an artificial bait is the key to success. Hard to beat in this line is the traditional cod fly, one or two dyed chicken feathers whipped to a cod hook. A modern version is the rubber squid, available in a range of hues which no mother squid ever expected its offsprings to adopt, but with soft pliable legs, or are they arms.

Thirdly there is the jig or lure, an elongated sinker armed with a treble hook at the business end. In fact the jig is an angling version of the "ripper" once used by commercial fishermen before that industry went high tech. Rippers as the name suggests were armed with a multitude of hooks. These were worked by pulling them swiftly up, before allowing them to drop to the sea bed and fish could be hooked on either the upward or the free falling down motion.

It would appear at first that fishing for codling means merely dropping the terminal tackle to the sea bed and winding in the fish as they are hooked. At times when shoals are dense this certainly can be the case. Yet at others there are anglers who take fish after fish while their neighbours remain blank.

Even when using similar baits it is not unusual for one angler to outfish all others onboard. More than anything else this boils down to presentation, the correct weight to hold the line vertical to the bottom with well baited hooks on snoods of a length to match the circumstances.

Similar instances are found when fishing with artificial baits, there are always those who are more successful than others. Yes even for the humble cod a certain sensitivity of touch is required.

To see your neighbour pulling in fish after fish while you yourself fail to register can be a harrowing experience. It is often the case when this happens that the fish are taking on the drop, or are feeding a few feet above the seabed. Hence the reason why an angler once having an initial success continues to outfish his companions.

Codling adopt two methods of feeding. One is to grub along the sea bed, the barbel below the chin is in fact a sensitive feeler to assist this manoeuvre. Here the fish chomps upon sundry lesser examples of marine life, worms, crabs and crustacea or even an unfortunate smaller member of its own species.

Again codling pursue shoals of small bait fish such as sandeels and herring fry, which may be swimming some distance above the sea bed. It is under these circumstances that artificial baits come into their own, the flash of the lure and movement of feather imitating the darting movement of the bait fish.

Whatever the artificial bait used they must be "worked" raising and lowering the rod tip drawing jigs and flies up then sent fluttering back down through the water.

One tip to remember when the boat contacts a shoal of fry-feeding codling is to always try and keep one set of tackle at least in the water. When fishing with the ripper, professional fishermen always considered that this was essential to maintain the shoal moving with the boat. Even if fish were already hooked, one line would be left down until the others were returned to the water.

Bottom grubbing codling are less likely to be taken with artificial baits as are the fish feeders. Nor is the fishing likely to be so intense as is the case with fry feeders when in the latter instance codling may be caught three at a time, or if a trace of six feathers is employed every hook filled.

Without codling, sea angling on the east coast at least would be a non starter. After a lean 1988 signs are that fishing is due to improve over the coming two years. Not only have catches of mature codling improved this year, but there are many juvenile fish on the ground. The basis for many sizzling home caught fish suppers in the future.

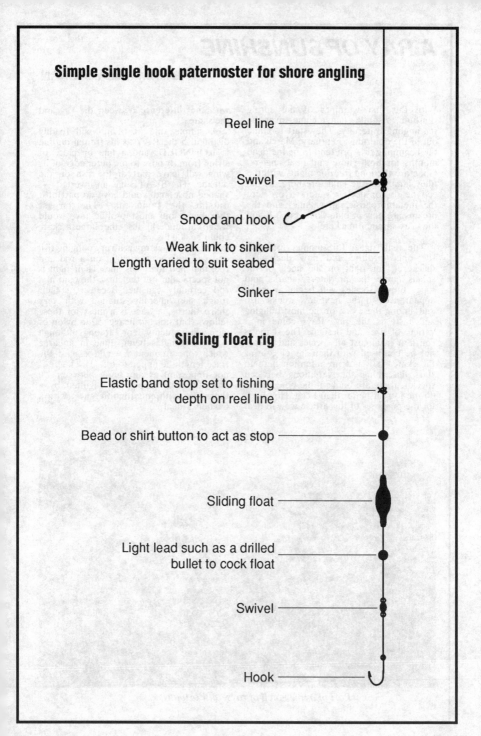

Simple single hook paternoster for shore angling

Reel line

Swivel

Snood and hook

Weak link to sinker
Length varied to suit seabed

Sinker

Sliding float rig

Elastic band stop set to fishing
depth on reel line

Bead or shirt button to act as stop

Sliding float

Light lead such as a drilled
bullet to cock float

Swivel

Hook

A RAY OF SUNSHINE

BY JIM MCLANAGHAN

With the first warnings of the spring sunshine, a subtle change comes over the sea angling fraternity. They start to come out of the doldrums. February, March and the beginning of April tend to be the dead months for both shore and boat anglers. Gone are the long freezing nights with the tilley lamps on the cold foreshore, as the cod heads for deeper waters. Now with the metamorphosis, all changes and the dreams are now of blue skies, big fish and the tasty summer mackerel.

The real trigger for summer fishing is the once prolific and now decimated mackerel, for right on the heels of the shoals come the predators, sharks and tope. Other species will begin to make appearances in the next few weeks also and among these one of the most obliging and tasty is the ray. Rays come in a variety of sizes and designs. The shape is constant in almost all species and should not be confused with their larger cousins the skate. It is not my intention here to start describing the variations between species, there are books to be bought that do the job far better than I can. However, for the purposes of this article we will deal with the difference between the ray and the skate.

A simple rule of thumb will readily distinguish the RAY as his frontal outline is ROUNDED, and a line or piece of string from its nose to the outer edge of its wing will leave part of the fish on the outside. The SKATE has an inverted 'V' shaped nose and would have no part of it outside the same line. The largest thornback, our most prolific ray, would weigh around 40 lbs, the largest skate could be 400 lbs.

The thornback ray is a very obliging fish and can give great delight on a rod and reel matched to 20 lbs line. Their fight is not spectacular but the curve they put in a rod certainly can be. Because of their rough skin liberally studded with very sharp thorns, a trace is a must for these fellows, but not too heavy. 50 lb nylon or wire will be plenty, 2 or 3 ft long, although if the angling is being done in an area which tope frequent I would suggest the trace length be upped to 6 ft. Hook size is not important as any hook between 1/0 and 10/0 will happily be engulfed by a thornback with equal indifference, with a 6/0 being ideal.

Part of a fine catch of rays, off Portpatrick.

Baits pose no problems when thinking of rays and any meal from a whole mackerel down to a few tasty lugworms will serve to whet the appetite of this prodigious eater. See what I mean about being obliging but the best is yet to come.

One of the biggest problems any angler faces is getting the fish to actually engulf the hook and strike before it rejects the offering. Hooking a ray is probably the most simple way of taking any fish I know, all it requires is more time and he'll hook himself. When a ray reaches a bait he flops down on it and pins it under him. This will cause your rod - which should be out of gear with the ratchet on - to give a good jump. At all costs leave the rod be, don't get fidgety or you may strike too soon. Remember at this stage he's only lying on the bait. He then has to get the bait to his mouth, which of course is on the underside of the fish, and starts turning and squirming to do so. The result is more rattles on your rod but, as before, leave it - have a cup of tea. When he at last manages to get the bait into his mouth the fish will then move off. This is your signal, so pick up the rod, put your reel in gear and hit him hard again and again remembering his mouth is very tough. A ray doesn't so much fight as put up a strong resistance and in a tide race you can be very surprised at the struggle put up by a medium size fish. Like a kite he catches the tide and uses it to his every advantage, stripping line off relentlessly in his wild surge away from the boat.

If the angler doesn't fancy a supper of ray wings, the fish should be returned to be caught another day or, as has happened to myself, twenty minutes later. That fish was thrown back a second time and it wasn't until much later - too late - I realized it would have been a Scottish record undulate ray. Ever felt a fool?

If you can find a recipe for rays or skates wings give them a try. Properly cooked, they are delicious and no bones to worry over. Only the wings need be used and care should be taken when skinning them - as I have already mentioned it is not called a thornback for nothing. It may seem incongruous to state the obvious, but never, never put your fingers in a skate or ray's mouth, even a dead one. Its lips are covered with hundreds of tiny teeth all pointing backwards and if your hold on the fish slips it can make a dreadful mess. That point apart, they are not dangerous fish and no-one, not even a boy, should view the prospects of a tussle with one of these most obliging fish with anything other than relish.

Dave Cardie handles a ray gently prior to returning it alive.

Luce Bay and the Mull of Galloway are two venues which produce these fish in good satisfying numbers to the visiting boat angler. They are also caught here from the shoreline with some hefty specimens to be taken close in. Top spots in the summer months will undoubtedly be Cailliness buoy off Drummore and the clean ground out from Portpatrick. Catches for a dinghy can often go into double figures, with fifteen pounders to be expected.

Commercial catches show that this fish can be caught all round Scotland, even in small sheltered bays. Anchoring is a favoured tactic for ray fishing for several reasons. Firstly, it allows the tide to wash the scent of the bait a long long way and these distant cousins of the shark have a prodigious sense of smell. They will come from afar. Secondly, since a long flowing trace is being utilised fished hard on the bottom, a drift could result in unacceptably high tackle losses. Thirdly, it is a lovely relaxing way to sit in the sun and watch and wait for that first nod of the rod tip to tell you dinner has come to call.

A worthwhile investment whilst angling in any ray waters is a book on identification. With so many separate species it is too easy to make a mistake and throw away a record - as I have discovered. Being conscious of the various species lends more interest to a day's angling and widens the angler's horizon. For a fish which does not "fight" well in the accepted sense of the word, the thornback and rays in general are much sought after. The thornback heralds the arrival of summer and after the bleak angling days of the spring they are in name and manner truly a Ray of Sunshine.

TAKE YOUR PLAICE

BY JIM MCLANAGHAN

One man's meat is another man's poison, an old saying which in general terms shows how each individual has his own tastes and preferences. Nowhere is this more true than in the sport of angling with each angler having his favourite tackle, baits, venues, etc. With all this specialisation it is somewhat of a surprise that the vast majority of sea anglers tend to go slightly glass eyed when we talk of a fish with an average weight of possibly only 2 lbs - the plaice.

It is hard to understand what the attraction of this little fish is. True, it makes lovely eating, it is a very obliging feeder and is a very handsome fish, but that's not it all. On all but the very lightest of tackle they have little or no sporting value but they can attract the big fish man as surely as a rubby dubby.

Plaice tend to be rather gregarious - or appear to be so - since they tend to congregate on their own particular patch of ocean, ideally a sandy gravelly bank over which a slight tide is running. This patch may be very small. Indeed, many are so small that they have never been properly realised as plaice marks. This anomaly can occur when a mark is fished on the drift and the baits may be across and past the mark before the fish can have a crack at the bait. On the other hand, I have taken one or two plaice in my local bay - on the drift - at a specific mark. If I were to anchor I feel I could produce some excellent bags or increase my catches.

Plaice are a very widespread species and can be taken from virtually any port in Scotland, a fact which is borne out by commercial catches. I feel it is possibly commercial influences which tend to keep anglers very quiet about any good plaice marks as a couple of sweeps with a trawler could obliterate a good mark. One mark I know of, which is safe from any trawler, is at Port Logan on the Mull of Galloway. The beach stretches from the harbour northwards to a small white house about ¾ mile and this is good plaice ground from both shore and boat up to about 600 yds out. Yet another spot is Lendalfoot south of Girvan. Large reefs here protect the fishing and one angler I know has taken 500 lbs of cod and plaice in two days, fishing from a small dinghy close inshore.

The most prolific mark of which I know is at Portpatrick and it has to be fished to be believed. The plaice average about 1½ lbs with occasional fish to 6 lbs showing, but for sheer quantity it must rate as one of the best plaice marks in Britain. The fishing is directly related to the tides and on most days will allow only 1½ hours fishing, but what fishing! On one occasion I timed an angler, local skipper Bryn Watson, who showed me the mark, and his bait rested on the bottom for an average of only 20 seconds before being scoffed. This hotspot is not too large, possibly 200 yds long, but I have seen 3 anglers take 2 boxes of fish in one day. That is 12 stone of good plaice. Since Bryn showed me this spot and for conservation reasons, I will not reveal the location. Bryn can be contacted on Portpatrick 681 if you want to try it firsthand.

As I mentioned earlier, each angler has his own ideas on how each species/situation should be tackled. Well, thankfully for plaice it doesn't matter too much. Being a bottom feeding species any reasonable presentation, as long as it is on or very near the bottom, will result in fish. Worm baits are an obvious favourite, with shellfish being useful as a standby or for cocktails. Mackerel I have found to be quite good. It has the added visual attraction but it must be fresh or it will be ripped off the hook.

As in most forms of fishing, a bit of movement is added incentive as it initially draws the fish's attention. To this end I always use a small 1" spoon on my terminal tackle with 18" of line either side to the hook and french boom. A small 3 oz lead, 10 lbs line, with matching multiplier and a 9½ ft spinning rod make up what is, in my opinion, the ideal outfit. Using this I cast well away, possibly 50 yds and, after settling the weight on the bottom, I start a very slow retrieve. Upon feeling the rattling bite I pay out a few feet of loose line and give it plenty of time. The next bite that takes up the slack I strike gently and proceed to play the fish. This is a technique that I use for all flatties as I find that they are not so fussy as other fish in their feeding habits. Give them the bait, the movement and the time and they're yours.

Another equally productive method, but one which can only safely be used at anchor, is the legered paternoster. This is a simple three hook paternoster style rig but legered right on the bottom with the weight above the hooks. This is a favourite rig with anyone who has a freezer to fill as two and three fish at a time are a probability rather than a possibility.

Some hotspots tend to produce big fish, others plenty of pan sized fish, although even in the latter, big fish do show occasionally. Two marks of which I know, Daly Bay and, just round the corner, at Lady Bay in Loch Ryan are good examples. Daly Bay seems to consist of mainly fish of 1 - 2½ lbs but plenty of them, whereas Lady Bay on the south side of Loch Ryan, has a smattering of fish but produces them up to 6 lbs. There does not appear to be any logical reason for this apparent division but both are equally good to fish.

Bryn Watson is, at present, trying to find a mark which one ancient mariner claims "is paved with plaice like dustbin lids". I hope it is and I hope Bryn finds it. The prospects of a plaice that size is enough to make any angler sign the pledge. The British Record for this species stands at over 10 lbs, a mindboggling fish taken from Gairloch in Wester Ross. It is one record which must be nigh on impossible to beat - OR IS IT?

If this mark ever materialises at Portpatrick, I shall be among the first looking for a "dustbin lid". As I said, no-one is immune from "plaice fever" and I have it just thinking of them.

Anchoring can produce good bags of plaice from even a small mark.

SCOTTISH FEDERATION OF SEA ANGLERS

OFFICIALS

President/Chairman Mr. Martin L. Rowlands,
9, Rosemount Crescent, Newcastle,
Glenrothes, KY6 2QQ. Tel: (0592) 751383

Vice-Presidents Mr. D.M. MacKay,
Flat 11B, Kirkmichael Road, Helensburgh
G84 7NH. Tel: (0436) 6980

Mr. R.B. Walker , Springvale Cottage,
Halket Road, Dunlop, Ayrshire KA3 4EE.
Tel: (050 585) 593

Hon. Treasurer Mr. R.F. Keltie,
76 Stewart Avenue, Bo'ness, West Lothian
EH51 9NW. Tel: (0506) 826274

**Secretary/
Administrator** Mrs. Helen C. Murray,
Caledonia House, South Gyle,
Edinburgh, EH12 9DQ. Tel: 031-317 7192.

Hon. Fish Recorder Mr. Gordon T. Morris,
8 Burt Avenue, Kinghorn, Fife.
Tel: (0592) 890055

REGIONAL SECRETARIES.

Clyde Mr. A.P. Brown, 32 Swisscot Walk, Fairhill,
Hamilton, ML3 8DX. Tel: (0698) 427085).

Central Mrs. Margaret McCallum,
58 Pottery Street, Kirkcaldy
KY1 3EU. Tel: (0592) 51710.

West Mr. David Neil,
30 Woodfield Road, Ayr.
Tel: (0292) 266549.

North East Mr. Paul King,
Harbour House, 69 Harbour Street,
Hopeman, Morayshire.

Eastern Mr. David G. Rice, 1/2 St. Leonards Street,
Edinburgh EH8 9RN.

Highlands & Islands Mr. J. McInnes, 24 Lochalsh Road,
Inverness. Tel: (0463) 222471.

Western Isles Mr. F.G. Jefferson, No. 1 Sheshader Point,
Isle of Lewis.

Why Not Join A Club?

THE FOLLOWING CLUBS AND ASSOCIATIONS ARE IN MEMBERSHIP OF THE FEDERATION.

Aberdeen Airport Angling Club
Hon. Sec. S. Cameron, Esq., 67 Fairview Circle, Bridge of Don, Aberdeen.
Aberdeen Thistle Sea Angling Club
Hon. Sec. J. Reid, Esq., 34 Gordon Place, Bridge of Don, Aberdeen AB2 8RA. (Tel. 0224 703429).
Albion Sea Angling Club
Hon. Sec. A. Semple Esq., 13 Ashgill Road, Lambhill, Glasgow G22 6QJ.
Ardrossan & District Sea Angling Club
Hon. Sec. I.B. McClymont Esq., 41 Corrie Crescent, Saltcoats, Ayrshire KA21 6JL. (Tel. 0294 61830).
Arran Sea Angling Association
Hon. Sec. Mrs. S. Alison, 7 Brathwic Terrace, Brodick, Arran KA27 8BW. (Tel. 0770 2613).
Atlantis Sea Angling Club
Hon. Sec. A. Barton, Esq., A Chomraich Duntrune, By Dundee DD4 0PP. (Tel. Kellas 374)
Ayr Sea Angling Club
Hon. Sec. S. Cresswell Esq., 25 Whitehall Avenue, Prestwick, Ayrshire KA9 1HT.
"856" Sea Angling Club
Hon. Sec. F. Leonard Esq., 64 High Street, Innerleithen, Peeblesshire EH44 6HF.
Beachcasters Sea Angling Club
Hon. Sec. Miss Joanne Simpson, 98 Glenkirk Drive, Glasgow G15.
Bell Rock Sea Angling Club
Hon. Sec. G. Harrison Esq., 35 St. Thomas Crescent, Arbroath, Angus DD11 1SR.
Bellshill Sea Angling Club
Hon. Sec. Gordon M. Sloan, Esq., 2 Strathview Road, Bellshill, Lanarkshire ML4 2UA.
Breakaway Sea Angling Club
Hon. Sec. A.N. Fennell Esq., 37 Broomhill Crescent, West Freeland, Erskine, Ayrshire.
Brechin Sea Angling Club
Hon. Sec. S. Melrose, Esq., 72 Caledonian Place, Montrose, Angus.
Britoil (Glasgow) Fishing Club
Hon. Sec. Don Anderson Esq., 301 St. Vincent Street, Glasgow G2 5DD.
Broughty Ferry Ex-Service Club Sea Angling Club
Hon. Sec. J. Croal Esq., 2 Strachan Avenue, West Ferry Park, Dundee DD5 1RE. (Tel. 0382 74223).
Bruntsfield Sea Angling Club
Hon. Sec. K.M. Gaffney Esq., 22 Baberton Mains Drive, Edinburgh EH14 3EA. (Tel. 031-442 1913).
Buckhaven & District Sea Angling Club
Hon. Sec. R. Paton, Esq., 46 West High Street, Buckhaven, Fife KY8 1AL.
Caithness Sea Angling Association
Hon. Sec. D.J. Proudfoot, Esq., 3 Bardnaclaven Place, Janetstown, Thurso. (Tel. 0847 64545).
Champion Shell, Rod & Gun Club
Hon. Sec. G. Boyd Esq., 2 Alexander Avenue, Stevenston, Ayrshire KA20 4BE.
Civil Service Sports Association
Hon. Sec. A. Ferguson Esq., Civil Service Sports Centre (Angling), Castle Road, Rosyth, Fife.
Clyde Specimen Hunters Sea Angling Club
Hon. Sec. J. Syme, Esq., 29 Dunbeth Court, Coatbridge ML5 3HF. (Tel. 0236 35076).
Cockenzie & Port Seton Royal British Legion Sea Angling Club
Hon. Sec. G. Strachan Esq., 11 Carlaverock Court, Tranent, East Lothian EH33 2PQ. (Tel. Tranent 610780).
Cupar, St. Andrews & District Sea Angling Club
Hon. Sec. J. O'Brien Esq., 40 King Street, Kirkcaldy, Fife. (Tel. Kirkcaldy 263065).
Daily Record & Sunday Mail Angling Club
Hon. Sec. J. McKie Esq., c/o Buying Dept., 40 Anderston Quay, Glasgow G3 8DA. (Tel. 041-242 3280).
Dalbeattie & District Sea Angling Club
Hon. Sec. J. Moran Esq., 12 Church Crescent, Dalbeattie, Kirkcudbrightshire
Dingwall British Legion Angling Club
Hon. Sec. D. Bruce Esq., Royal British Legion (Scotland), High Street, Dingwall, Ross-shire.
"Drifters" Sea Angling Club
Hon. Sec. A. Kelly, Esq., 19 Woodburn Grove, Dalkeith, Midlothian.
Drumfork Sea Angling Club
Hon. Sec. W. Donald Esq., 12 Pladda Way, Clyde Arran Estate, Helensburgh, Dunbartonshire.
Dysart Sailing Club Sea Angling Section
Hon. Sec. Mrs. Yuonne R.E. Brown, 56 Woodend Road, Auchterderran, Cardenden KY5 0NH. (interim)
Eastern Sea Angling Club
Hon. Sec. J. Gordon Esq., 42 Pennelton Place, Bo'mains, Bo'ness, West Lothian.
East Kilbride Inland Revenue Angling Club
Hon. Sec. T. McCormick, Esq., 59 Silvertonhill Avenue, Hamilton, Lanarkshire ML3 7NB.
East Sutherland Sea Angling Club
Hon. Sec. E. Cousins Esq., 10 Tower Street, Golspie, Sutherland KW10 6SB. (Tel. 04083 3168).
Edina Sea Angling Club
Hon. Sec. R. Combe Esq., 38 Craiglockhart Terrace, Edinburgh EH14 1AJ. (Tel. 031-443 7209).
Edinburgh Masonic Club Sea Angling Section
Hon. Sec. D.H. Fairbairn Esq., The Lodge House, 200 Piersfield Terrace, Edinburgh EH8 7BN. (Tel. 031-669 2118).
Edinburgh Post Office Angling Club
Hon. Sec. D.M. Cox, Esq., 4 Merchiston Grove, Edinburgh EH11 1PP. (Tel. 031-346 1187).
Ellon & District British Legion Angling Club
Hon. Sec. A.J. Barker, Esq., 163 Western Avenue, Meiklemill, Ellon, Aberdeenshire AB4 9FX.
Fereneze Sea Angling Club
Hon. Sec. H. Kennedy, Esq., 4 Killoch Drive, Barrhead, Renfrewshire G78 2UU.
Ferranti Sea Angling Club
Hon. Sec. J. Christie Esq., 331 South Gyle Road, Edinburgh. (Tel. 031-443 7039).

Firth of Clyde Sea Angling Association
Hon. Sec. J. Galt Esq., 22 Helmsdale Avenue, Blantyre G72 3NY.
Flounders Sea Angling Club
Hon. Sec. Ian King, Esq., 60 Dundee Road, West Ferry, Dundee, Angus.
Forfar Seahawks Angling Club
Hon. Sec. I.C. Hardie Esq., 8 Western Sunnyside, Forfar, Angus DD8 1ED.
Forth Sea Angling Club
Hon. Sec. J. Ryan, Esq., 3 Cruickness Road, Inverkeithing, Fife. (Tel. 0383 419170).
Galloway Rodbenders Sea Angling Club
Hon. Sec. P. Paterson Esq., 65 Dalrymple Street, Stranraer, Wigtownshire. (Tel. 2344).
Gareloch & Loch Long Civil Service Angling Club
Hon. Sec. J.D. Blenkinsop, Esq., 16 Argyll Road, Rosneath, Helensburgh G84 0RP. (Tel. Clynder 831610).
Glaxo Sports & Social Club Angling Section
Hon. Sec. W. Philips Esq., 27 Grampian View, Ferryden, Montrose, Angus DD10 9SU.
Glenrothes Royal British Legion Sea Angling Club
Hon. Sec. P. Grehan Esq., 113 Inveraray Avenue, Glenrothes, Fife KY7 4QR.
Glen Urquhart Sea Angling Club
Hon. Sec. R. MacGregor Esq., 'Bernera' West Lewiston, Drumnadrochit, Highland Region.
Grange Hotel Sea Angling Club
Hon. Sec. M. Bennison Esq., Crosby Cottage, by Woodhead Farm, Dalry Road, West Kilbride.
Hamilton & District Sea Angling Club
Hon. Sec. A.P. Brown Esq., 32 Swisscot Walk, Fairhill, Hamilton ML3 8DX. (Tel. 427085).
Highland Sea Angling Club
Hon. Sec. D.J. MacKay Esq., 35 Dell Road, Inverness (Tel. Inverness 230136).
Hillside Sea Angling Club
Hon. Sec. B.H. Watt Esq., 3 Turnstone Court, Newtonhill, Stonehaven AB3 2QG. (Tel. 0569 30865).
Innes Angling Club
Hon. Sec. J. McInnes, Esq., 24 Lochalsh Road Inverness IV3 6HS. (Tel. 0463 222471).
Inveraray & District Sea Angling Club
Hon. Sec. J.B. Cullen, Esq., 22 Donich Park, Lochgoilhead, Argyll PA24 8AB. (Tel. 03013 430).
Irvine Sea Angling Club
Hon. Sec. W.R. Findlay, Esq., 54 Frew Terrace, Irvine, Ayrshire. (Tel. 0294 79582).
Isle of Skye Sea Angling Club
Hon. Sec. G. Smith Esq., 8 Urquhart Place, Portree, Isle of Skye IV51 9HJ. (Tel. 0478 2573).
Johnstone Castle Sea Angling Club
Hon. Sec. Mrs. E. Walker, Springvale Cottage, Halket Road, Lugton Dunlop, Ayrshire KA3 4EE. (Tel. 050 585 593).
Kelvin Sea Angling Club
Hon. Sec. D.A. Darroch Esq., 12 Hermitage Avenue, Knightswood, Glasgow G13 3QP.
Kinghorn Sea Angling Club
Hon. Sec. G.T. Morris Esq., 8 Burt Avenue, Kinghorn, Fife. (Tel. 0592 890055).
Kingsmills Sea Angling & Sporting Club
Fishing Convener, J. MacAulay, Esq., 12 Pict Avenue, Inverness. (Tel. 0463) 225398).
Leachkin Angling Club
Hon. Sec. W. Mackintosh, Esq., 16 Glengarry Road, Inverness IV3 6NJ.
Leith Sea Angling Club
Hon. Sec. W.A. Lyall, Esq., 35 McDonald Road, Edinburgh EH7 4LY. (Tel. 031-556 2925).
Leukaemia Unit Fund Angling Club
Hon. Sec. Mrs. J. Lambert, 47 Gyle Park Gardens, Edinburgh EH12 8NG.
Lochaber Sea Angling Club
Hon. Sec. A. Pyper Esq., 16 Farrow Drive, Corpath, Fort William, Inverness-shire PH33 7JW.
Locharbriggs & District Social Club Limited Sea Angling Club.
Hon. Sec. J. Kerr Esq., 70 Gledhill Crescent, Locharbriggs, Dumfries DG1 1XD.
Lochryan Sea Angling Association
Hon. Sec. T. Harrison Esq., 18 Brickfield Road, Stranraer DG9 7QZ.
Lothian & Borders Police, Sea Angling Section
Hon. Sec. P.C. A. McCreadie, Gayfield Square Police Station, Gayfield Square, Edinburgh 1.
Mates Sea Angling Club
Hon. Sec. R. Frain, Esq., 3 Wolseley Terrace, Edinburgh EH8 7AB.
Moorpark Sea Angling Club
Hon. Sec. S. Spalding, Esq., 12A Laggan Terrace, Kirklandneuk, Renfrew PA4 9DW.
Nairn Thistle Angling Club, Kirkcaldy
Hon. Sec. A. McCallum, Esq., 58 Pottery Street, Kirkcaldy, Fife KY1 3EU.
Norscot Angling Association
Hon. Sec. V. Goudie Esq., c/o Norscot Base, P.O. Box No. 6, Lerwick, Shetland. (Tel. 2983).
North Berwick Sea Angling Club
Hon. Sec. A. Macdonald, Esq., 2 Redhouse Cherries, Dirleton, East Lothian EH39 5EP.
Northfield Sea Angling Club
Hon. Sec. D. Thomson, Esq., 10 Rosevale Terrace, Edinburgh EH6 8AR.
Orkney Islands Sea Angling Association
Hon. Sec. J. Geddes Esq., Quarryfield Orphir, Orkney. (Tel. 085681 311).
Ormlie Lodge Angling Club
Hon. Sec. I. Myles Esq., 32 Sweyn Road, Thurso, Caithness KW14 7NW. (Tel. 0847 62000).
Park Bar Sea Angling Club
Hon. Sec. C. McDonald, Esq., 26 Forres Avenue, Kirkton, Dundee DD3 0EJ.
Peebles County Hotel Angling Club
Hon. Sec. W. Bisset, Esq., c/o County Hotel, 33 High Street, Peebles. (Tel. 0721 20595).
Philips Sea Angling Club
Hon. Sec. Mrs. A. Donnelly, 12 Avon Road, Larkhall, Strathclyde ML9 1PG. (Tel. 885790).
Possilpark Garage Angling Club
Hon. Sec. J. Elliott, Esq., 12 Glenkirk Drive, Glasgow G15 6DH.
Prestwick Sea Angling Club
Hon. Sec. Mrs. M. Templeton, 'Trebor', 15 Teviot Street, Ayr. (Tel. 0292 268072).
Quaich Sea Angling Club
Hon. Sec. J. Connell Esq., 9 Balfour Court, Leithington Avenue, Shawlands, Glasgow.
R.A.F. Kinloss Sea Angling Club
Hon. Sec. Cpl. A. Tilley, N.M.S.U., 4 Team, RAF Kinloss, Forres IV36 0UH.
R.A.F. Lossiemouth Sea Angling Club
Hon. Sec. J.W. Courtnell (WO) Officer, IC Sea Angling Eng. Wg. H.Q. Royal Air Force, Lossiemouth, Moray IV31 6SD.

R.A. Range Hebrides Sea Angling Club
Hon. Sec. Capt. D. Thorington, R.A. Range Hebrides, Isle of Benbecula, Outer Hebrides PA88.
Ross-shire Sea Angling Club
Hon. Sec. Mrs. W. Dowie, 43 MacKenzie Place, Maryburgh, Conon Bridge, Ross-shire. (Tel. 0349 61850).
Saltcoats Argyle Seahawks Sea Angling Club
Hon. Sec. Tony Kelly, Esq., 5 Ailsa Gardens, Ardrossan, Ayrshire. (Tel. 62550).
Saltcoats Sea Angling Association
Hon. Sec. P.J. Allwell, Esq., 12 Sidney Street, Saltcoats, Ayrshire KA21 5DD. (Tel. 0294 64012).
Scottish Aviation Sea Angling Club
Hon. Sec. W. Clark, Esq., 11 Avon Place, Kilmarnock, Ayrshire. (Tel. 39865).
Scottish Police Sea Angling Association
Hon. Sec. A. Sutherland, Esq., Police Station, Bridge Road, Balerno, Edinburgh.
Sea Pirates Sea Angling Club
Hon. Sec. C. Mains, Esq., 7 Holm Place, Larkhall ML9 1QX.
Shetland Association of Sea Anglers
Hon. Sec. Mrs. B. Cummings, Windward, Port Arthur, Scalloway, Shetland. (Tel. 0595 88517).
Silver Lure Sea Angling Club
Hon. Sec. D. McNair, Esq., 4 Haining Road, Renfrew PA4 0JJ. (Tel. 041-886 4412).
South Queensferry Angling Club
Hon. Sec. R. Perrett, Esq., 129 Baberton Mains Drive, Edinburgh EH14 3EA.
Spinningdale Angling Club
Hon. Sec. D. Young, Esq., 12 Weavers Avenue, Paisley PA2 9DR. (Tel. 041-848 1962).
Stornoway Fire Brigade Sea Angling Club
Hon. Sec. C. Nixon, Esq., 15 Cearn Shiaraim, Stornoway, Isle of Lewis. (Tel. 0851 3808).
Stornoway Sea Angling Club
Hon. Sec. F.G. Jefferson, Esq., No.1 Sheshader Point, Isle of Lewis. (Tel. 0851 870214).
Strathclyde Police Recreation Association Sea Angling Section
Hon. Sec. F. Kirkham Esq., Greenock Police Office, Rue End Street, Greenock, Renfrewshire.
Tower Angling Club
Hon. Sec. Miss E. Tulloch, 4 Ardross Terrace, Inverness. (Tel. 0463 232765).
Towerlands Sea Angling Club
Hon. Sec. W. McLennan, Esq., 38 Gigha Place, Broomlands, Irvine, Ayrshire. (Tel. Irvine 216779).
Troon Sea Angling Club
Hon. Sec. W. Wallis, Esq., 4 Pladda Avenue, Broomlands, Irvine, Ayrshire KA11 1DR.
Whitfield Labour Club Angling Section
Hon. Sec. A. Perrie, Esq., 69 Blacklock Crescent, Dundee, Angus.

JUNIOR CLUB MEMBERSHIP (HONORARY)
Crookston Castle Secondary School Sea Angling Club
Hon. Sec. T. Craig, Esq., Science Dept., 126 Brockburn Road, Glasgow G53 5RX.
Mid Craigie & Linlathen Junior Sea Angling Club
Hon. Sec. J. Gordon, Esq., 44 Longtown Road, Dundee, Angus. (Tel. 451649).
Rosehall High School Angling Club
Hon. Sec. R. MacDonald, Esq., Rosehall High School, Woodhall Avenue, Coatbridge, Strathclyde (Tel. 31166).
Stevenston Sea Angling Club
Hon. Sec. P. McGill, Esq., 5 Annanhill Place, Whitehurst Park, Kilwinning, Ayr.

Cleaning part of the catch off the Mull of Galloway

SEA ANGLING – REGULATIONS

MINIMUM QUALIFYING SIZES OF FISH PRESENTED FOR WEIGH-IN FROM 1 JANUARY 1989.

1. Bass (Dicentrarchus labrax) — 36 cm. (14.2 in)
   Brill (Scophthalmus rhombus) — 30 cm. (11.8 in)
   Coalfish (Pollachius virens) — 35 cm (13.8 in.)*
   Cod (Gadus morhua) — 35 cm. (13.8 in)*

N.B. In U.K. Fishery area V11a from 1st October to 31 December the minimum size for Cod will be 45 cm. (17.7 in.)*

Species	Size	
Dab (Limanda limanda)	23 cm.	(9.06 in)*
Dogfish – all species (Scyliorhinus, Squalius sp)	35 cm	(13.8 in)
Eel Common (Anguilla anguilla)	35 cm	(13.8 in)**
Eel Conger (Conger conger)	58 cm	(22.8 in)*
Flounder (Platichthys flesus)	25 cm	(9.8 in)*
Haddock (Melanogrammus aeglefinus)	30 cm	(11.8 in)*
Hake (Merluccius merluccius)	30 cm.	(11.8 in)
Halibut (Hippoglossus hippoglossus)	35 cm	(13.8 in)
Ling (Molva molva)	58 cm	(22.8 in)**
Megrim (Lepidorhombus wiffiagonis)	25 cm	(9.8 in)
Pollack (Pollachius pollachius)	35 cm	(13.8 in)
Plaice (Pleuronectes platessa)	27 cm	(10.6 in)*
Rays (Raja sp)	35 cm	(13.8 in)
Seabream, Red (Pagellus bogaraveo)	25 cm	(9.8 in)*
Seabream, Black (Spondyliosoma cantharus)	23 cm	(9.05 in)*
Shad Twaite (Alosa Fallax)	30 cm	(11.8 in)*
Skates (Raja batis, alba, oxyrinchus sp)	11.35 kg	(25 lbs)
Sole Lemon (Microstomus kitt)	25 cm	(9.8 in.)*
Sole (Solea solea)	24 cm	(9.4 in)*
Tope (Galeorhinus galeus)	9.10 kg.	(20 lbs)
Turbot (Scophthalmus maximus)	30 cm	(11.8 in.)
Whiting (Merlangius merlangus)	27 cm	(10.6 in)
Witches (Glyptocephalus gynoglossus)	28 cm.	(11.0 in)
All other species	20 cm	(7.9 in)

* Denotes brought into line with E.E.C. Legislation.
** These sizes may be altered when the European Community determine the new limit for the species.

2. A maximum of three mackerel may be presented for weigh-in.

3. TOPE and SKATE: (R. batis); long-nosed (R. oxyrhinchus) or white (R. alba) are not to be brought ashore during events designated as TOPE or SKATE festivals. They are to be weighed immediately after capture and returned to the sea.
(This rule does not apply to potential national record fish which must be brought ashore for weighing.) In designated TOPE competitions no minimum size for weighing will be applied as long as fish are weighed on board and returned alive.

4. Any obviously undersized fish for the weigh-in will result in the entrant being disqualified.

SCOTTISH BOAT AND SHORE (rod and line caught)
MARINE FISH RECORDS

B - Boat Records   S - Shore Records   Spec. - Speciman Qualifying Weight

Species		lb.	oz.	dm.	kg.	Place of Capture	Angler	Year	Spec. lb.
ANGLERFISH	B	45	0	0	20.412	Sound of Mull	D. Hopper	1978	20
Lophius piscatorius	S	38	0	0	17.237	Blairmore Pier Loch Long	L. C. Hanley	1970	15
ARGENTINE	B		5	3	0.147	Arrochar	I. Millar	1978	4oz.
Argentina sphyraena	S	OPEN AT ANY WEIGHT							
BARRACUDINA	B	OPEN AT ANY WEIGHT							any
(Paralepis coreganoides borealis)	S	0	1	14	0.054	Newton Shore	D. Gillop	1987	1¹/₂oz
BASS	B	8	14	3	4.025	Balcary Bay	D. Shaw	1975	6
Dicentrarchus labrax	S	13	4	0	6.010	Almorness Point	G. Stewart	1975	6
BLACKFISH	B	3	10	8	1.658	Heads of Ayr	J. Semple	1972	2¹/₂ oz
Centrolophus niger	S	OPEN AT ANY WEIGHT							any
BLENNY, SHANNY	B	OPEN AT ANY WEIGHT							any
Blennius pholis	S	0	1	10	0.046	Carolina Port Dundee Docks	M. S. Ettle	1983	1oz.
BLENNY, TOMPOT	B	OPEN AT ANY WEIGHT							any
Blennius gattorugine	S		2	12	0.078	Portpatrick	G. Dods	1977	2oz.
BLENNY VIVIPAROUS	B		10	0	0.283	Craigendoran	T. Lambert	1977	7oz.
Zoarces viviparus	S		11	3	0.317	Craigendoran	D. Ramsay	1975	7oz.
BLENNY, YARREL'S	B	OPEN AT ANY WEIGHT							any
Chirolophis ascanii	S		2	1	0.059	Gourock	D. McEntee	1979	1¹/₂oz.
BLUEMOUTH	B	3	2	8	1.431	Loch Shell	Mrs. A. Lyngholm	1976	2¹/₂oz
Helicolenus dactylopterus	S	OPEN AT ANY WEIGHT							any
BREAM, BLACK	B	2	9	0	1.162	Kebock Head Lewis	T. Lumb	1974	1
Spondyllosoma cantharus	S	1	13	8	0.836	Gareloch	A. L. Harris	1973	1
BREAM, GILTHEAD	B	OPEN AT ANY WEIGHT							any
Sparus aurata	S	1	1	5	0.490	Dunnet Head	W. Thornton	1988	1
BREAM, RAYS	B	6	3	13	2.829	West of Barra Head	J. Holland	1978	4
Brama brama	S	6	6	8	2.905	Portobello	G. Taylor	1973	4
BREAM RED	B	4	10	0	2.097	Ardnamurchan	R. Steel	1969	1
Pagellus bogaraveo	S	OPEN AT ANY WEIGHT							any
BRILL	B	1	4	0	0.567	Portpatrick	J. Dickson	1984	1
Scophthalmus rhombus	S	1	2	0	0.510	Killintrinnan Lighthouse	P. Baisbrown	1971	1
BULL HUSS	B	20	3	8	9.171	Mull of Galloway	J. K. Crawford	1971	15
Scyliorhinus stellaris	S	15	8	0	7.031	West Tarbet Mull of Galloway	A. K. Paterson	1976	10
BUTTERFISH	B	OPEN AT ANY WEIGHT							any
Pholis gunnellus	S		1	2	0.032	Gourock	D. McEntee	1978	1oz
CATFISH, COMMON	B	13	12	11	6.256	Burnmouth	D. Brown	1985	7
Anachichas lumpus	S	12	12	8	5.797	Stonehaven	G. M. Taylor	1978	4
COALFISH	B	28	4	0	12.814	Eyemouth	L. Gibson	1982	12
Pollachius virens	S	11	7	8	5.202	Loch Long	S. Mather	1976	7
COD	B	46	0	8	20.879	Gantocks	B. Baird	1970	25
Gadus morhua	S	40	11	8	18.470	Balcary Point	K. Robinson	1988	15
DAB	B	2	12	4	1.254	Gairloch	R. Islip	1975	1¹/₂
limanda limanda	S	2	5	0	1.049	Cairnryan	A. Scott	1969	1¹/₂
DAB LONG ROUGH	B		6	6	0.180	Helensburgh	J. Napier	1984	1¹/₂
Hippoglossoides platessoides	S		5	8	0.155	Coulport	I. McGrath	1975	4oz
DOGFISH, BLACK-MOUTHED	B	2	13	8	1.288	Loch Fyne	J. H. Anderson	1977	1¹/₂
Galeus melastromus	S	OPEN AT ANY WEIGHT							any
DOGFISH LESSER-SPOTTED	B	3	15	12	1.807	Portpatrick	R. I. Carruthers	1987	3
Scyliorhinus caniculus	S	4	15	3	2.246	Abbey Burnfoot	S. Ramsay	1988	3
DRAGONET COMMON	B		5	0	0.142	Gareloch	T. J. Ashwell	1985	4oz.
Callionymus lyra	S		5	0	0.143	Loch Long	J. Crawford	1985	4¹/₂

Species		lb.	oz.	dm.	kg.	Place of Capture	Angler	Year	Spec lb.
EEL, COMMON	B	1	13	7	0.834	Gareloch	P. Fleming	1976	1$\frac{1}{2}$
Anguilla anguilla	S	3	0	0	1.360	Ayr Harbour	R. W. Morrice	1972	2^2
EEL, CONGER	B	48	1		21.820	Largs	R. Bond	1985	30
Conger conger	S	45	0	0	20.411	Scrabster Pier	P. G. Bell	1966	25
FLOUNDER	B	2	13	11	1.295	Portnockie	K. F. Mackay	1985	2$\frac{1}{2}$
Platichthys flesus	S	4	11	8	2.140	Musselburgh	R. Armstrong	1970	2$\frac{1}{2}$
GARFISH	B	1	11	8	0.799	Brodick	R. Stockwin	1970	1
Belone belone	S	1	11	0	0.764	Bute	Miss McAlorum	1971	1
GOBY BLACK	B		1	4	0.035	Cairnryan	J. Price	1976	1oz
Gobius niger	S		2	4	0.063	Inveraray	F O'Brien	1980	1oz
GURNARD, GREY	B	2	7	0	1.105	Caliach Point	D. Swinbanks	1976	1$\frac{3}{4}$
Eutrigla gurnardus	S	1	5	0	0.595	Peterhead	A. Turnbull	1973	1
		1	5	0	0.595	Port William	J. W. Martin	1977	1
GURNARD, RED	B	2	8	8	1.148	Tobermory	D. V. Relton	1985	1$\frac{1}{2}$
Aspitrigla cuculus	S	1	2	5	0.519	Gareloch	G. Smith	1981	12oz.
GURNARD STREAKED	B		10	10	0.301	Isle of Mull	J. Duncan	1985	any
Trigloporus lastoviza	S	1	6	8	0.637	Loch Goil	H. L. Smith	1971	1
GURNARD, TUB	B	5	5	0	2.409	Luce Bay	J. S. Dickinson	1975	3$\frac{1}{2}$
Trigla lucerna	S	1	1	0	0.481	Carrick Bay	A. E. Maxwell	1978	12oz.
HADDOCK	B	9	14	12	4.501	Summer Isles	M. Lawton	1980	6
Melanogrammus aeglefinus	S	6	12	0	3.061	Loch Goil	G. B. Stevenson	1976	3
HAKE	B	18	5	8	8.321	Shetland	B. Sinclair	1971	10
Merluccius merluccus	S		11	7	0.324	Gourock	S. Moyes	1979	8oz
HALIBUT	B	234	0	0	106.136	Scrabster	C. Booth	1979	50
Hippoglossus hippoglossus	S	OPEN AT ANY WEIGHT							any
HERRING	B	1	2	0	0.510	Loch Long	R. C. Scott	1974	14oz.
Culpea harengus	S		11	11	0.331	Port Logan	R. Smith	1984	10oz.
LING	B	57	8	0	26.082	Stonehaven	I. Duncan	1982	20
Molva molva	S	12	4	0	5.557	Scrabster	A. Allan	1984	6
LUMPSUCKER	B	4	11	4	2.133	Innellan	G. T. Roebuck	1976	3
Cyclopterus lumpus	S	5	12	10	2.626	Cruden Bay	M. Rennie	1987	3
MACKEREL	B	3	12	0	1.701	Ullapool	E. Scobie	1965	2
Scomber scombrus	S	2	5	9	1.063	Wick	W. Richardson	1969	2
MEGRIM	B	3	12	8	1.715	Gareloch	P. Christie	1973	2
Lepidorhombus whiffiagonis	S	OPEN AT ANY WEIGHT							any
MULLET, GOLDEN GREY	B	OPEN AT ANY WEIGHT							any
Lisa aurata	S		11	0	0.312	Fairlie	I. McFadyen	1972	8oz.
MULLET, THICK LIPPED GREY	B	3	6	0	1.531	Luce Bay	R. Williamson	1976	3$\frac{1}{2}$
Crenimugil labrosus	S	6	7	8	2.934	Ayr Harbour	D. A. Smith	1984	4$\frac{1}{2}$
NORWAY HADDOCK	B	1	1	0	0.482	Shetland	Mrs. E.W.M. Watt	1984	14oz.
Sebastes viviparus	S	OPEN AT ANY WEIGHT							any
PIPEFISH, GREATER	B	OPEN AT ANY WEIGHT							any
Sygnathus acus	S		0	13	0.023	Coulport	H. Holding	1975	any
PLAICE	B	10	3	8	4.635	Longa Sound	H. Gardiner	1974	5
Pleuronectes platessa	S	5	8	0	2.494	Arrochar	A. Holt Jnr.	1971	3$\frac{1}{2}$
POLLACK	B	18	0	0	8.165	Scrabster	N. Carter	1971	10
Pollachius pollachius	S	13	14	0	6.293	Furnace	J. Arthur	1974	8
POOR COD	B	1	4	0	0.567	Arbroath	F. Chalmers	1969	1
Trisopterus minutus	S	1	0	0	0.453	Loch Fyne	F. Johnstone	1970	12oz.
POUTING	B	3	8	0	1.587	Gourock	J. Lewis	1977	2
Trisopterus luscus	S	3	3	7	1.458	Kirkcudbright	R. Cartwright	1984	1$\frac{1}{2}$
RAY BLONDE	B	26	11	0	12.105	Caliach Point	B. Swinbanks	1977	15^2
Raja brachyura	S	OPEN AT ANY WEIGHT							any
RAY CUCKOO	B	5	4	4	2.388	Gairloch	A. Bridges	1979	4
Raja naevus	S	4	11	0	2.126	Gourock	R.A.H. McCaw	1973	3$\frac{3}{4}$
RAY SPOTTED	B	7	1	8	3.227	Loch Roag	P. Rayner	1985	4
Raja montagui	S	5	12	0	2.608	Cairnryan	G.C. Styles	1975	4
RAY, THORNBACK	B	29	8	10	13.399	Luce Bay	A. McLean	1982	15
Raja clavata	S	21	12		9.866	Kirkcudbright	S. Ramsay	1985	4

52

B - Boat Records   S - Shore Records   Spec - Specimen Qualifying Weight

Species		lb.	oz.	dm.	kg.	Place of Capture	Angler	Year	Spec. lb.
ROCKLING, FIVE BEARDED	B	OPEN AT ANY WEIGHT							any
Ciliata mustela	S		7	0	0.198	Balcarry Point	K. Greason	1988	4½oz.
ROCKLING, FOUR BEARDED	B		1	7	0.040	Gourock	S. Hodgson	1981	1¼oz.
Rhinomenus cimbrius	S	OPEN AT ANY WEIGHT							any
ROCKLING SHORE	B	OPEN AT ANY WEIGHT							any
Gairdropsarus mediterraneus	S		14	8	0.411	Loch Long	A. Glen	1982	7oz.
ROCKLING, THREE BEARDED	B	1	14	4	0.857	Stonehaven	W. Murphy	1972	1¼
Gairdropsaus vulgaris	S	2	11	9	1.235	Kircudbright	A. Johnstone	1981	1½
SANDEEL, GREATER	B		8	0	0.227	Caliach Point	T.J. Ashwell	1984	6oz.
Hyperoplus lanceolatus	S	0	4	4	0.120	Isle of Lewis	R. McMillan	1987	3oz.
SCAD (HORSE MACKEREL)	B	1	7	0	0.652	Loch Shell	D. MacNeil	1976	1
Trachurus trachurus	S	3	0	14	1.384	Cockenzie	R. Dillon	1981	1
SEA SCORPION, LONGSPINED	B		3	6	0.096	Rhu Narrows	C. Heath	1985	2½oz.
Taurulus bubalis	S		5	9	0.157	Aberdeen	T.J. Ashwell	1982	2½oz.
SEA SCORPION SHORTSPINED	B	2	3	0	0.992	Kepple Pier	R. Stevenson	1973	1¾
Myoxocephalus scorpius	S	2	3	0	0.992	Cloch, Gourock	W. Crawford	1979	1½
SHAD, TWAITE	B	OPEN AT ANY WEIGHT							any
Alosa fallax	S	2	12	0	1.247	Garlieston	J.W. Martin	1978	1½
SHARK, BLUE	B	85	8	0	38.781	Stornoway	J. Morrison	1972	50
Prionace glauca	S	OPEN AT ANY WEIGHT							any
SHARK PORBEAGLE	B	404	0	0	183.244	Sumburgh Head	P. White	1976	300
Lamna nasus	B	404	0	0	183.244	Sumburgh Head	P. White	1978	300
	S	OPEN AT ANY WEIGHT							any
SKATE, COMMON	B	227	0	0	102.967	Tobermory	R. Banks	1986	100
Raja batis	S	154	0	0	69.854	Achiltibuie	M.J. Traynor	1971	50
SMELT	B	OPEN AT ANY WEIGHT							any
Osmerus Eperlanus	S		5	4	0.149	Riverside, Dundee	M. Ettle	1988	4½oz.
SMOOTHHOUND STARRY	B	OPEN AT ANY WEIGHT							any
Mustelus asterias	S	7	12	14	3.540	Kirkcudbright	M. Roberts	1987	5
SOLE, DOVER	B	1	12	0	0.793	Killintrinnon	W. Hannah	1974	1
Solea Solea	S		9	12	0.276	Portpatrick	G. Griffiths	1977	8oz.
SOLE LEMON	B	2	2	0	0.963	Lochgoilhead	J. Gordon	1976	1
Microstomus kitt	S	1	6	2	0.627	Peterhead	B.N. Davidson	1982	12oz.
SPURDOG	B	18	14	0	8.560	Tobermory	J. Bean	1988	14
Squalus acanthias	S	12	8	12	5.691	Millport	R. Paterson	1983	8
TADPOLE FISH	B		14	14	0.421	Firth of Clyde	R. Donnelly	1981	8oz.
Raniceps raninus	S	1	3	0	0.538	Dunbar	W. Dickson	1977	10oz.
TOPE	B	62	0	0	28.122	Drummore	F. Bristow	1975	45
Galeorhinus galeus	S	54	4	0	24.606	Loch Ryan	D. Hastings	1975	30
TOPKNOT	B	OPEN AT ANY WEIGHT							any
Zeugopterus punctatus	S		8	8	0.241	Peterhead	G.M. Taylor	1975	6oz.
TORSK	B	15	7	2	7.006	Pentland Firth	D.J. Mackay	1982	8
Brosme brosme	S	OPEN AT ANY WEIGHT							any
TURBOT	B	25	4	0	11.453	Mull	I. Jenkins	1982	15
Scophthalmus maximus	S	1	3	1	0.540	Troon	A. Crowther	1976	1
WEAVER, GREATER	B	OPEN AT ANY WEIGHT							any
Trachinus draco	S	1	1	14	0.508	Mull of Galloway	Mr. W. Allison	1984	1
WHITING	B	6	8	0	2.948	Girvan	A.M.Devay	1969	3
Merlangius merlangus	S	3	0	0	1.360	Gourock	D. McTehee	1970	2
WHITING, BLUE (POUTASSOU)	B	1	12	0	0.793	Loch Fyne	J.H. Anderson	1977	8oz.
Micromesistius	S	OPEN AT ANY WEIGHT							any

B - Boat Records   S - Shore Records   Spec - Specimen Qualifying Weight

Species		lb.	oz.	dm.	kg.	Place of Capture	Angler	Year	Spec lb.
WRASSE BALLAN	B	4	12	4	2.161	Calgary Bay, Mull	K.F.J. Hall	1983	3$^{1}/_{2}$
Labrus bergylta	S	5	0	0	2.268	Girvan	T. McGeehan	1971	3$^{1}/_{2}$
WRASSE, CORKWING	B	OPEN AT ANY WEIGHT							any
Crenilabrus melops	S		5	12	0.163	Portpatrick	K. Grey	1986	4oz.
WRASSE, CUCKOO	B	3	0	0	1.361	Scrabster	Mrs. H. Campbell	1969	1$^{1}/_{4}$
Labrus mixtus	S	1	2	0	0.510	Neist Point, Skye	Q.A. Oliver	1972	12oz.
WRASSE GOLDSINNY	B	0	0	12	0.021	Lochaline	D. D. Morrison	1983	1oz.
Ctenolabrus rupestris	S		1	13	0.051	Loch Goil	T. Lambert	1977	1$^{1}/_{2}$oz.
			1	13	0.051	Mull of Galloway	G.V.R. Griffiths	1985	1$^{1}/_{2}$oz.
WRASSE SMALL MOUTHED ROCK COOK	B	OPEN AT ANY WEIGHT							any
Centrolabrus exoletus	S		2	0	0.056	Achitibuie Pier	D.F. McKendrick	1985	1$^{1}/_{2}$oz.
WRASSE, SCALE RAYED	B	0	10	15	0.310	Tobermory	J. Teal	1986	8oz.
Acantholabrus palloni	S	OPEN AT ANY WEIGHT							any

The above records are based on information received up to 30th September, 1988, by the S.F.S.A. Honorary Fish Recorder, G. T. Morris, 8 Burt Avenue, Kinghorn, Fife.

USEFUL ADDRESSES IN SCOTTISH SPORT FISHERIES

Scottish Tourist Board, 23 Ravelston Terrace, Edinburgh EH4 3EU. Tel: 031-332 2433.

Department of Agriculture & Fisheries for Scotland, Pentland House, 47 Robb's Loan, Edinburgh EH14 1TW. Tel: 031-556 8400.

Inspector of Salmon Fisheries, Pentland House (Room 227), 47 Robb's Loan, Edinburgh EH14 1TW. Tel: 031-244 6227.

Freshwater Fisheries Laboratory, Secretary, G. Struthers, "Torshavn", Lettoch Road, Pitlochry PH16 5AZ. Tel: (Home) 0796 2846. (Work) 0796 2060.

Marine Laboratory, P.O. Box 101, Victoria Road, Aberdeen AB9 8DB. Tel: (0224) 876544.

Secretary, Scottish River Purification Boards Association, City Chambers, Glasgow G2 1DU. Tel: 041-227 4190.

Scottish Sports Council, Caledonia House, South Gyle, Edinburgh EH12 9DQ. Tel: 031-317 7200.

Nature Conservancy Council, 12 Hope Terrace, Edinburgh. Tel: 031-447 4784.

Forestry Commission, Jill Mackay, Information Officer, 231 Corstorphine Road, Edinburgh EH12 7AT. Tel: 031-334 0303.

North of Scotland Hydro-Electric Board, 16 Rothesay Terrace, Edinburgh EH3 7SE. Tel: 031-225 1361.

Institute of Fisheries Management, Secretary (Scottish Branch), Gordon Struthers, c/o Freshwater Fisheries Laboratory, Faskally, Pitlochry, Perthshire.

Anglers' Cooperative Association, Secretary, Malcolm Thomson, 21 Heriot Row, Edinburgh EH3 6EN. Tel: 031-225 6511.

The Salmon and Trout Association, 2 Queen's Road, Aberdeen AB9 8BD. Tel: (0224) 644276.

Scottish Anglers' National Association, Secretary, Mr. A.D. Jamieson, 5 Cramond Glebe Road, Edinburgh EH4 6ND. Tel: 031-229 9292, ext. 2559.

Central Scotland Anglers' Association, Secretary, Kevin Burns, 53 Fernieside Crescent, Edinburgh. Tel: 031-664 4685.

Federation of Highland Angling Clubs, Secretary, W. Brown, Coruisk, Strathpeffer, Ross-shire. Tel: (0997) 21446.

Department of Forestry and Natural Resources, University of Edinburgh, Kings Buildings, Mayfield Road, Edinburgh EH9 3JU. Tel: 031-667 1081.

Institute of Aquaculture, University of Stirling, Stirling FK9 4LA. Tel: (0786) 73171.

54

TRADES DESCRIPTION ACT

The accommodation mentioned in this holiday guide has not been inspected, and the publishers rely on information provided. The publishers have every confidence in their advertisers but cannot be held responsible for the accuracy of the descriptions published.

GAME FISHING HOLIDAYS IN CAITHNESS

The River Thurso is one of Scotland's finest "fly only" Salmon rivers, having both a Spring and Autumn run. The water is controlled by a dam at Loch More, which was built solely for the improvement of the Salmon fishing.

The river is divided into 13 beats so that it is possible to fish the whole river during a 2 week holiday. Ghillies arranged if required.

Sea angling is well catered for from different harbours round the county. Well equipped boats can be hired by the day with the necessary bait and tackle.

All arrangements for these fishings can be made through the ULBSTER ARMS HOTEL, HALKIRK. The hotel has long been a favourite with anglers and stands on the banks of the River Thurso. The ULBSTER has lately been improved to meet the demands of today's sportsmen. The hotel and its many sporting packages are easily accessible by regular air services, rail or road.

All enquiries given the personal attention of the General Manager, Christopher Pern, Ulbster Arms Hotel, Halkirk, Caithness KW12 6XY. Tel: (084783) 641.

Ask your bookshop for Pastime Publications other Holiday Guides Scotland Home of Golf Scotland for Motorist

LADY JANET'S WOOD CARAVAN & CAMPING SITE
THURSO
Telephone Thurso (0847) 62611 or 64588

Hard standings for caravans and caravanettes - showers, shop, recreation room with pool table. 4-6 berth caravans for hire (electric light).

CARAVANS ALSO AVAILABLE ON THURSO MUNICIPAL SITE

FREE FISHING

For salmon, sea trout and brown trout when you stay at Warmanbie Hotel

Warmanbie, a Georgian country house hotel is set in secluded woodland grounds overlooking the River Annan. Here you'll find an ideal place to relax and enjoy old fashioned service, fine wine and creative cooking. All our spacious bedrooms have private bathroom, telephone, colour TV and radio alarm. Fishing is free (except from 9th September until 15th November when it is £5.00 per person per day) on the hotel's private stretch (only 100 yards away). Fishing on other stretches also arranged. Special rate for three or more nights or weekends-Sunday trout fishing can be arranged. Holiday cottage also available.

For further details write to:
Warmanbie Hotel, Annan DG12 5LL
or telephone Rod Duncan on Annan (046 12) 4015/6

A SMALL HOTEL WITH A BIG WELCOME

THE ESKDALE HOTEL
★★ AA ★★ RSAC ★★ RAC

The Eskdale Hotel, a former coaching house, stands in Langholm's market place, a prominent position in one of Scotland's most attractive Border towns. There are 16 modernised, comfortable bedrooms, single, twin, double and family, 10 with shower and toilet en-suite. The hotel is fully licensed and the restaurant provides a wide selection of good food and wines in a relaxed and pleasant atmosphere. The Eskdale is a family-run hotel, with the emphasis very much on personal service. Excellent salmon and trout fishing on River Esk 100 yds. from hotel. Fishing permits available from hotel.

For further details, please contact:
The Eskdale Hotel, Langholm, Dumfriesshire. Telephone: (03873) 80357

Lockerbie, Dumfries-shire.
Tel: Lockerbie (05762) 2427

Privately owned and managed hotel set in 7 acres. Comfortable bedrooms most with private bathrooms, all with TV and telephone. A la carte restaurants, also appetising bar meals. Ideal touring situation. Riding, shooting, fishing, golf available. Fishing on several beats on the Annan, also good coarse fishing in locality. Johansen and Ashley Courtenay recommended.

RIVER AND LOCH
FISHING

Mid-Annandale, with easy access from the A74 or A75 in a country area. Salmon, Trout, Pike and Coarse fishing on River Annan and in stocked lochs. Terms on request for fishing on Nith and Cairn.

Contact Mrs. M. Vaughan.

Braehead Farmhouse, Heck, Lockerbie, Dumfriesshire Tel. Lochmaben (0387) 810444. Own meat, eggs, vegetables, home baking, parties up to six persons £98-£115 per person weekly, full board, including packed lunches and fishing.

Three day break including all above from £44-£55.

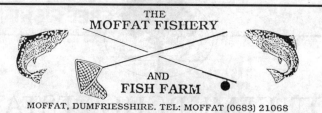

DUMFRIESSHIRE

FIFE

The Kirklands Hotel
Kinross

Telephone (0577) 63313

A.A.★★   R.A.C.★★
S.T.B. ♛♛♛ Commended

Situated near historical Loch Leven, only half a mile from M90 (Junction 6) this family-run charming old coach-house has recently been completely refurbished to the highest standard. All bedrooms now have en suite facilities, colour TV, direct dial telephone, tea/ coffee tray.

The Kirklands now hosts the Gallery Restaurant for your dinner/supper (beautiful paintings by local artists). Bar lunches daily. We are centrally situated making The Kirklands an ideal venue for the golfer, fisher motorist alike.

20 High Street, Kinross KY13 7AN.

A REAL FAMILY ATMOSPHERE

---- S T A K I S ----

Dunkeld House

---- H O T E L ----

Built at the turn of the century by the 7th Duke of Atholl, today Dunkeld House retains all the elegance of its heritage, along with one thing the Edwardians overlooked. A modern leisure facility complete with indoor pool, all-weather tennis courts, a Turkish steam room, a solarium and a whirlpool spa.

We can, however, think of a number of good reasons why guests might prefer not to visit the leisure club at all. Namely, our private two mile salmon beat on the River Tay, seasonal game shooting, stalking and the nearby golf courses at Gleneagles, St Andrews and Carnoustie.

An inspired decision.

Dunkeld, Perthshire PH8 0HX. Telephone: (03502) 771

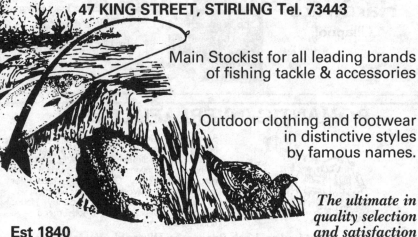

SUTHERLAND

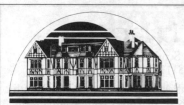

Uist landscape

Area Tourist Board
Scottish Borders Tourist Board

Director of Tourism
Scottish Borders Tourist Board
Municipal Buildings
High Street
Selkirk TD7 4JX.
Tel: Selkirk (0750) 20555

RIVER PURIFICATION BOARD
TWEED RIVER PURIFICATION BOARD
Burnbrae
Mossilee Road
Galashiels.
Tel: Galashiels 2425

RIVERS

Water	Location	Species	Season	Permit available from	Other Information
Blackadder	Greenlaw	Brown Trout	1 Apr. to 6 Oct.	Greenlaw Angling Club J. Purves, 9 Wester Row, Greenlaw. Doigs Store. Post Office. All Hotels.	No bait fishing till 15 Apr. Sunday fishing. No spinning. No Sunday competitions.
Eden Water	Kelso	Brown Trout	1 Apr. to 30 Sept.	Forrest & Sons, 35 The Square, Kelso. Tel: 24687. Redpath & Co., Horsemarket, Kelso. Intersport, 43 The Square, Kelso. River Watchers, Springwood Caravan Park, Kelso TD5 8LS. Tel: (0573) 24596. Border Temperance Hotel	Fly only. No spinning. Restricted to 3 rods.
	Gordon	Brown Trout	15 Mar. to 6 Oct.	Mr. W. Halliday, 46 Glebe Park, Gordon. J.H. Fairgrieve, Burnbank, Gordon. Tel: 357.	No Spinning. No Sunday fishing.
Ettrick & Yarrow	Bowhill	Salmon Trout	1 Feb.-30 Nov. 15 Mar.-30 Sep.	Buccleuch Estates, Bowhill, Selkirk. Tel: (0750) 20753.	
	Selkirk	Brown Trout	1 Apr. to 30 Sept.	Selkirk & District Angling Association. A. Murray, 40 Raeburn Meadow, Selkirk. Gordon Arms Hotel. Cross Keys Inn, Tel: (0750) 21283. P.O.'s at Ettrick, Yarrowford, Yarrow, Ettrickbridge.	Night fishing 15 May-14 Sept. Week ticket only. No minnows or spinning. No Sundays.
Ettrick	Ettrick Bridge	Brown Trout Salmon	Apr.-30 Sep. 1 Feb.-30 Nov.	Ettrickshaws Hotel, Tel: (0750) 52229.	Packed Lunches and flask for residents. Permits also available for other waters.
Eye Water	Eyemouth	Brown Trout	15 Mar. to 6 Oct.	R. Grieve, 21 High Street, Eyemouth.	Fly only. No spinning. No Sundays. Catch limit 6.
Gala Water	Stow	Trout	1 Apr. to 30 Sept.	Royal Hotel, Stow. Post Office, Stow.	No Spinning. Fishing to cease 1 hour after sunset until 1 hour before sunrise.
	Galashiels	Trout	1 Apr. to 30 Sept.	Gala Angling Association (as for Tweed entry)	Sunday fishing.

Water	Location	Species	Season	Permit available from	Other Information
Jed/Oxnam Waters	Jedburgh	Trout	1 Apr. to 30 Sept.	Jedforest Angling Association, Game & Country Enterprises, 6/8 Canongate, Jedburgh. (Trout permits only). W. Shaw, Canongate, Jedburgh.	1-30 Apr. fly only. 1-30 Sept. no spinning, no spinning reels, no floats, no minnows. Minimum size 9in. No Sundays.
Kale Water	Eckford	Trout Grayling	1 Apr. to 30 Sept.	Gamekeeper, No. 4 Eckford. Mr. Graham, Eckford Cottage, Eckford, Kelso. Tel: (083-55) 255.	No Sundays.
	Morebattle	Trout Grayling	15 Mar. to 6 Oct.	D.Y. Gray, 17 Mainsfield Avenue, Morebattle. The Garage, Morebattle.	No ground baiting. No Sunday fishing.
Leader Water	Lauderdale	Trout	15 Mar. to 6 Oct.	Lauderdale Angling Association, D.M. Milligan, 1 Newbyth House Stables, East Linton. Lauder Post Office. Tower Hotel, Oxton. A. Hogarth, Ivy Cottage, West High Street, Lauder. Newsagent, Market Place, Lauder. Lauderdale Hotel. The Chip Shop. Anglers Choice, High Street, Melrose. Committee Members.	No Spinning. Sunday fishing. No Grayling fishing.
Leader Water/ Tweed	Earlston	Trout	15 Mar. to 30 Sept.	Earlston Angling Association P. Hessett, 2 Arnot Place, Earlston. Tel: 577. E. & M. Browne, Newsagent, Earlston. Ian's Videos, Earlston. L. Wilson, Newsagent, Earlston. Anglers Choice Hotel, Melrose. Tel: (089 682) 3070. Wilson, Saddlers, Dalkeith. Tweed Permits from J. Yule, Huntspool, Eastgreen, Earlston. Tel: 216.	No Sunday fishing. Other restrictions as per permit.
Leet	Coldstream	Trout Grayling	15 Mar. to 6 Oct.	Coldstream Angling Association Tweed Fishing Tackle, Market Square, Coldstream.	Fly only. No spinning.
Liddle Water	Newcastleton	Salmon	1 Feb. to 31 Oct.	R.J.B. Hill, Solicitor, Langholm. Tel: Langholm 80428.	Spinning allowed when water is above markers at Newcastleton and Kershopfoot Bridge. Tickets also available for Esk, Liddle and Tributaries. Full details on association pamphlet available from Mr. Hill, Bank of Scotland Buildings, Langholm.
		Sea Trout	1 May to 30 Sept.	J.D. Ewart, Fishing Tackle Shop, Newcastleton. Tel: Liddlesdale 257	
		Brown Trout	15 Apr. to 30 Sept.	Mrs. B. Elliot, Thistlesyke, Newcastleton. Tel: Liddlesdale 200.	

Water	Location	Species	Season	Permit available from	Other Information
Lyne Water	Tweed Junction to Flemington Bridge	Trout Grayling	1 Apr. to 30 Sept.	Peebleshire Trout Fishing Association D.G. Fyfe, 39 High Street, Peebles. Tel: 20131. I. Fraser, Northgate, Peebles. Tel: 20979. Tweed Valley Hotel, Walkerburn. J. Dickson & Son, 21 Frederick Street, Edinburgh. Tel: 031-225 4218. Post Office, Stobo. The Luckenbooth, High Street, Innerleithen. Crook Inn, Tweedsmuir. Sonny's Sports Shop, 29 High Street, Innerleithen.	No Sundays. No spinning. No bait fishing April & Sept. Tickets also cover Tweed.
Teviot	Kelso	Trout Grayling	1 Apr. to 30 Sept.	Kelso Angling Association C. Hutchison, 53 Abbotseat, Kelso. Tel: Kelso 23340. Forrest & Sons, 35, The Square, Kelso. Tel: Kelso 24687. Redpath & Co., Horsemarket, Kelso. Tel: Kelso 24578. Intersport, 43, The Square, Kelso. Border Temperance Hotel. Springwood Caravan Park.	No Sundays. Restrictions on spinning. No maggots or ground bait. Size limit 9in.
	Eckford	Salmon Sea Trout Brown Trout	1 Feb.-30 Nov. 15 Mar. to 30 Sep.	Gamekeeper, No. 4, Eckford Mr. Graham Eckford Cottage, Eckford, Kelso. Tel: (083-55) 255.	No Sundays. Limited to 4 day permits. Bait and spinning 15 Feb.-15 Sept. only. Spinning for Trout and Grayling prohibited.
	Jedforest	Salmon	1 Feb. to 31 Nov.	Jedforest Angling Association J.T. Renilson, 4 Canongate, Jedburgh.	No Sundays. Salmon: 3 rods per day only. Spinning allowed from 15 Feb. to 14 Sept. Fly only 15 Sept. to 30 Nov.
		Trout Grayling	1 Apr. to 30 Sept.	Game & Country Enterprises, 6/8 Canongate, Jedburgh. (Trout permits only) W. Shaw, Canongate, Jedburgh.	No spinning for trout. Salmon day permits n/a on Saturdays.
Teviot (and Ale Slitrig Borthwick Rule)	Hawick	Brown Trout	15 Mar. to 30 Sept.	Porteous & Newcombe, Howgate, Hawick.	All rules and regulations on ticket.
		Salmon	1 Feb. to 30 Nov.	The Pet Store, Union Street, Hawick.	
		Grayling	1 Jan. to 30 Sept.	Club Premises, 5 Sandbed, Lindsays Grocers, Denholm.	

Please mention this Pastime Publications Guide

Water	Location	Species	Season	Permit available from	Other Information
Teviot	Above Chesters	Salmon Sea Trout	1 Feb. to 30 Nov.	The Pet Store, Union Street, Hawick.	All rules and regulations on ticket. Limited to 4 rods per day. 6 visitors tickets only now available on application to: The Secretary, Hawick Angliing Club, Mr. R.A. Sutherland, (Waiting List), 20 Longhope Drive, Hawick TD9 0DU. Tel: 0450 75150.
Tweed	Tweedsmuir	Salmon Brown Trout Grayling	1 Oct. to 30 Nov.	Crook Inn, Tweedsmuir. Tel: (08997) 272.	All rules and regulations on permits.
	Peebleshire (substantial stretch of river)	Trout Grayling	1 Apr. to 30 Sept.	Peebleshire Trout Fishing Association D.G. Fyfe, 39 High Street, Peebles. Tel: 20131. Ian Fraser Sports, 1 Bridgegate, Peebles. Tel: 20979. Tweed Valley Hotel, Walkerburn. Tel: 220. George Hotel, Walkerburn. Tel: 219. Sonny's Sports Shop, 29 High Street, Innerleithen. Tel: 830806. The Luckenbooth, High Street, Innerleithen. Tel: 830877. The Crook Inn, Tweedsmuir. Tel: 272. F. & D. Simpson, 28 West Preston Street, Edinburgh. Tel: 031-667 3058. J. Dickson & Son, 21 Frederick Street, Edinburgh. Tel: 031-225 4218.	No spinning. No bait fishing, Apr. & Sept. No Sunday fishing. Tickets also cover Lyne Water. Waders desirable. Fly only on Tweed from Lynefoot upstream.
	Peebles (Wire Bridge Pool to Nutwood Pool - excluding Kailzie)	Salmon	21 Feb. to 30 Nov.	Peebleshire Salmon Fishing Association Seasons: Blackwood & Smith, W.S., 39 High Street, Peebles. Tel: 20131. Days: I. Fraser, Northgate, Peebles. Tel: 20979.	Fly fishing only. No Sundays. Other regulations on tickets.
	Peebles	Salmon	21 Feb. to 30 Nov.	Residents: Tweeddale District permit applies. Visitors: I. Fraser, Northgate, Peebles. Tel: 20979.	Restricted to 20 per day. No seasons for visitors. Advance booking advisable Sept. to Nov. No Sundays. No swivels. Other regulations as Peebleshire Salmon Fishing Association.

Water	Location	Species	Season	Permit available from	Other Information
Tweed contd.	Walkerburn	Salmon Trout Sea Trout	1 Feb.-30 Nov. 1 Apr. to 30 Sep.	Tweed Valley Hotel, Walkerburn. Tel: (089687) 636. Telex: 94013344 Ref: TWEEG.	Salmon tickets for hotel guests only after 14 Sept. Special salmon and trout weeks, tuition. Trout and grayling permits available to all.
	Peel	Salmon Sea Trout	15 Sept.-30 Nov. 1 Feb.-31 Aug.	Tweed Valley Hotel, Walkerburn. Tel: (089687) 636. Telex: 94013344 Ref: TWEEG.	Private 2-rod salmon beat on south bank.
	Nest	Salmon Sea Trout	1 Feb-14 Sept. 15 Sept-30 Nov.	Tweed Valley Hotel, Walkerburn. Tel: (089687) 636. Telex: 94013344 Ref: TWEEG.	Private salmon/sea trout beat approx. 1¾ miles, 4 rods. Fly only 15 Sept. to 30 Nov.
	Ashiestiel (Nest and Peel)	Salmon Sea Trout Trout	15 Feb. to 30 Nov. 1 Apr. to 30 Sept.	Tweed Valley Hotel, Walkerburn. Tel: (089687) 636 Telex: 94013344 Ref: TWEEG	2½ miles south bank. Week or day lets Spring/Summer. Week lets only October and November. Angling Course September. Angling course for both trout and salmon fishing spring and autumn both fly and bait casting, single handed, two handed and spinning rods.
	Haystoun	Salmon	1 Feb. to 30 Nov.	I. Fraser Sports, Northgate, Peebles. Tel: 20979.	Spinning allowed 15 Feb. to 14 Sept. 1½ miles in length. 8 named salmon pools.
	Kingsmeadow	Salmon	1 Feb. to 30 Nov.	I. Fraser Sports, Northgate, Peebles. Tel: 20979.	Spinning allowed. 15 Feb to 14 Sept. 3/4 miles in length. 5 named salmon pools.
	Glenormiston	Salmon	1 Feb. to 30 Nov.	I. Fraser Sports, Northgate, Peebles. Tel: 20979.	Fly only. 1 mile in length. 5 named salmon pools.
	Galashiels	Trout	1 Apr. to 30 Sept.	Gala Angling Association Messrs. J. & A. Turnbull, 30 Bank Street, Galashiels. Tel: 3191. Kingsknowes Hotel, Galashiels. Tel: (0896) 58375. Clovenfords Hotel, Clovenfords. Tel: 203.	No Sundays. Day tickets available on Saturdays. No spinning.
	Boleside	Grayling Brown Trout	1 Feb. to 10 Sept.	N. Fell, Fisherman's Cottage, Boleside. Tel: Galashiels 2972.	
	Melrose	Trout Grayling	1 Apr.to 6 Oct. 7 Oct.to 15 Mar.	Melrose & District Angling Association Anglers Choice Hotel, High Street, Melrose. Tel: 3070.	No spinning. No ground baiting. No Sundays. Minnow fishing not permitted. Spinning reels of all types prohibited.
		Grayling and Brown Trout only available	1 Apr. to 6 Oct.	The Brother Superior, St. Aidans, Gattonside, Melrose.	No spinning. Bait and fly only. Sunday fishing restrictions on number of rods. See permit for full details.

Water	Location	Species	Season	Permit available from	Other Information
Tweed contd.	Melrose (Ravenswood Tweedswood)	Brown Trout	1 Apr. to 30 Sept.	Anglers Choice Hotel, High Street, Melrose. Tel: 3070.	
	Melrose (Pavilion)	Salmon Sea Trout	1 Feb. to 30 Nov.	Anglers Choice Hotel, High Street, Melrose. Tel: 3070.	Fly only - 1 to 15 Feb. and 15 Sept. to 30 Nov. Feb. 16 to Sept. 14 fly and spinning.
	St. Boswells	Brown Trout Trout	1 Apr. to 30 Sept.	St. Boswells Angling Association Mr. Law, Main Street, St. Boswells. C.D. Grant, Newsagent, Newton, St. Boswells. Mr. Geddes, Fisherman's House, Mertoun Mill, Dryburgh. Dryburgh Abbey Hotel, St. Boswells. Tel: (0835) 22261. Anglers Choice Hotel, Melrose. Miss A. Laing, Newsagent, St. Boswells.	Fly only 1 Apr. to 1 May. No ground baiting. No bait fishing until May 1. No Sundays. No spinning tackle. No coarse fishing allowed outside season. Full details of local rules on permit. Access to restricted beats by special permits only. Full details shown on permit.
Tweed (and Teviot)	Kelso	Trout	1 Apr. to 30 Sept.	Kelso Angling Association C. Hutchison, 53 Abbotseat, Kelso.	No Sundays. Size limit 10in. Fly only 1-30 April.
		Grayling	1 May-31 Aug. 1 Dec.-31 Jan.	Forrest & Sons, 35, The Square, Kelso. Tel: (0573) 24687. Redpath & Co., Horsemarket, Kelso. Intersport, 43, The Square, Kelso. River Watchers. Borders Temperance Hotel. Springwood Caravan Park. Tweedside Tackle, Woodside.	Spinning restrictions. No maggots or ground bait. No fishing above Roxburgh Viaduct between 15 & 30 Sept. both dates incl.
Tweed	Kelso	Brown Trout Coarse Fish	1 Apr to 30 Sept.	Forrest & Sons, 35, The Square, Kelso. Tel: (0573) 24687.	
	Coldstream	Brown Trout Grayling Roach	Varies according to best. Details on permit.	Coldstream Angling Association Tweed Fishing Tackle, Market Street, Coldstream. Crown Hotel, Market Square, Coldstream. Tel: Coldstream 2558.	Fly only. No Sunday or night fishing. No spinning.
	Cornhill	Salmon Sea Trout Brown Trout	Salmon 1 Feb. to 30 Nov.	Tillmouth Park Hotel, Tel: Coldstream 2255.	No Sundays. No worming. Boats and ghillies available. Special terms for residents.
	Ladykirk	Brown Trout	19 Mar. to 8 Oct.	Ladykirk & Norham Angling Association Masons Arms, Norham. Tel: (0289) 82326. Victoria Hotel, Norham, Tel: (0289) 82237.	No spinning. No ground baiting. Fly only above Norham Bridge to West Ford. No Sundays.
	Horncliffe (Tidal)	Trout, Grayling, Roach, Dace and Eel.		No permit required.	
Whiteadder & Dye & Tributaries	30 miles	Brown/ Rainbow Trout	15 Mar. to 30 Sept.	Whiteadder Angling Association Mr. Cowan, Crumstane, Duns. (Bailiff). R. Welsh, Abbey St. Bathans, Duns. Peter Grzeszuk, Whitchester, Ellemford.	No Sundays. Fly only before 15 Apr. Worm from 15 Apr. only. Minnow from 1 May only. Tickets in advance. Size limit 8 inches. River stocked annually.

Water	Location	Species	Season	Permit available from	Other Information
Whiteadder	Allanton	Trout	15 Mar. to 30 Sept.	Berwick & District Angling Association. Mr. D. Cowan, 3 Church Street, Berwick. Tel: (0289) 330145. Bus parties limited in numbers and prior arrangement only with Hon. Secretary. Messrs. Jobson, Marygate, Berwick. Messrs. Game Fair, Berwick. Allanton Inn Allanton.	Fly only before May. No spinning (rod and/or reel). No threadline. No maggot fishing. No ground baiting. 9 inch min. Max bag of 12 brown trout per day. No Sundays.
	Abbey St. Bathans	Brown Trout	15 Mar. to 30 Sept.	Head Keeper Abbey St. Bathans Trout Farm, Tel: (03614) 237.	4½ miles private stretch. Fly only.

LOCHS AND RESERVOIRS

Water	Location	Species	Season	Permit available from	Other Information
Acreknowe Reservoir	Hawick	Brown/ Rainbow Trout	15 Mar. to end Sept.	Porteous & Newcome, Howgate, Hawick. The Pet Shop, Union Street, Hawick. Mr. R.A. Sutherland, 20 Longhope Drive, Hawick. Tel: (0450) 75150.	Ticket covers all other trout waters managed by Hawick Angling Club. Boats available from Pet Shop.
Alemoor Loch	Hawick	Brown Trout Perch Pike		As Acreknowe	Bank fishing only.
Coldingham Loch	Coldingham	Brown/ Rainbow Trout	15 Mar. to 30 Oct.	Dr. E.J. Wise, West Loch House, Coldingham. Tel: 71270.	Fly only. 4 boats (max. 8 rods). 4 bank rods. Sunday fishing, 10 am-Dusk. Bag limit 4 per rod full day. Min. size 12 in. Advance booking essential. Full details on leaflet.
Fruid Reservoir	Tweedsmuir	Brown Trout	1 Apr. to 30 Sept.	Boat and bank permits from Reservoir Superintendent. Tel: Tweedsmuir 225.	Sunday fishing. Two boats to be booked in advance. Bus parties can be accommodated. Prior notice to water keeper preferred.
Heatherhope Reservoir	Morebattle	Trout	1 Apr. to 30 Sept.	Mr. H. Fox Orchard Cottage, Morebattle.	No ground baiting. No Sunday fishing.
Hellmoor Loch	Hawick	Brown Trout		As Acreknowe	No Boat.
Loch of the Lowes and St. Mary's Loch	Selkirk	rown Trout	1 Apr. to 30 Sept.	St. Mary's A.C., per secretary, J. Miller, 8/5 Craighouse Gardens, Edinburgh. Tel: 031-447 0024.	Fly fishing only, until 30th April thereafter spinning and bait allowed.
		Pike Perch Eels	1 May to 30 Sept.	The Glen Cafe, Cappercleuch. Tibbiesheils Hotel (Loch side). Anglers Choice Hotel, High Street, Melrose. Keeper, Henderland East Cottage, Cappercleuch. Tel: Cappercleuch 42243. Rodono Hotel (Loch side).	Club fishing apply in advance to Secretary or keeper. Sunday fishing allowed. Weekly permits are obtainable from the keeper. Permits must be obtained before commencing to fish. No

Water	Location	Species	Season	Permit available from	Other Information
Loch of the Lowes and St. Mary's Loch contd.	Selkirk			Sonny's Sports Shop, 29 High Street, Innerleithen.	float fishing. Boats from keeper only. River Tweed Protection Order applies. Club memberships available.
Megget Reservoir	Selkirk	Brown Trout	1 Apr. to 30 Sept.	Boat and bank permits from Mrs. Baigrie, 2 Gillwood, Cappercleuch. Tel: (0750) 42265.	Sunday fishing. Fly only. 6 boats & bank fishing.
Peebleshire Lochs	Tweed Valley	Brown/ Rainbow Trout	Apr. to Oct.	Tweed Valley Hotel, Walkerburn. Tel: (089687) 220. Telex: 946240 Ref: TWEEG	Stocked private lochans.
Synton Loch	Hawick	Brown Trout		As Acreknowe Reservoir.	Boats available from Porteous & Newcome, Howgate, Hawick.
Talla Reservoir	Tweedsmuir	Brown Trout	1 Apr. to 30 Sept.	Boat and bank permits from Reservoir Superintendent, Tel: Tweedsmuir 209.	Sunday fishing, fly only. Two boats may be booked in advance. Bus parties can be accommodated. Prior notice to water keeper preferred.
Upper Loch	Bowhill	Brown/ Rainbow Trout	1 Apr. to 5 Oct.	Buccleuch Estate, Bowhill, Selkirk. Tel: (0750) 20753.	Fly only. 2 rods per boat and limit of 8 fish per boat.
Watch Reservoir	Longformacus	Brown/ Rainbow Trout	15 Mar.- 30 Sept. All year	Watch Fly Reservoir, W.F. Renton, Tel: (03617) 331 & (0289) 306028.	Sunday fishing.
Whiteadder Reservoir	Cranshaws	Brown Trout	Boat fishing 1 Apr. to 30 Sept. Bank fishing 1 Jun. to 30 Sept.	Boat and bank permits from waterkeeper. Tel: Longformacus 257.	Sunday fishing. Fly only. 3 boats may be booked in advance. Bus parties can be accommodated. Prior notice to waterkeeper preferred.
Williestruther Loch	Hawick	Brown/ Rainbow Trout		As Acreknowe Reservoir.	Limit of 2 rainbow per day. No limit of brown trout.
Wooden Loch	Eckford	Brown Trout / Rainbow Trout	1 Apr. to 30 Sept. 1 Apr. to 31 Oct.	Gamekeeper, No. 4 Eckford Mr. Graham Eckford Cott. Eckford, Kelso. Tel: (083-55) 255	One boat. No bank fishing. Only rainbow trout after 30 Sept. Only 3 rods at any time. Advance booking necessary.

BORDERS
Sea Angling

The Scottish Borders provide some of the best sea angling in the UK. Based on Eyemouth and the smaller fishing villages of Burnmouth and St. Abbs, the clear unpolluted waters are well stocked with a wide variety of sea fish. It should be noted that sea angling is not permitted off St. Abbs Head National Reserve (Petticowick – Long Carr).

Eyemouth is only nine miles north of Berwick-upon-Tweed. Well known for its excellent rock fishing, the town is also a useful point of access to shoreline to the north and south. Boat fishing has developed over the years due to the efforts of Eyemouth Sea Angling Club who now run a number of shore and boat competitions throughout the season.

The club operates the coast from Burnmouth harbour to St. Abbs harbour.

Types of fish: Shore – cod, mackerel, coalfish, flounder, plaice, sole, haddock, whiting, catfish, ling and wrasse.
Boat – same species but larger.

Boats: Fishing boats are usually available from Eyemouth, St. Abbs and Burnmouth for parties at weekends. For bookings and further information write c/o F.M.A., Harbour Road, Eyemouth or J. Weatherhead and Sons, Harbour Road, Eyemouth. (50382).

Area Tourist Board
Dumfries and Galloway Tourist Board

Director of Tourism,
Dumfries and Galloway Tourist Board
Douglas House,
Newton Stewart,
Wigtownshire DG8 6DQ.
Tel: Newton Stewart (0671) 2549

RIVER PURIFICATION BOARD
SOLWAY RIVER PURIFICATION BOARD
River's House, Irongray Road,
Dumfries DG2 0JE.
Tel: Dumfries 720502.

RIVERS

Water	Location	Species	Season	Permit available from	Other information
Annan	Newbie Estate	Salmon Sea Trout	25 Feb. to 15 Nov.	Mr. Bailey, Newbie Mill, Annan. Tel: Annan 2608.	Fly fishing all season. Spinning when above mark on Galabank Bridge. Worm fishing in flood.
	Hoddom & Kinmount Estates Ecclefechan	Salmon Sea Trout Brown Trout	25 Feb. to 15 Nov.	Miss Marsh, Bridge Cottage, Hoddom. Tel: (05763) 488.	No Sunday fishing. Fly water unless the spinning mark is covered.
	Halleaths Estate Lockerbie	Salmon Sea Trout	25 Feb. to 15 Nov.	Messrs. McJerrow & Stevenson, Solicitors, Lockerbie, Dumfriesshire. Tel: Lockerbie 2123.	Limited number of tickets.
	Royal Four Towns Water Lockerbie	Salmon Sea Trout Brown Trout Harling Chub Griese	25 Feb. to 15 Nov.	Clerk and Commissions, Royal Four Towns Fishing K. Ratcliffe, 'Jay-Ar', Preston House Road, Hightae, Lockerbie. Tel: Lochmaben 220.	Boats prohibited. Fly and spinning. Worm fishing 15/3/89. No Sunday fishing.
	St. Mungo Parish	Salmon Sea Trout	25 Feb. to 15 Nov.	Castle Milk Estates Office, Norwood, Lockerbie.	Fly fishing only. No Sunday fishing.
		Brown Trout	15 Mar. to 6 Oct.	Tel: Kettleholm 203/4.	
	Kinmount Estate Lockerbie	Salmon Sea Trout Brown Trout	25 Feb. to 15 Nov.	Miss Marsh, Bridge Cottage, Hoddam. Tel: (05763) 488.	No Sunday fishing. Fly water unless the spinning mark is covered.
	Moffat	Salmon Sea Trout	25 Feb. to 15 Nov.	Upper Annandale Angling Association J. Black. 1 Rosehill, Grange Road, Moffat. Tel: Moffat 20104.	Limited number of seasons available.
		Brown Trout	1 Apr. to 15 Sept.		
Bladnoch	Newton Stewart	Salmon	1 Mar. to 30 Sept.	Newton Stewart Angling Association Galloway Guns & Tackle, Arthur Street, Newton Stewart. Tel: (0671) 3404.	
Cairn	Dumfries	Salmon Sea Trout	25 Feb. to 31 Oct.	Dumfries & Galloway Angling Association Secretary, R. Marcucci, 64 Georgetown Road, Dumfries DG1 4DF. Tel: (0387) 62868 (Evenings). D. McMillan, 6 Friars Vennel, Dumfries. Tel: Dumfries 52075.	Limited number of permits. No Sunday fishing. Restrictions depend on Water level. Visitors Mon.-Fri. only.
		Brown Trout	15 Mar. to 31 Aug.		

Water	Location	Species	Season	Permit available from	Other Information
Cree (and Pencill Burn)	Newton Stewart	Salmon Sea Trout	1 Mar. to 14 Oct.	Newton Stewart Angling Association Galloway Guns & Tackle, Arthur Street, Newton Stewart. Tel: (0671) 3404.	No Sunday fishing.
Cross Waters of Luce	New Luce	Salmon Sea Trout	1 May to 31 Oct.	Stranraer & District Angling Association. McDiarmid Sports Shop, 90 George Street, Stranraer. Tel: (0776) 2705. And local hotels.	No Sunday fishing.
Dee	New Galloway	Salmon Sea Trout Brown Trout Roach Perch Pike	15 Mar. to 31 Oct. 15 Mar. to 30 Sept.	Shops and hotels in New Galloway.	Surcharged if permit bought from bailiffs.
Black Water of Dee	Mossdale	Salmon	11 Feb. to 31 Oct.	New Galloway Angling Association, Secretary, N. Birch, Galloway View,	
		Trout Pike Perch	15 Mar. to 30 Sept.	Balmaclellan, Castle Douglas. Tel: New Galloway 404. Local Hotels.	
Esk	Langholm Canonbie	Salmon	1 Feb. to 31 Oct.	Esk and Liddle Fisheries Association.	Spinning allowed until 14 Apr. and from 1 Oct., otherwise only when water is above markers at Willow Pool, Canonbie Bridge, Skippers Bridge and River Liddle markers. No Sunday fishing.
Liddle and Tributaries	Newcastleton (All waters ticket)	Sea Trout	1 May to 30 Sept.	Secretary, R.J.B. Hill, Solicitor, Bank of Scotland Buildings, Langholm, Dumfriesshire. Tel: Langholm 80428. Mr. P. Lillie, 19 Rowanburn, Canonbie. Tel: Canonbie 224.	
Ewes, Wauchope, Tarras		Brown Trout	15 Apr. to 30 Sept.	George Graham, Hagg-Old School, Canonbie, Dumfriesshire. Tel: Canonbie 71416.	
	Canonbie Ticket			Secretary	No Sunday fishing.
	Langholm Ticket			Secretary and George Graham, Hagg-Old School, Canonbie. Tel: Canonbie 71416.	Spinning allowed until 14 Apr. & from 1 Oct., otherwise only when water is above marker at Skippers Bridge. No Sunday fishing.
	Canonbie Lower Liddle Ticket			Secretary and George Graham, Hagg-Old School, Canonbie. Tel: Canonbie 71416.	Spinning allowed until 14 Apr. & from 1 Oct., otherwise only when water is above marker at Canonbie Bridge. No Sunday fishing.

Water	Location	Species	Season	Permit available from	Other Information
Ewes, Wauchope, Tarras cont.	Newcastleton Ticket	Salmon Sea Trout Brown Trout	15 Apr.-31 Oct. 1 May-30 Sept. 15 Apr.-30 Sept.	Secretary and J.D. Ewart, Drapers, Newcastleton. Tel: Liddlesdale 257.	Spinning allowed when water is above markers at Newcastleton and Kershopelfoot Bridges. No Sunday fishing.
	Langholm Area Tributaries Ticket	Salmon Sea Trout Brown Trout	15 Apr. to 30 Sept.	Secretary and George Graham, Hagg-Old School, Canonbie, Dumfriesshire. Tel: Canonbie 71416.	No spinning. No Sunday fishing.
	River and Tributaries	Coarse Fishing	Nov. to 31 Jan.	R.J.B. Hill, Bank of Scotland Buildings, Langholm, Dumfriesshire.	Club applications.
Fleet	Gatehouse of Fleet	Salmon Sea Trout Brown Trout	1 Jun. to 31 Oct.	Murray Arms Hotel, Gatehouse of Fleet. Tel: (05574) 207.	
Kelhead Quarry	Hoddom & Kinmount Estate, Lockerbie	Coarse Fishing	No close season	Kelhead Bungalow, Cummertrees. Tel: Cummertrees 344.	
Ken	New Galloway	Salmon Sea Trout Brown Trout	11 Feb. to 31 Oct. 15 Mar. to 3 Sept.	New Galloway Angling Association N. Birch, Galloway View, Balmaclellan, Castle Douglas. Tel: New Galloway 404. Local Hotels.	
	Dalry	Salmon Sea Trout Brown Trout	1 Apr. to 30 Sept.	Dalry Angling Association T. & A. Kirk, Glenkens Cafe, Dalry.	
Milk	Scroggs Bridge	Sea Trout Brown Trout	1 Apr. to 30 Sept.	Castle Milk Estates Office, Norwood Lockerbie. Tel: Kettleholm 203/4.	Fly fishing only. No Sunday fishing.
Nith	Dumfries	Salmon Sea Trout Brown Trout	25 Feb. to 30 Nov. 15 Mar. to 6 Oct.	Director of Finance, Nithsdale District Council, Municipal Chambers, Dumfries. Tel: Dumfries 53166.	
				Dumfries & Galloway Angling Association Secretary, R. Marcucci, 64 Georgetown Road, Dumfries DG1 4DF. Tel: (0387) 62868 (evenings). D. McMillan, 6 Friar's Vennel, Dumfries.	Limited number of permits. Weekly permits from Mon.-Fri. Advance booking possible. Spinning restrictions.
	Thornhill	Salmon	25 Feb.-30 Nov.	Mid Nithsdale Angling Association.	No day permits on Saturdays. Spinning and worming allowed, only in flood conditions. Advisable to book for autumn fishing.
		Sea Trout Brown Trout	1 Apr. to 30 Sept.	I.R. Milligan, 123 Drumlanrig Street, Thornhill. Tel: (0848) 30555.	
	Thornhill	Salmon Sea Trout Brown Trout	April to 30 Nov.	Buccleuch Estates Ltd., Drumlanrig Mains, Thornhill. Tel: (08486) 283.	Three beats - weekly lets. Two rods per beat with optional third rod. One beat-daily let-three rods. Two trout lochs with boat on each.

Water	Location	Species	Season	Permit available from	Other Information
Nith (and Tributaries Kello Crawick Euchan Mennock)	Sanquhar	Salmon Sea Trout Brown Trout Grayling	15 Mar. to 30 Nov. Jan., Feb.	Upper Nithsdale Angling Club. W. Forsyth, Solicitor, 100 High Street, Sanquhar, Dumfriesshire. Tel: Sanquhar 50241.	No Saturday/Sunday fishing. Visitors to district and bona fide residents.
Nith and Afton	New Cumnock	Brown Trout	15 Mar. to 6 Oct.	New Cumnock Angling Association, T. Basford, 1 Pathhead, New Cumnock.	
Tarf	Kirkcowan	Sea Trout Brown Trout	Easter - 30 Sept.	A. Brown, Three Lochs Caravan Park, Kirkcowan, Newtown Stewart, Wigtownshire. Tel: Kirkcowan 304.	
	Kirkcowan	Salmon Brown Trout Pike	18 Feb to 31 Oct.	Derek Lynch Torwood House Hotel, Glenluce, Newton Stewart. Tel: (05813) 463.	Sunday fishing for pike only. Salmon best 1 Sep. to 31 Oct.
Urr	Dalbeattie	Salmon Sea Trout Brown Trout	25 Feb. to 29 Nov. 15 Mar. to 6 Oct.	Castle Douglas and District Angling Association Tommy's Sport Shop, King Street, Castle Douglas. Tel: (0556) 2861. Dalbeattie Angling Association Ticket Sec., M. McCowan & Son, 43 High Street, Dalbeattie. Tel: (0556) 610270.	
White Esk	Eskdalemuir	Salmon Sea Trout	15 Apr. to 30 Sept.	Hart Manor Hotel, Eskdalemuir, by Langholm. Tel: Eskdalemuir 73217.	Fly and spinner only.

LOCH AND RESERVOIRS

Water	Location	Species	Season	Permit available from	Other Information
Barnbarroch Loch	Whauphill	Bream Carp Roach Tench Rudd	No close season	Derek Lynch, Torwood House Hotel, Glenluce, Newton Stewart. Tel: (05813) 469.	Day tickets available to matches. Up to 20 pegs.
Barscobe Loch	Balmaclellan	Brown/ Rainbow Trout	15 Mar. to 6 Oct.	Sir Hugh Wontner, Barscobe, Balmaclellan, Castle Douglas. Tel: (064 42) 245/294.	
Black Esk Reservoir	Eskdalemuir	Brown Trout	1 Apr. to 30 Sept.	Hart Manor Hotel, Eskdalemuir, by Langholm. Tel: Eskdalemuir 73217.	Fly and spinner only.
Black Loch	Newton Stewart	Brown Trout (stocked)	15 Apr. to 30 Sept.	Forestry Commission, Creebridge. Tel: (0671) 2420. Galloway Deer Museum, New Galloway, Tel: (064 42) 285.	Fly only until 1 July.
Brack Loch	Dalry	Brown/ Rainbow Trout	1 Apr. to 30 Sept.	Milton Park Hotel, Dalry. Tel: (064 43) 286.	1 Boat. Sunday fishing.
Bruntis Loch	Newton Stewart	Brown/ Rainbow Trout	15 Mar. to 30 Sept.	Newton Stewart Angling Association. Galloway Guns & Tackle, Arthur Street, Newton Stewart. Tel: Newton Stewart 3404.	Bank fishing only. Sunday fishing.
Castle Loch	Lochmaben	Bream Perch	No close season	Mr. Armstrong, Lochside Cottage, Lochmaben. Tel: Lochmaben 340.	
Clattering-shaws Loch	6 miles west of New Galloway	Trout Pike Perch	Open all year for coarse fish	Permits at Deer Museum.	

Water	Location	Species	Season	Permit available from	Other Information
Dalbeattie Reservoir	Dalbeattie	Brown/ Rainbow Trout	15 Apr. to 30 Sept.	Dalbeattie Angling Association M. McCowan & Son, 43 High Street, Dalbeattie. Tel: (0556) 610270.	Bank fishing. Fly only.
Loch Dee	New Galloway	Brown Trout	15 Mar. to 6 Oct.	Forestry Commission, Creebridge. Tel: (0671) 2420 or Castle Douglas Tel: (0556) 3626. Galloway Deer Museum, New Galloway. Tel: (064 42) 285.	Fly fishing only, sunrise to sunset. No boats. Sunday fishing.
Dernagler Loch	Glenluce	Pike Perch	No close season	Derek Lynch, Torwood House Hotel, Glenluce, Newton Stewart. Tel: (05813) 469.	
Dindinnie Reservoir	Stranraer	Brown Trout	15 Mar. to 30 Sept.	Stranraer & District Angling Association. McDiarmid Sports Shop, 90 George Street, Stranraer. Tel: (0776) 2705. Local hotels.	Fly fishing only. Sunday fishing.
Ervie Estate Fishings	Castle Douglas	Brown/ Rainbow Trout	1 Apr. to 30 Sept.	G.M. Thomson & Co. Ltd., 27 King Street, Castle Douglas. Tel: (0556) 2701.	Bank fishing only. Limited rods. Sunday fishing. Bag limit - 6 fish.
Glenkiln Reservoir	Dumfries	Brown Trout (stocked) Rainbow Trout	1 Apr. to 30 Sept.	Director of Water & Sewerage, Dumfries & Galloway Regional Council, 70 Terregles Street, Dumfries DG2 9BB. Tel: (0387) 61234.	
Hightae Mill Loch	Lochmaben	Bream Carp Tench Rudd Chub Roach		J. Wildman, Annandale Cottage, Greenhill, Lockerbie. Tel: Lochmaben 478.	Fishing by boat only. No restrictions.
Jericho Loch	Dumfries	Brown Trout Rainbow Trout Brook Trout	1 Apr. to 30 Sept.	Pattie's of Dumfries, 103 Queensberry Street, Dumfries. Tel: (0387) 52891. Thistle Stores, Locharbriggs. Sunday tickets, Tourist Information, Dumfries.	Bank fishing only. Fly fishing only. Sunday fishing.
Loch Ken	Parton	Pike	All year	G.M. Thomson & Co. Ltd., 27 King Street, Castle Douglas. Tel: Castle Douglas 2701/2973.	Self Catering Accommodation available throughout Galloway.
	West Bank Lochside Aird's (Viaduct)	Salmon Trout and coarse fish	Open all year for coarse fish	Shops, hotels in New Galloway	Surcharged if permits bought from bailiffs.
		Pike Perch	All year.	Galloway View, Balmaclellan, Castle Douglas. Tel: New Galloway 404. Local hotels.	
Mossdale Loch	Mossdale	Brown/ Rainbow Trout	15 Mar. to 30 Sept.	Garry House, Mossdale.	Fly fishing from boat only.

Please mention this Pastime Publications Guide

Water	Location	Species	Season	Permit available from	Other Information
Loch Mossrodick	Dalry	Brown/ Rainbow Trout	1 Apr. to 30 Sept.	Milton Park Hotel, Tel: (06442) 286.	Fly only. 2 Boats. Sunday fishing.
Kirriereoch Loch	Newton Stewart	Brown Trout	15 Mar. to 6 Oct.	Newton Stewart Angling Association. Galloway Guns & Tackle, Arthur Street, Newton Stewart. Tel: Newton Stewart 3404.	Bank fishing only. Fly fishing only. Sunday fishing.
Knockquassan Reservoir	Stranraer	Brown Trout	15 Mar. to 30 Sept.	Stranraer & District Angling Association. McDiarmid Sports Shop, 90 George Street, Stranraer. Tel: (0776) 2705. Local hotels.	Bank fishing only. Fly and spinner. Sunday fishing.
Lairdmannoch Loch	Twynholm	Brown Trout	1 Apr. to 30 Sept.	G.M. Thomson, & Co. Ltd., 27 King Street, Castle Douglas. Tel: (0556) 2701.	Boat fishing only. Limited rods. Limited days. 2 boats included in house rent.
Lillies Loch	New Galloway	Brown Trout	15 Mar. to 6 Oct.	Forestry Commission, Creebridge. Tel: (0671) 2420. Galloway Deer Museum, New Galloway, Tel: (06442) 285.	Bank fishing only. Any legal method. Sunday fishing.
Lochenbreck Loch	Lauriston	Brown/ Rainbow Trout	1 Apr. to 30 Sept.	Watson McKinnel, 15 St. Cuthbert Street, Kirkcudbright. Tel: (0557) 30693. M. & E. Brown, Gatehouse of Fleet, Tel: 222.	8.30 am to 10 pm. Bank fishing. Five boats. Sunday fishing.
Lochinvar Loch	Dalry	Brown Trout	1 Apr. to 30 Sept.	Mr. Armour, Lochinvar Lodge, Dalry. Tel: (06443) 355.	Sunrise to sunset. Bank fishing. Two boats. Fly fishing only.
Loch of the Lowes	Newton Stewart	Brown trout (stocked)	15 Mar. to 6 Oct.	Forestry Commission Creebridge. Tel: (0671) 2420.	Fly only. Sunday fishing.
Lochmaben	Lochmaben	Bream Roach Tench Vendace	No close season	The Warden, Lochfield, Lochmaben. Tel: Lochmaben 340.	Matches can be arranged.
Loch Ochiltree	Newton Stewart	Brown Trout Brook Trout Pike	15 Mar. to 6 Oct. All year	Newton Stewart Angling Association.	Fly, spinning and bait. Bank fishing and two boats. Sunday fishing. No live bait.
Penwhirn Reservoir	Stranraer	Brown Trout	15 Mar. to 30 Sept.	Stranraer & District Angling Association. McDiarmid Sports Shop, 90 George Street, Stranraer. Tel: (0776) 2705. Local hotels.	Fly fishing and spinning. Bank fishing. Sunday fishing.
Purdom Stone Reservoir	Hoddom & Kinmount Estates, Lockerbie	Brown Trout	1 Apr. to 15 Sept.	The Water Bailiff, 2 Bridge End Cottage, Hoddom, Lockerbie. Tel: Ecclefechan 488.	Fly fishing only.
Loch Roan	Castle Douglas	Brown/ Rainbow Trout	1 Apr. to 6 Oct.	Tommy's Sports Shop, King Street, Castle Douglas. Tel: (0556) 2851.	Fly fishing only. Four boats.
Soulseat Loch	Stranraer	Brown/ Rainbow Trout	15 Mar. to 30 Sept.	Stranraer & District Angling Association. McDiarmid Sports Shop, 90 George Street, Stranraer. Tel: (0776) 2705. Local hotels.	Fly, spinning and bait. Bank fishing and two boats. Sunday fishing.

Water	Location	Species	Season	Permit available from	Other Information
Loch Stroan	Castle Douglas	Pike Perch	15 May to 23 Oct.	Forestry Commission, 21 King Street, Castle Douglas. Tel: (0556) 3262.	Bank fishing only. Any legal method. Sunday fishing.
Torwood Lochs	Glenluce	Trout Bream Tench Carp Roach Rudd Perch	No close season	Derek Lynch, Torwood House Hotel, Glenluce, Newton Stewart. Tel: (05813) 469.	
Loch Whinyeon	Gatehouse of Fleet	Brown Trout	1 Apr. to 30 Sept.	M. & E. Brown, Gatehouse of Fleet. Tel: 222.	8 am to 10 pm. Bank and fly fishing only.
Whitefield Loch	Glenluce	Pike Perch	No close season	Derek Lynch, Torwood House Hotel, Glenluce, Newton Stewart. Tel: (05813) 469.	

DUMFRIES AND GALLOWAY
Sea Angling

Solway Firth to Mull of Galloway and Loch Ryan
An area of many headlands and off-shore reefs with strong tidal runs which can give rise to dangerous sea conditions with rising winds. Small boat anglers should always seek local advice before putting to sea. The Solway Firth area is noted for its many fine shore marks, many of which produce species such as bass, bullhuss and tope in far greater numbers than marks further north. Shore marks on the Kirkcudbrightshire coast regularly produce large cod during the winter months.

Kippford by Dalbeattie
Kippford is a well known yachting centre on the Solway Firth which offers some very good fishing, especially for flatfish.
Types of fish: Cod, flounder, plaice from the shore. Flatfish (including turbot), cod, tope, mackerel, and pollack from boats.
Tackle: Available from M. McCowan & Son, 43 High Street, Dalbeattie. M. Pattie, Dumfries, Dumfriesshire.
Bait: Lugworm can be dug locally. Cockles and mussels from the shore at low water. M. McCowan and Son can supply prepack baits.
Season for fishing: Best May-October. Some winter fishing for cod to 30lb.

Further information and boat details from: Ticket Secy: Mr. Eric McCowan, 43, High Street, Dalbeattie. Tel: (0556) 610270

Kirkcudbright
Kirkcudbright is a picturesque town with a very good but tidal harbour. It is approximately three miles from fishing grounds, which offer excellent tope as well as good general fishing. The coast is rugged and not recommended for dinghy or small boat fishing.

Types of fish: Cod, coalfish, conger, bass, plaice, flounders, pollack and dogfish from the shore. Cod, coalfish, conger, dogfish, mackerel, haddock, tope, pollack, all types of flatfish and whiting from the boats. Local sea angling clubs hold regular outings and competitions, where visitors are welcome. Information in Harbour Square.

Boats: S. Unsworth, "Raasay Cottage", 4 Bourtree Crescent, Kirkcudbright. Tel: 0557 30337.
Tackle: Available from W. McKinnel, 15 St. Cuthbert Street, Kirkcudbright. M. McCowan & Son, 43 High Street, Dalbeattie, Tel: (0556) 610270 and 52 King Street, Castle Douglas, Tel: (0556) 2009. Patties, 109 Queensferry Street, Dumfries, Dumfriesshire. Castle Douglas Guns & Tackle, 9 St. Andrews Street, Castle Douglas. Tommy's Sports Shop, 178 King Street, Castle Douglas. Tel: (0556) 2851
Bait: Lugworm can be dug locally. Mussels available at low water.

Season for fishing: May- October. Some winter fishing.
Further information from: Tourist Information Centre, Tel: Kirkcudbright (0557) 30494.

Garlieston
Garlieston has a potentially good but undeveloped tidal harbour on the east side of the Machars Peninsula in Wigtownshire with several square miles of water, sheltered by the land from prevailing winds and therefore suitable for trailed and car-top dinghies. Access from the A75 Dumfries to Stranraer road is by the A714 and B7004 from Newton Stewart.
Types of fish: Mackerel, cod, pollack and coalfish from the shore. Mackerel, cod, pollack, ray, plaice, dab, flounder and coalfish from boats.
Bait: Lugworm may be dug and mussels gathered from the foreshore.
Season for fishing: June-September.
Further information from: Mr A. Houston, The Crescent, Garlieston, Newton Stewart. Tel: Garlieston (098-86) 238.

Isle of Whithorn
This picturesque old seaport on the souht-west corner of Wigtown Bay has an excellent redesigned harbour with a flourishing local sailing club. It tends to be busy in summer and is a port for 'Queenie' boats. The Isle Bay itself offers nearly a mile of sheltered water in all but severe weather conditions. There are

many good rock fishing marks.
Tope festivals are held here twice
a year, also shore and boat fishing
competitions throughout the
season. Local weather forecasts
can be obtained from HM
Coastguard Station in the centre
of the village.
Types of fish: Cod, coalfish,
dogfish, conger, pollack,
mackerel, wrasse from the shore.
Cod, rays, flatfish, spurdog,
dogfish, mackerel, conger and
tope from boats.
Boats: C. Mills, 14 Main Street,
Isle of Whithorn, Tel: 098 85 393.
"Haley Lorraine", Ken Rush,
Dunbar House, Isle of Whithorn,
Tel: 098 85 336 W.F. McCreadie,
1 Barrhill Avenue, Newton
Stewart, Tel: 0671 2466. Various
Boats, Bryce Walker, Balcraig,
Port William. Tel: 098 87 249.
Tackle: Available from J.
McWilliam, Grocer, Main Street,
Isle of Whithorn. Tel: (098-85)
246. A. McGhie, Radio Shop,
George Street, Whithorn, R.
McDowell, George Street,
Whithorn, M. E. Clark, George
Street, Whithorn. The Shop,
Burrow-Head, Holiday Farm.
"Morning Star" and "Connie
Barr", c/o Sam Archer,
Fishmonger, Whithorn. Tel: 098
85 630. **Bait:** Lugworm and
ragworm, mussels and limpets can
be gathered on the shore. Good
bait can also be bought from E.
McGuire, Burnside Cottage, Isle
of Whithorn, at a reasonable
price (order in advance).
Season for fishing:
June-September.
Further information from: Mr.
E.C. McGuire, Burnside Cottage,
Isle of Whithorn, Wigtownshire
DG8 8LN. Tel: Whithorn (098-
85) 468.

Luce Bay
There are some good shore
marks, namely Sandhead Sands
for Flatfish, Dogfish and Bass in
season, Terrally Bay for these
species plus Codling, Whiting,
Spurdogfish.
Around East and West Tarbet
bays at the Mull of Galloway
good rock fishing may be had for
Lesser Spotted Dogfish, Bull
Huss, Spurdogfish, Conger Eels,
Wrasse, Whiting, Pollack,
Coalfish, Flatfish and Mackerel in
season, normally from late April
to December.

Boats: W. Carter, Castle Daly
Angling Centre, Auchenmalg,
Glenluce. Tel: 058 15 250.
(Self drive boats for hire & hotel
accommodation). ˙

Port William
Port William is situated on the
east side of Luce Bay and has a
good though tidal harbour. It is
the starting point for many
anglers wishing to fish the lower
part of Luce Bay. The once
famous shore mark of Monreith
Bay, still a good bass beach, lies
just to the south of Port William.
Types of fish: Tope, spurdog,
rays, cod, pollack, flatfish from
boats. Bass, wrasse, codling and
pollack from the shore.
Boats: James Brawls, Port
William. Tel: 098 87 464.
Tackle: Available in village.
Bait: Lugworm, shellfish and
molluscs along beach. Mackerel
in bay.
Season for fishing: May- October.

Drummore
Drummore, the main port for
anglers wishing to fish the western
side of Luce Bay lies 5 miles
north of the Mull of Galloway.
Hotels and guest houses cater for
anglers. There are many good
shore marks on sandy beaches
north of Drummore, while the
Mull of Galloway provides
excellent shore fishing over rocky
ground. The Mull, the most
southerly part of Scotland, is an
area of very strong tides and is
not recommended as a fishing
area to anglers with small boats
incapable of at least 10 knots,
especially during ebb tides.
Types of fish: Pollack, wrasse
from rocky shores, flatfish, bass,
mullet, porbeagle shark and rays
from sandy beaches. Pollack,
coalfish, cod, whiting, wrasse,
lesser, spotted dogfish, bullhuss,
spurdog, tope, rays, conger from
boats.
Boats: S. Woods, Clachanmore
House, Ardwell, Drummore, Tel:
0776 86 297. S. Ilett, Bryces
Corner, Drummore. Tel: 0776 84
337.
Bait: All types available on shore
at low tide. Mackerel from Mull
of Galloway shore marks.

Port Logan
Port Logan is the small

community which is situated
about 7½ miles north of the Mull
of Galloway on the west side of
the Galloway Peninsula. An area
with many good shore marks both
to the north and south of the
village. It is one of the few
relatively easy launching sites on
this coastline south of
Portpatrick. A good alternative
for the angler with his own boat
when easterly winds prevent
fishing in Luce Bay. Like the
Mull of Galloway an area of
strong tides, especially off
Crammoc Head, to the south of
Port Logan Bay.
Types of fish: As for the southern
part of Luce Bay with occasional
haddock. Herring in June and
July.

Portpatrick
The small fishing port and holiday
resort of Portpatrick lies on the
west coast of Wigtownshire, 8
miles from Stranraer. There is
good shore fishing from the many
rocky points north and south of
the resort, the best known being
the Yellow Isle, ½ mile north of
the harbour. Sandeel Bay, a little
further north, and Killintringan
Lighthouse are also worth fishing.
Types of fish: Pollack, coalfish,
plaice, flounder, codling,
mackerel, dogfish, conger,
wrasse, and tope occasionally.
Boats: B. Watson, 1 Blair
Terrace, Portpatrick. Tel: 0776 81
468, P. & M. Green, Hawthorn
View, Lochans, Portpatrick. Tel:
0776 81 534, M. Wood, Ard
Choille, Guest House, 1 Blair
Terrace, Portpatrick,
Wigtownshire.
Tel: (077681) 468.
Bait: None sold locally. Lugworm
and some ragworm can be dug
east of the railway pier,
Stranraer.
Season for fishing:
May-December.
Further information from: Mr R.
Smith, 24 Millbank Road,
Stranraer. Tel: Stranraer (0776)
3691.

Stranraer & Loch Ryan
Stranraer, at the head of Loch
Ryan, offers the angler, as a rail
and bus terminal, a good stepping
off point for many sea angling
marks and areas in this part of
Scotland, with Sandhead on Luce
Bay (8 miles) to the south,

Portpatrick (8 miles) to the west and Lady Bay (8 miles) on the west side of Loch Ryan with Cairnryan (6 miles) and Finnart Bay (10 miles) on the opposite side of the loch. Best Shore marks being Cairnryan Village, South of Townsend Thoresen ferry terminal. Old House Point and Concrete Barges north of Cairnryan Village, Finnart Bay on East Mouth of Loch, Wig Bay, Jamiesons Point and Lady Bay on west side of Loch Ryan. Boats may be launched at Wig Bay Slipway, Lady Bay and at Stranraer Market Street.

Types of fish: Cod, pollack, mackerel, whiting, flatfish, (Gurnard, conger, dogfish and occasional tope.

Boats: Mr. Steve Dutton, "Auld Haim", Main Street, Cairnryan, Tel: 058-12-248. Mike Watson, 32 Main Street, Kirkcolm, Tel: 0776-853225.

Tackle: The Sports Shop, George Street, Stranraer. (Frozen bait stocked).

Bait: Excellent lugworms can be dug at low tide from the sands exposed to the east side of the railway pier at low tide.

Further information from: Mr S. Dutton, "Auld Haim", Main Street, Cairnryan, Tel: 058-12-248. Mr. R. Smith, 24 Millbank Road, Stranraer, Tel: Stranraer (0776) 3691.

A good catch of pollack on only 6 lb line proving the days of the billiard cue sea anglers have gone.

Please mention this Pastime Publications Guide

99

Constituent Area Tourist Boards

Ayrshire and Burns Country Tourist Board
Director of Tourism,
Ayrshire & Burns Country Tourist Board,
39 Sandgate, Ayr KA7 1BG.
Tel: Ayr (0292) 284196.

Ayrshire Valleys Tourist Board
Tourist Officer,
Ayrshire Valleys Tourist Board,
62 Bank Street,
Kilmarnock,
Ayrshire KA1 1ER.
Tel: Kilmarnock (0563) 39090.

Clyde Valley Tourist Board
Tourism Officer,
Clyde Valley Tourist Board,
Horsemarket,
Ladyacre Road,
Lanark ML11 7LQ.

Cunninghame District Council
Tourist Officer,
Cunninghame District Council,
Tourist Information Centre,
Largs,
Ayrshire KA30 8BG.
Tel: Largs (0475) 673765

Isle of Arran Tourist Board
Area Tourist Officer,
Isle of Arran Tourist Board,
Information Centre, The Pier,
Brodick, Isle of Arran KA27 8AU.
Tel: Brodick (0770) 2140/2401.

Greater Glasgow Tourist Board
Chief Executive,
Greater Glasgow Tourist Board,
39 St. Vincent Place,
Glasgow G1 2ER.
Tel: 041-227 4885/4880.

Other Tourist Organisations

**CUMBERNAULD AND KILSYTH
INVERCLYDE
MONKLANDS
EAST KILBRIDE
EASTWOOD**

**RIVER PURIFICATION BOARD
CLYDE RIVER PURIFICATIN BOARD**
River House, Murray Road, East Kilbride,
Tel: East Kilbride 38181.

RIVERS

Water	Location	Species	Season	Permit available from	Other information
Annick (and Irvine)	Irvine	Salmon Sea Trout Brown Trout	15 Mar. to 30 Oct. 15 Mar. to 6 Oct.	Irvine & District Angling Club, Secretary. A. Sim, 51 Rubie Crescent, Irvine. Currie Sports, 32 High Street, Irvine. Tel: Irvine 78603.	
Annick	Irvine	Salmon Sea Trout Brown Trout	15 Mar. to 31 Oct. 15 Mar. to 6 Oct.	Dreghorn Angling Club, Dr. D.D. Muir, 6 Pladda Avenue, Broomlands, Irvine. Alexander's, Fishmongers, 10 Bank Street, Irvine. (Tues-Sat).	
Annick (and Glazert)	Kilmaurs	Brown Trout	15 Mar. to 6 Oct.	Kilmaurs Angling Club, J. Watson, 7 Four Acres Drive, Kilmaurs.	
Avon	Strathaven	Brown Trout Grayling	15 Mar. to 6 Oct.	Avon Angling Club. Local tackle shops. R. & K. Sports, Strathaven. Sportsman Emporium, Hamilton. Country Lines, 29 Main Street, The Village, E. Kilbride. Tel: (03552) 28952. P. & R. Torbet, 15 Strand Street, Kilmarnock. Tel: (0563) 41734.	

Water	Location	Species	Season	Permit available from	Other Information
Ayr	Mauchline	Salmon Sea Trout Brown Trout	15 Mar. to 31 Oct. 15 Mar. to 15 Sept.	Linwood & Johnstone Newsagent, The Cross, Mauchline.	
Ayr (Cessnock Lugar)	Mauchline	Salmon Sea Trout Brown Trout	11 Feb. to 31 Oct. 15 May-6 Oct.	Mauchline Ballochmyle Angling Club. Linwood & Johnstone Newsagents, The Cross, Mauchline.	
Ayr (Lugar)	Mauchline	Salmon Sea Trout Brown Trout	15 Mar. to 30 Oct. 15 Mar.-15 Sept.	Linwood & Johnstone Newsagents, The Cross, Mauchline.	
Cessnock	Mauchline	Brown Trout	15 Mar. to 15 Sept.	Mauchline Ballochmyle Angling Club. Linwood & Johnstone, Newsagents, The Cross, Mauchline. The Post Office, Main Street, Ochiltree.	
Clyde (and Douglas	Motherwell & Lanark Carstairs, Roberton & Crawford	Brown Trout Grayling	15 Mar. to 30 Sept. All year.	United Clyde Angling Protective Association, Secretary, Joseph Quigley, 39 Hillfoot Avenue, Wishaw. Permits widely available in tackle shops in Glasgow and Lanarkshire.	
Clyde	Lanark	Brown Trout Grayling	15 Mar. to 6 Oct.	Lanark & District Angling Club William Frood, 82 Rhyber Avenue, Lanark. (S.A.E. please).	
	Thankerton & Roberton	Brown Trout Grayling	15 Mar. to 6 Oct. All year.	Lamington & District Angling Association, Secretary, B.F. Dexter, 18 Boghall Park, Biggar. Bryden Newsagent, Biggar, or Bailiffs.	No Sunday fishing.
Doon	Patna	Salmon Sea Trout Brown Trout	15 May to 31 Oct. 15 Mar. to 6 Oct.	Drumgrange and Keir's Angling Club. Mr. Thomas Cosgrove, The Waterside Store Inn, Waterside, Patna, Ayrshire. Tel: (0292) 531204.	No Sunday fishing.
Douglas (and Clyde)	Douglas Water	Brown Trout Grayling	15 Mar. to 30 Sept.	United Clyde Angling Protective Association, Secretary, Joseph Quigley, 39 Hillfoot Avenue, Wishaw. Permits widely available in tackle shops in Glasgow and Lanarkshire.	
Fenwick (and local waters)	Kilmarnock	Brown Trout	15 Mar. to 6 Oct.	Kilmarnock Angling Club, Messrs McCuricks, 39 John Finnie Street, Kilmarnock.	
Forth and Clyde Canal	Whole Canal	Pike Perch Roach Tench Carp	No close season	British Waterways Board, Canal House, Applecross St., Glasgow. Tel: 041-332 6936.	
	Wyndford	Pike Perch Roach Tench Carp	No close season	Central Match Anglers C. Palmer, 64 Dawson Place, Bo'ness. Tel: Bo'ness 823953.	

Water	Location	Species	Season	Permit available from	Other Information
Garrell Burn	Kilsyth	Brown Trout	15 Mar. to 6 Oct.	Kilsyth Fish Protection Assoc., P. Brown, Colzium Sales & Services Station, Stirling Road, Kilsyth. Coachman Hotel, Kilsyth.	
Garnock	Kilbirnie	Brown Trout Salmon Sea Trout	15 Mar. to 6 Oct. 15 Mar.-31 Oct.	Kilbirnie Angling Club I. Johnstone, 12 Grahamston Avenue, Glengarnock, KA14 3AF. Tel: (0505) 682154.	No Sunday fishing after July 1.
	Dalry	Brown Trout	15 Mar. to 6 Oct.	Dalry Garnock Angling Club. David Morton, Newsagent, Main Street, Dalry.	
Garnock (and Lugton)	Kilwinning	Salmon Sea Trout Brown Trout	15 Mar. to 31 Oct. 15 Mar.-6 Oct.	R. Irvine, 88 Duddingston Avenue, Kilwinning. John Gordon Sports, 118 Main Street, Kilwinning. Tel: (0294) 52264. Abbey Newsagent & Off Sales, 40 Main Street, Kilwinning.	
Girvan	Girvan	Salmon Sea Trout Brown Trout	25 Feb. to 31 Oct.	Carrick Angling Club, T.L. Wilson, 1 Church Square, Girvan.	
Glenrosa (and other waters)	Arran	Sea Trout Brown Trout		Arran Angling Club. A.J. Andrews, Park House, Corriecravie, Arran. Shops and Post Offices on Island.	
Gryfe	Bridge of Weir	Brown Trout	15 Mar. to 6 Oct.	Bridge of Weir Angling Club, J. Milne, 8 Beach Avenue, Bridge of Weir.	
	Kilmacolm	Brown Trout	15 Mar. to 6 Oct.	Strathgryfe Angling Association, Mr. K. Wood, 6 Beauly Crescent, Kilmacolm. Cross Cafe, Kilmacolm.	
Iorsa	Isle of Arran	Sea Trout Brown Trout	1 June to 15 Oct.	The Estate Office, Dougarie, Isle of Arran. Tel: (0770-84) 259.	
Irvine	Hurlford and Crookedholm	Salmon Sea Trout Brown Trout	15 Mar. to 31 Oct. 15 Mar. to 6 Oct.	Hurlford, Crookedholm Angling Club, Sec. D. Baird, 17 Lomond Avenue, Hurlford. P. & R. Torbet, 15 Strand Street, Kilmarnock. Tel:(0563) 41734.	
Irvine (and Annick)	Irvine	Salmon Sea Trout Brown Trout	15 Mar. to 6 Oct.	Irvine & District Angling Club, Secretary, A. Sim, 51 Rubie Crescent, Irvine. Currie Sports, 32 High Street, Irvine.	
	Dreghorn	Salmon Sea Trout Brown Trout	15 Mar. to 31 Oct. 15 Mar.-6 Oct.	Dreghorn Angling Club. Dr. D.D. Muir, 6 Pladda Avenue, Broomlands, Irvine. Alexander's Fishmongers, 10 Bank Street, Irvine. (Tues.-Sat.)	

Water	Location	Species	Season	Permit available from	Other Information
Irvine (and Cessnock)	Galston	Salmon Sea Trout Brown Trout	15 Mar. to 31 Oct. 15 Mar.-6 Oct.	Galston Angling Club, Sec. J. Steven, 12 Millands Road, Galston. P. & R. Torbet, 15 Strand Street, Kilmarnock. Tel: (0563) 41734.	
Machrie	Arran	Salmon Sea Trout	1 June to 15 Oct.	Strathtay Estate Office, Strathtay, Aberfeldy, Perthsire. Tel: (0887) 20496.	No Sunday fishing. Booking: Jan.-Feb.
Stinchar	Colmonell	Salmon Sea Trout	25 Feb. to 31 Oct.	Boars Head Hotel, Colmonell. Tel: (046588) 272. Queen's Hotel, Colmonell.	

LOCHS AND RESERVOIRS

Water	Location	Species	Season	Permit available from	Other Information
Banton Loch	Kilsyth	Brown Trout	15 Mar. to 6 Oct.	Kilsyth Fish Protection Assoc. P. Brown, Colzium Sales & Services Station, Stirling Road, Kilsyth.	Boats from: Coachman Hotel, Kilsyth. Boat session: 9 am-5 pm 6 pm-midnight.
Loch Belston	Sinclairston	Brown Trout Rainbow Trout	15 Mar-15 Sept. All year round	Mauchline Ballochmyle Angling Club. H. Goodwin, 76 Sunnyside Crescent, Mauchline. Linwood & Johnstone Newsagents, The Cross, Mauchline.	Boats available.
Loch Bradan	Straiton	Brown Trout (Stocked)	15 Mar. to 6 Oct.	Forestry Commission, Straiton, Tel: (065 57) 637. Mr. R. Heaney, Tallaminnoch, Straiton. Tel: (065 57) 617.	Five Boats
Loch Brecbowie	Straiton	Brown Trout	15 Mar. to 6 Oct.	Forestry Commission, Straiton. Tel: (065 57) 637. Mr. R. Heaney, Tallaminnoch, Straiton. Tel: (065 57) 617.	Fly fishing advised. Boats available.
Castle Semple Loch	Lochwinnoch	Pike Perch Roach Eels	No close season	St. Winnochs Angling Club, 19 Glenpark Road, Lochwinnoch. Rangers Centre at the loch.	Day permits for bank fishing. North shore only.
Daer Reservoir	Crawford	Brown Trout	Easter to 6 Oct.	Kilbryde Angling Club, John Mills, Mills McGraw & Co., 1 Orchard Street, Motherwell. Tel: (0698) 68511. D.T. Cormie, 6 MacAdam Place, East Kilbride. Tel: (03552) 22808.	Four boats. Fly fishing only. No bank fishing. Outboard engines essential.
Loch Doon	Dalmellington	Brown Trout Char	15 Mar. to 6 Oct.	No permit required.	Bank fishing only. Sunday fishing.
Hillend Reservoir	Caldercruix	Brown/ Rainbow Trout	15 Mar. to 6 Oct.	Airdrie Angling Club, Roy Burgess, 21 Elswick Drive, Caldercruix, Lanarkshire. Tel: (0236) 842050.	All legal methods. Bag limit - 6 trout. Bank and boat fishing. No ground bait. Sunday fishing.
Kilbirnie Loch	Kilbirnie	Brown Trout Roach	15 Mar. to 6 Oct.	Kilbirnie Angling Club, I. Johnstone, 12 Grahamston Avenue, Glengarnock KA14 3AF. Tel: (0505) 682154.	All legal methods.

Water	Location	Species	Season	Permit available from	Other Information
Lanark Loch	Lanark	Carp	No close season	Clydesdale District Council, Lanark Moor Country Park.	
Linfern Loch	Straiton	Pike		Forestry Commission, Straiton. Tel: (065 57) 637. Mr. R. Heaney, Tallaminnoch, Straiton. Tel: (065 57) 617.	
Plan or Pundeavon Reservoir	Kilbirnie	Brown/ Rainbow/ Brook Trout	15 Mar. to 6 Oct.	Kilbirnie Angling Club, I. Johnstone, 12 Grahamston Avenue, Glengarnock KA14 3AF. Tel: (0505) 682154.	Fly and spinning only. Brown trout no limit. Rainbow and brook trout 4 fish limit.
Loch Skelloch	Straiton	Brown Trout (Stocked)	15 Mar. to 6 Oct.	Forestry Commission, Straiton. Tel: (065 57) 637. Mr. R. Heaney, Tallaminnoch, Stration. Tel: (065 57) 617.	Fly fishing only. Boats available.
Strathclyde Country Park Loch (and adjacent River Clyde)	Motherwell	Carp Bream Roach Pike Perch Dace	No close season	Booking Office, Strathclyde Country Park, 366 Hamilton Road, Motherwell. Tel: Motherwell 66155.	Regulations on permit. No fly fishing. Lead-free weights recommended.
		Grayling Trout	15 Mar. to 29 Sept.		
Loch Thom and compensations 6,7 & 8	Greenock	Brown Trout	15 Mar. to 6 Oct.	Greenock & District Angling Club, Secretary, J. McMurthie, 45 Whinhill Court, Greenock. Tel: (0475) 27551. Findlay & Co., 58 Lynedoch Street, Greenock. Tel: (0475) 24056. Jenny Baird, Cornalees Farm, Jean Caskie, Garvocks Farm, Jimmy Rankin, Watermans Cottage.	Fly and bank fishing only.

STRATHCLYDE SOUTH
Sea Angling

Loch Ryan to Ardrossan
The angling potential of much of the coast between Loch Ryan and Girvan remains unknown, the many rocky shores, small headlands and sandy beaches probably only attracting the anglers in an exploratory mood, or those seeking solitude in pursuit of their hobby.

Girvan
Girvan has a sheltered port and is a family holiday resort. From the end of the pier good fishing can be had for fair-sized plaice and flounders. Night fishing is good for rock cod. Just one mile to the south of the town and close to the Haven Hotel lies the noted 'Horse Rock', only about 50 yards from the main Stranraer road. Access to the rock may be gained from about half-tide. Except during very high tides and during storms it is a good shore mark providing access to water of about 20 feet on the sea-side even at low tide.

Types of fish: Haddock, plaice, hake, codling, rays, flounder, whiting, and gurnard (mostly from boat).

Tackle: Available from J.H. Murray, 3 Dalrymple Street, Girvan.

Boats: Contact A. Ingram, Tel: Girvan (0465) 2320 for information.
Boats leave harbour 10 am, 2 pm, 6 pm.

Ayr
Ayr is a popular holiday town on the estuaries of the Rivers Ayr and Doon, 32 miles south-west of Glasgow. Good shore fishing can be had on the Newton Shore, north of the harbour, from the harbour jetty and from the rocky coastline at the Heads of Ayr. Boat fishing in the bay can be very productive with good catches of cod, haddock, thornbacks, spurdogs and flatfish. Tope have also been taken from around the Lady Isle.

Types of fish: Cod, mackerel, ling, plaice, dab and pollack are the main type of fish being caught in Ayr Bay over the past few year.

Boats: Available from Mrs M. Semple, Ayr Marine Charters, 92 Dalmilling Crescent, Ayr KA8

0QJ, Tel: (0292) 281638. T.
Medina, 10 Brittania Place, Ayr
KA8 9AQ, Tel: Ayr 285297.
Tackle: Available from James
Kirk, Unit 5, Union Arcade, Ayr.
Games Sport, 60 Sandgate, Ayr.
Bait: Lugworm and ragworm
from Ayr and Newton shore. Mrs
M. Semple, Ayr Marine Charters,
92, Dalmilling Crescent, Ayr
KA8 0QJ, Tel: (0292) 281638 can
supply herring, mussels and
mackerel. Bait available on
request from T. Medina, Tel:
(0292) 285297.

Prestwick
Prestwick is a pleasant seaside
holiday town on the coast
between Troon and Ayr. Shore
fishing is best after dark.
Temporary membership of
Prestwick SAC can be obtained.
Types of fish: Shore – cod,
flounder, plaice, dab, coalfish,
dogfish and mullet. Boat – as
above plus tope and rays,
thornbacks and mackerel, except
mullet.
Boats: 14ft skippered boat
available from Prestwick Sea
Angling Club and boats can also
be chartered from Troon and
Ayr. J. Wilson, 27 Wallace
Avenue, Barassie, Troon,
Ayrshire.
Tackle: T.G. Morrison, 117 Main
Street, Prestwick, Ayrshire.
Bait: Lugworm and ragworm can
be dug on Prestwick shore.
Season for fishing: Shore –
October-March. Boat – all year.
Further information from: Mrs
Templeton, Prestwick Sea
Angling Club, 'Trebor', 15 Teviot
Street, Ayr. Tel: Ayr 68072.

Troon
Troon is a popular holiday town
between Ayr and Irvine with
good public transport for coastal
fishing points. There is good pier
fishing from the harbour. Cod
and flatfish can be taken at low
tide from Barassie shore. Local
skippers have many good marks
out on the bay, with a small
wreck off the Lady Isle.
Type of fish: Shore – cod, plaice,
flounder, coalfish, rays, dogfish,
conger, whiting, pollack. Boat –
as above plus thornback, and
gurnard.
Boats: There are numerous boats
available. *'Dusky Maid'* – Mr J.
Wilson, 27 Wallace Avenue,
Barassie, Troon, Ayrshire. Tel:
Troon 313161. M. V. Talisman.

Tel: Prestwick 76543.
Tackle: P. & R. Torbet, 15 Strand
Street, Kilmarnock. McCririck &
Sons, 38 John Finnie Street,
Kilmarnock, Ayrshire.
Bait: Lugworm, ragworm and
mussels from shore only.
Lugworm from the Barassie shore
at low tide.
Season for fishing: All year.
Further information from:
Glacier Angling Club, Mr N.
Lindsay, 5 Ayr Road,
Kilmarnock, Ayrshire.

Irvine
Irvine on the Ayrshire coast, is a
rapidly developing New Town on
the River Irvine. The sea is
relatively shallow, with long
sandy beaches. It is a good boat
fishing area. Irvine was previously
a very busy port, but now the
river anchorage is used by a
greater number of small craft.
The estuary has, in the past two
years come up trumps for flatfish,
dabs, flounders and plaice. South
of Irvine Estuary is a small island
called 'The Lady Isle'. In the past
year the pollack have increased
not only in number but also in
size. Just off this Isle pollack can
be taken with ragworm on a long
flowing trace. Pollack to 10 lbs.,
are not an unusual sight at some
club matches. For cod, close
inshore is best and small coloured
beads are preferred to spoon and
lures. The best bait by far is a
cocktail of lugworm and cockle or
ragworm and cockle, all of which
can be obtained locally.
Types of fish: Flounder and cod
from the shore. Cod, flounder,
plaice, conger, haddock, ling,
whiting, and coalfish.
Boats: Irvine Water Sports Club,
126 Montgomery Street, Irvine, J.
Wilson. Tel: Troon (0292)
313161. J. Wass, 22 Templeland
Road, Dalry. Tel: Dalry (029-
483) 3724.
Tackle: Irvine Water Sports Club;
Sports Shop, High Street, Irvine;
Gilmour Sports, Bridgegate,
Irvine; J.W. Fishing Shop,
Seagate, Irvine.
Bait: Lugworm can be dug from
foreshore at low tide and mussels
under wharves.
Season for fishing: All year.
Further information from: Irvine
SAC, Hon. Sec., W.R. Findlay,
40 Frew Terrace, Irvine. Tel:
Irvine 79582.

Saltcoats & Ardrossan
Saltcoats with the neighbouring
towns of Stevenston and
Ardrossan, is situated on the
Ayrshire coast 30 miles south-
west of Glasgow. Shore fishing is
possible in the South Bay and
around the harbours.
Approximately 3 miles north is
Ardneil Bay which is prolific cod
ground.
Types of fish: Cod, rays, flounder,
coalfish, dogfish, conger, whiting
and pollack from shore, plus
haddock, dab, gurnard and
thornback from boats.
Boats: Available from G. Dickie,
27 Braes Road, Saltcoats, Tel:
0294 61867. Mr A.S. Wass, 22
Templeland Road, Dalry,
Ayrshire. Tel: Dalry (029-483)
3724. There are no professional
hirers at Ardrossan but private
owners are willing to help.
Tackle: Available from Saltcoats
& Leisure Time, 42 Hamilton
Street, Saltcoats.
Bait: Limited supplies of
ragworm, lugworm, sandgapers
and crab are available at the
tanker berth, while lugworm can
be found on the north and south
shores. N. Gibson can supply
fresh or preserved bait.
Season for fishing: All year round
from shore. March-October from
boats.
Further information from: Bud
McClymont, Hon. Sec. Ardrossan
and District SAC, 1 Hill Street,
Ardrossan.

Largs
Largs is within easy reach of
several good fishing banks,
including the Piat Shoal, the
Skelmorlie Patch and the east
shore of Cumbrae.
Types of fish: Dogfish, flounders,
gurnard, grey sole, haddock,
hake, pollack, mackerel, plaice.
Boats: Are readily available from
local hirers.
Tackle: Hastie of Largs Ltd,
Department Store, 109 Main
Street, Largs. Tel: Largs 673104
Bait: Mussels are available from
Fairlie Flats.

Gourock
The coastline from Largs to
Greenock is probably the most
popular area in Scotland for shore
angling, with many anglers from
the Midlands of England and
beyond making regular trips
north. At Wemyss Bay, angling is

not permitted from the pier, but good catches can be had to the south, and the Red Rocks, about a mile to the north, are noted for codling and other species. At Inverkip there is a sandy beach around the entrance to the marina where large flounders and other flatfish can be taken. Cloch Point, where the Firth turns east, is well known for its fishing potential, although the current can be fierce, and because of the rough bottom, relatively heavy lines are necessary. The coastline from Cloch along Gourock Promenade to the swimming pool car park provides good fishing and is easily accessible. Further inland, at Greenock Esplanade, codling and flatfish are among the species available, although the water here is shallower, and this area is more productive at night. This stretch of coastline provides the dinghy angler with easy access to many of the Clyde marks, including the Gantocks, where outsize cod and coalfish have been taken, mainly on pirks. The bay beside the power station holds large flatfish and the ground off Greenock Esplanade is popular for codling. Dinghy owners should note that no anchoring is permitted in the main navigation channels, and several other regulations must also be adhered to. Full details are given in 'The Small Boat Owner's Guide to Clydeport' which may be obtained, free of charge, from: The Control Tower, Clyde Port Authority, Greenock.

Types of fish: Coalfish (known locally as saithe), cod, conger eel, dab, dogfish, flounder, occasional ling, plaice, pollack (lythe), pouting, whiting and wrasse. Grey mullet, herring and mackerel can also be caught during the summer months.

Tackle: K.A. Binnie, 29 Kempock Street, Gourock; Findlay & Co., 58 Lyndedoch Street, Greenock; SK 8, 27 Kempock Street, Gourock; Brian Peterson & Co., 12 Kelly Street, Greenock.

Bait: Lug, rag, mussels, cockles and crabs are easily obtainable from the shoreline.
Boats: J. Crowther, Inverclyde Boat Owners Association, 164

Burns Road, Greenock. Tel: (0475) 34341 can advise.

Isle of Arran
The island of Arran, lying in the outer Firth of Clyde, may be reached from the mainland by ferries running from Ardrossan to Brodick, the largest community on the island. Good shore fishing is found around the whole of the island, much of which remains unexplored.

Lamlash
Lamlash is the main centre for sea angling on the island, probably because of its situation on the shores of Lamlash Bay, the large horse-shoe shaped bay which is almost landlocked by the Holy Isle. This gives excellent protection to the bay from easterly winds. Lamlash is also the starting point for boat trips to the excellent fishing grounds off Whiting Bay and those around Pladda to the south.
Types of fish: Cod, haddock, whiting, coalfish, pollack, conger, rays, flatfish, mackerel, dogfish.
Boats: Dinghies are available from the Arran Sea Angling Centre, Brodick (Tel: Brodick (0770) 2192); N.C. McLean, Torlin Villa, Kilmory (Tel: Sliddery (077 087) 240); Johnston Bros, Old Pier Shop, Lamlash (Tel: Lamlash (07706) 333). Mr Ambler, Kilmory Post Office, (Tel: Sliddery (077 087) 237.
Tackle: Available from Johnstone Bros, Pierhead Shop, Lamlash.
Bait: Obtainable from many beaches. May also be purchased from N.C. McLean.
Season for fishing: March-November.
Further information from: Mr N.C. McLean, Torlin Villa, Kilmory, Tel: Sliddery (077 087) 240.

Corrie
Corrie is situated on north east coast of the island.
Types of fish: Cod, haddock, conger, skate, dogfish, tope, turbot, ling, pollack, gurnard and garfish.

Whiting Bay
This bay, which takes its name from the whiting, is very open to the sea. There are excellent fishing banks from Largiebeg Point to King's Cross Point.
Boats: Dinghies can be hired from the Jetty, Whiting Bay or by

arrangement with Jim Ritchie, Tel: Whiting Bay (07707) 382.
Bait: Cockles, mussels, lugworm, ragworm, limpets and crabs are abundant on the banks from half-tide.

Lochranza
Lochranza is situated at the northern end of the island. The loch is surrounded by hills opening out on to Kilbrennan Sound.
Types of fish: Cod, conger, and haddock from the shore. Cod, conger, haddock from boats.
Tackle: Available from boat hirers.
Bait: Mussels, cockles, lugworm and ragworm obtainable; scallops from Mr F. Murchie.

Brodick
Good fishing in Brodick Bay from Markland Point to Clauchlands Point.
Types of fish: Codling, plaice and other flatfish, conger, wrasse and pollack, can be had from the shore while cod, haddock, conger, skate, dogfish, tope, turbot, ling, pollack, gurnard, garfish and other round fish can be fished from boats.
Boats: Boats can be hired from Arran Sea Angling Centre, The Beach, Brodick. Tel: (0770) 2192. Bait, tackle and freezer facilities.
Bait: Mussels are obtainable from the rocks around Brodick Pier or may be purchased from boat hirers.

Isle of Cumbrae Millport
There is good fishing at a bank between the South East Point of Millport Bay (Farland Point) and Keppel Pier. Fintry Bay and Piat Shoal provide good sport. West of Portachur Point in about 15/20 fathoms and in Dunagoil Bay, S.W. Bute are good. Fairlie Channel directly seaward of Kelburn Castle is about 12/15 fathoms. East shore northwards about 10 fathoms line.
Types of fish: Saithe, conger, coalfish, haddock, dogfish and mackerel.
Boats: Mr W.S. McIntyre, Tel: Millport (0475) 530566. Mr Wright, Tel: Millport (0475) 530692. Mr A. Roberts, Tel: Millport (0475) 530465 or 530723.
Tackle: Available locally from boat hirers.
Bait: Mussels, worms, etc. on shore. Boat hirers and local shops provide bait.

Constituent Area Tourist Boards

Dunoon and Cowal Tourist Board
Area Tourist Officer,
Dunoon and Cowal Tourist Board,
Information Centre,
7 Alexandra Parade,
Dunoon, Argyll PA23 8AB.
Tel: Dunoon (0369) 3755.

Oban, Mull and District Tourist Board
Area Tourist Officer,
Oban, Mull and District Tourist Board,
Boswell House, Argyll Square,
Oban, Argyll PA34 4AN.
Tel: Oban (0631) 63122/63059.

Mid Argyll, Kintyre and Islay Tourist Board
Area Tourist Officer,
Mid Argyll, Kintyre and Islay Tourist
Board,
The Pier, Campbeltown,
Argyll PA28 6EF.
Tel: Campbeltown (0586) 52056.

Isle of Bute Tourist Board
Area Tourist Officer,
Isle of Bute Tourist Board,
The Pier, Rothesay,
Isle of Bute PA20 9AQ.
Tel: Rothesay (0700) 2151.

RIVER PURIFICATION BOARD
CLYDE RIVER PURIFICATION BOARD
Rivers House,
Murray Road,
East Kilbride.
Tel: East Kilbride 38181.

RIVERS

Water	Location	Species	Season	Permit available from	Other information
Aray	Inveraray	Salmon Sea Trout Brown Trout	May to Mid-Oct.	Argyll Estates Office, Cherry Park, Inveraray. Tel: Inveraray (0499) 2203.	No Sunday fishing. Fly fishing only.
Aros	Mull	Salmon Sea Trout	End June to Mid Oct.	Tackle and Books, Main Street, Tobermory, Isle of Mull. Tel: (0688) 2336.	
Awe	Taynuilt	Salmon Sea Trout	June to Sept.	Inverawe/Taynuilt Fisheries, Argyll. Tel: (08662) 446.	Rod hire. Casting tuition.
Bellart	Mull	Salmon Sea Trout	June to End Oct.	Tackle & Books, Main Street, Tobermory, Isle of Mull. Tel: (0688) 2336.	No Sunday fishing.
Crinan Canal	Lochgilphead	Trout		Lochgilphead & District Angling Club.	No permit required.
Cur	13 miles from Dunoon	Salmon Sea Trout Brown Trout	1 Apr. to 31 Oct.	Dunoon & District Angling Club, Purdies of Argyll, 112 Argyll Street, Dunoon. Tel: Dunoon 3232.	Fishing by all legal methods permitted. For advanced bookings please contact: The Hon. Sec. D. & D.A.C., 7 Blair Lane, Stewart Street, Dunoon. Tel: Dunoon 5732.
Douglas	Inveraray	Salmon Sea Trout	May to Mid-Oct.	Argyll Caravan Park, Inveraray, Argyll. Tel: (0499) 2285.	No Sunday fishing. Fly fishing only.
Euchar	Kilninver	Salmon Sea Trout Brown Trout	1 June to 15 Oct.	Mrs. Mary McCorkindale, 'Glenann' Kilninver, by Oban, Argyll.	No Sunday fishing.
	Kilninver	Salmon Sea Trout	Mid-July to Mid-Oct.	J.T.P. Mellor, Barncromin Farm, Knipoch, by Oban, Argyll. Tel: Kilninver 273.	3 days per week.
	Kilinver (Lagganmore)	Salmon Sea Trout Brown Trout	June to 14 Oct.	Lt. Col. P.S. Sandilands, Lagganmore, Kilninver, by Oban. Tel: Kilninver 200.	Not more than 3 rods per day. Fly fishing only. No Sunday fishing.

Water	Location	Species	Season	Permit available from	Other Information
Finnart	Ardentinny	Salmon Sea Trout	1 Apr. to 15 Oct.	Dunoon & District Angling Club. Purdie's of Argyll, 112 Argyll Street, Dunoon. Tel: Dunoon 3232. Warden's House, Glen Finnart.	No Sunday fishing. For details and advanced bookings contact: The Hon. Sec. D. & D.A.C., 7 Blair Lane, Stewart Street, Dunoon. Tel: Dunoon 5732.
Forsa	Mull	Salmon Sea Trout	Mid-June to Mid-Oct.	Tackle and Books, Main Street, Tobermory. Tel: (0688) 2336.	No Sunday fishing.
		Salmon Sea Trout	Early July to Mid-Oct.	Glenforsa Hotel, by Salen. Tel: (06803) 377.	No Sunday fishing.
Goil	Lochgoilhead	Salmon Sea Trout	May to End-Oct.	R. Kennedy, Drimsyniebeag, Lochgoilhead. Tel: (03013) 273.	No Sunday Fishing.
Laggan	Bowmore	Salmon	Mid-June to Mid-Oct.	Mrs. Lucy Stewart, Kynagary, Bowmore. Tel: Bowmore 204.	
Machrie	Islay	Salmon Sea Trout	25 Feb. to 31 Oct.	Machrie Hotel, Port Ellen, Islay, Argyll PA42 7AN. Tel: (0496) 2310.	
Massan	6 miles from Dunoon	Salmon Sea Trout	1 Apr. to 31 Oct.	Dunoon & District Angling Club. Purdies of Argyll, 112 Argyll Street, Dunoon. Tel: Dunoon 3232.	All legal methods permitted. For advanced booking contact: The Hon. Sec. D. & D.A.C., 7 Blair Lane, Stewart Street, Dunoon. Tel: Dunoon 5732.
Orchy	Dalmally	Salmon	11 Feb. to 15 Oct.	W.A. Church, Croggan Crafts, Dalmally, Argyll. Tel: Dalmally 201.	
Ruel	Glendaruel	Salmon Sea Trout		Glendaruel Hotel, Clachan of Glendaruel, Argyll PA22 3AA. Tel: (036982) 371.	No Sunday fishing.
Ruel	Glendaruel	Salmon Sea Trout		Glendaruel Hotel, Clachan of Glendaruel, Argyll PA22 3AA. Tel: (036982) 371.	No Sunday fishing.
Shira	Inveraray	Salmon Sea Trout	May to Mid-Oct.	Argyll Estates Office, Cherry Park, Inveraray, Argyll. Tel: Inveraray 2203.	Fly fishing only. No Sunday fishing.

LOCHS AND RESERVOIRS

Water	Location	Species	Season	Permit available from	Other Information
Loch Ascog	Argyll	Brown Trout Rainbow Trout	15 Mar. to 5 Oct.	Kyles of Bute Angling Club. Shops Kames. Tighnabruaich	Fly only.
Loch Assopol	Mull	Salmon Sea Trout	April to beg. Oct.	Argyll Arms Hotel, Bunessan, Isle of Mull. Tel: Fionnphort 240.	Fly and spinner only. No Sunday fishing.
Loch Avich	Taynuilt	Brown Trout	15 Mar. to 6 Oct.	S. Davren, 40 Dalavich, by Taynuilt, Argyll. Tel: Lochavich 216.	
Loch Awe	Taynuilt	Salmon Sea Trout Brown Trout Rainbow Trout	12 Feb. to 15 Oct. 15 Mar. to 6 Oct.	S. Davren, 40 Dalavich, by Taynuilt, Argyll. Tel: Lochavich 216.	

Water	Location	Species	Season	Permit available from	Other Information
Loch Awe contd.		Sea Trout Brown Trout Salmon Pike Perch Char	12 Feb.-15 Oct. 15 Mar.-6 Oct.	Forestry Commission, Loch Awe Forest District, Whitegates, Lochgilphead, Argyll. Tel: Lochavich 211.	
	Ford	Brown Trout	15 Mar. to 6 Oct.	Ford Hotel, Ford, Argyll. Tel: (054 681) 273.	
	South Lochaweside Nr. Dalmally	Salmon Brown Trout Sea Trout Rainbow Trout Pike Perch Char	15 Mar.-15 Oct. 15 Mar.-6 Oct.	The Portsonachan Hotel, Nr.Dalmally, Argyll PA33 1BL. Tel: (086 63) 224/225/356/328.	
	Dalmally	Salmon Brown Trout Rainbow Trout	15 Mar. to 6 Oct.	Carraig Thurra Hotel, Lochawe Village by Dalmally. Tel: Dalmally 210.	
		Salmon Sea Trout Brown Trout Rainbow Trout Pike	12 Feb. to 15 Oct. All year.	Ardbrecknish House, by Dalmally, Argyll. Tel: (08663) 223.	Self Catering flats. Rods, tackle & ghillie available. Boats.
		Salmon Brown Trout Rainbow Trout	15 Mar. to 6 Oct.	Dalmally Hotel, Dalmally.	
	Kilchrennan	Salmon Brown Trout Rainbow Trout		Taychreggan Hotel, Kilchrennan.	
		Trout Salmon Pike	All year	Cuil-Na-Sithe Hotel, Kilchrennan Tel: 234	Boat hire Dawn/dusk
Barnluasgan Loch	Lochgilphead	Brown Trout	15 Mar. to 6 Oct.	Mrs. Robertson, Barnluasgan, Lochgilphead.	
Coll Estate Lochs	Coll	Brown Trout	1 Apr. to 30 Sept.	Factor, Coll Estate House, Aringour, Isle of Coll. Tel: Coll 367.	
Coille Bhar	Lochgilphead	Brown Trout	1 Apr. to 6 Oct.	Mrs. Robertson, Barnluasgan, Lochgilphead.	Four boats
Dubh Loch	Inveraray	Salmon Sea Trout Brown Trout	15 Apr. to 6 Oct.	Argyll Estates Office, Cherry Park, Inveraray. Tel: Inveraray 2203.	
	Kilninver	Loch Leven Trout Brown Trout	April to Mid-Oct.	J.T.P. Mellor, Barndromin Farm, Knipoch, by Oban. Tel: Kilninver 273.	
Dunoon Reservoir	Dunoon	Rainbow Trout	15 Mar. to 31 Oct.	Dunoon & District Angling Club. Purdies of Argyll, 112 Argyll Street, Dunoon. Tel: Dunoon 3232.	Fly fishing from bank only. Other rules on permit.
Loch Eck	Dunoon	Salmon Sea Trout Brown Trout Char Powan	16 Mar. to 31 Oct.	The Whistlefield Inn, Loch Eck, by Dunoon, Argyll. Tel: (036 986) 250.	Seven boats. Ghillie available.

Water	Location	Species	Season	Permit available from	Other Information
Loch Fad	Bute	Brown Trout Rainbow Trout	1 Apr.-6 Oct. 1 Apr.-1 Nov.	Bailiff in attendance at the loch. Tel: (0700) 4871.	Bank fishing and ten boats. Fly methods from boats. All legal methods from bank. Double sessions: 8 am to 5 pm, 5 pm to 10 pm.
		Rainbow Trout (fish farm)		Carleol Enterprises Angling Holidays, 3 Alma Terrace, Rothesay. Tel: (0700) 3716.	Trout fishing package holidays. Accommodation and permits are available. Full details on application.
Loch Finlaggan	Islay	Brown Trout		Brian Wiles, Islay House, Bridgend. Tel: Bowmore 293.	Two boats.
Loch Gleann A'Bhaerradch	Lerags by Oban	Brown Trout	15 Mar. to 6 Oct.	Cologin Homes Ltd., Lerags, by Oban, Argyll. Tel: Oban 64501. The Barn Bar, Cologin, Lerags.	One boat available.
Glen Dubh Reservoir	Connel	Brown Trout Rainbow Trout	15 Mar. to 6 Oct.	J. Lyon, Appin View, Barcaldine.	Fly only.
Loch Gorm	Islay	Brown Trout	15 Mar. to 6 Oct.	Brian Wiles, Islay House, Bridgend. Tel: Bowmore 293	Boat and bank fishing.
Inverawe Fisheries	Taynuilt	Rainbow Trout	Mar. to Nov.	Inverawe Fisheries, Taynuilt, Argyll. Tel: (08662) 446.	
Kilmelford Lochs	Kilmelford	Brown Trout		Oban & Lorne Angling Club.	Numerous Lochs
Lochgilphead Lochs	Lochgilphead	Brown Trout	15 Mar. to 6 Oct.	Lochgilphead and District Angling Club, H. McArthur, The Tackle Shop, Lochnell Street, Lochgilphead.	Numerous lochs.
Loch Loskin (The Lochan)	Dunoon	Brown/ Sea Trout	1 Apr. to 30 Sept.	Dunoon & District Angling Club. Purdies of Argyll, 112 Argyll Street, Dunoon. Tel: Dunoon 3232.	Fishing from boat only. Please enquire about other rules.
Loch Lussa	Campbeltown	Brown Trout	15 May to 6 Oct.	McCrory & Co., Main Street, Campbeltown.	
Mishnish & Aros Lochs	Mull	Brown Trout	15 Mar. to 30 Sept.	Tobermory Angling Association. Brown's Shop, Tobermory. Tel: (0688) 2020.	No Sunday fishing.
Loch Nant	Kilchrenan	Brown Trout	15 Mar. to 8 Oct.	Kilchrenan Trading Post, Kilchrenan, Tel: (08663) 232.	
Loch Nell	Oban	Brown Trout	15 Mar. to 6 Oct.	Oban & Lorne Angling Club.	
Powderworks Reservoir	Argyll	Brown/ Rainbow Trout	15 Mar. to 5 Oct.	Kyles of Bute Angling Club. Several shops in Kames and Tighnabruaich.	Fly and bait only, no spinning.
Lochquien	Bute	Brown Trout	1 Apr. to 6 Oct.	Bute Estate Office, Rothesay, Isle of Bute. Tel: Rothesay 2627.	Fly only. Salmon and trout fishing in sea around Bute.

Water	Location	Species	Season	Permit available from	Other Information
Loch Scammadale	Kilninver	Salmon Sea Trout Brown Trout	1 June to 15 Oct. 15 Mar.-6 Oct.	Mrs. McCorkindale 'Glenann', Kilninver, by Oban, Argyll. Tel: Kilninver 282.	No Sunday fishing.
Loch Seil	Kilninver	Sea Trout Brown Trout	Apr. to Mid-Oct.	J.T.P. Mellor, Barndromin Farm, Knipoch, by Oban, Argyll. Tel: Kilninver 273.	
Loch Squabain	Mull	Salmon Sea Trout Brown Trout		Tackle & Books, Main Street, Tobermory, Mull. Tel: (0688) 2336.	Boat fishing only.
Loch Tarsan	Dunoon	Brown Trout	1 Apr. to 30 Sept.	Dunoon & District Angling Club. Purdies of Argyll, 112 Argyll Street, Dunoon. Tel: Dunoon 3232.	Fly only and Sunday fishing is permitted.
Tighnabruaich Reservoir	Tighnabruaich	Brown Trout	15 Mar. to 5 Oct.	Kyles of Bute Angling Club. Several shops in Kames and Tighnabruaich, Argyll.	
Torr Loch	Mull	Sea Trout Brown Trout Rainbow Trout		Tackle and Books, Main Street, Tobermory, Mull. Tel: (0688) 2336.	Fly only.
Loch Tulla	Tyndrum	Brown Trout		Royal Hotel, Tyndrum.	

STRATHCLYDE NORTH
Sea Angling

Isle of Bute Rothesay
The holiday resort of Rothesay, situated on the island of Bute, only a 30 minute crossing by roll-on/ roll-off ferry from Wemyss Bay, is sheltered from the prevailing south- westerly winds. Several boat hirers cater for sea anglers. There are also many excellent shore marks. The deep water marks at Garroch Head can be productive for both shore and boat anglers.
Types of fish: Shore – cod, coalfish, pollack, plaice, mackerel, wrasse. Boat – cod, pollack, plaice, mackerel, conger, spurdog, coalfish, wrasse and whiting.
Boats: Peter McIntyre (Clyde) Ltd., Port Bannatyne (0700) 3171. Keith Todd, Carleol, Alma Terrace, (0700) 3716. 1 fishing cruiser and boarding house. Advance booking necessary. 'Marion', 35ft cobble. Mr. Bob Heatley Tel: 83–615.
Tackle: Available from Bute Tools, Montague Street, Rothesay.
Bait: Low water at Port Bannatyne for cockles, Lugworm and ragworm. Herring is also useful bait. Mussel bait can be obtained on shore.
Season for fishing: May-October.

Kilchattan Bay
Sheltered bay waters at the south end of the Isle of Bute renowned for its good all year round fishing.
Types of fish: Cod, pollack, plaice, mackerel, conger, dogfish, wrasse, whiting.
Boats: Mr C. Kay, St. Blanes Hotel, Kilchattan Bay, Isle of Bute (070 083) 224.
Tackle: Mr C. Kay, St. Blanes Hotel, Kilchattan Bay, Isle of Bute.
Bait: Worm, fresh cockle available locally.
Season for fishing: All year.

Mainland Ardentinny
Ardentinny is a small unspoiled village picturesquely situated on the west shore of Loch Long, 12 miles from Dunoon by car.
Types of fish: Cod, mackerel, from the shore. Cod, conger, haddock, ray, plaice, flounder, whiting, coalfish and mackerel from boats.
Bait: Cockles. mussels, lug and ragworm easily dug in bay.
Season for fishing: All year, winter for large cod.

Dunoon
Types of fish:
Most of the shoreline around Dunoon provides catches of cod, coalfish, pollack, flounder, mackerel, plaice. Using ragworm & lugworm, cockle, mussel, razorfish & Peeler crab. Boat fishing takes mostly cod, pollack, coalfish, dogfish, dabs, plaice, flounder. Also conger over wrecks or rough ground at night
Winter fishing: Also produces fair sized cod. Also haddock and whiting. So anglers can fish all year round from boat or shore.
Boats: Gourock skippers fish Dunoon waters. Approx. 3 miles from Dunoon is Holy Loch.
Tackle: Argyll Marine Sports, 60 Argyll Street, Dunoon; Purdies Fishing Tackle & Sports, 112 Argyll Street, Dunoon. Tel: Dunoon (0369) 3232.
Bait: Can be bought at these shops most of the year or obtained in East Bay shore.
Further information from: Mr. W. Wilson, Sec. D.S.A.C., 35 Spence Court, Queen Street, Dunoon, PA23 8EZ.

Tighnabruaich and Kames
Tighnabruaich, on the Kyles of Bute is famed for its beauty and highland scenery. There is access

to some good fishing banks on the west side of Bute and around Inchmarnock.

Types of Fish
Mackerel and coalfish from the shore. Cod, haddock, flatfish, whiting, dogfish, pollock, gurnard and several species of wrasse. Conger fishing can be arranged. The winter run of big cod is well known, haddock and whiting are also caught.

Bait
Supplies of fresh bait (lug, cockle, mussel, clams etc) are locally available.

Boats
Motor dinghies available for hire. Local fishermen can take parties of anglers by arrangement. Contact Andy Lancaster, Kames Hotel. Tel (0700) 811489.

Season
Spring to Autumn, plus winter cod.

Loch Fyne
This is the longest sea-loch in Scotland, penetrating into the Highlands from the waters of the lower Firth of Clyde. The depth of the water within the loch varies enormously with depth of around 100 fathoms being found not only at the seaward end but also at the head of the loch of Inveraray. Much of the shore angling potential remains unknown although access to both shores is made relatively easy by roads running down each side. Boat launching facilities are less easy to find because of the rugged shoreline. Best side is Inveraray to Furnace. Quarry is now out of bounds.

Types of fish: Mackerel, cod, pollack, flatfish, conger (at night).

Inveraray
Inveraray stands on its west shore near the head of Loch Fyne.

Types of fish: Cod, mackerel, pollack, coalfish, ling, dogfish, conger eel, hake and plaice.

Tackle: Available from Ironmonger Store, Inveraray.

Bait: Mussels and worms available from shore at low tide.

Season for fishing: June-September.

Tarbert (Loch Fyne)
The sheltered harbour and the adjacent coast of the loch near the lower end of the loch on the west shore are good fishing grounds for the sea angler.

Types of fish: Cod, mackerel, coalfish, and sea trout from the shore. Mackerel, cod, coalfish, rays, haddock and whiting from boats.

Boats: Evening out with the boats of the herring fleet can be arranged. Boats available from Dugald Cameron, McCulloch Buildings, Lochgilphead, Argyll (Tel: Lochgilphead 2773).

Tackle: Available from Alex Mackay & Son, Ironmonger, Tarbert; and other local shops.

Bait: There is an abundance of shellfish and worms on the mud flats.

Season for fishing: June, July and August.

Further information from: Mr. A. MacKay, Barmore Road, Tarbert.

Oban
Good catches can be occasionally taken in Kerrera Sound near the Cutter Rock and the Ferry Rocks. Fishing is much better off the south and west coasts of Kerrera Island, particularly near the Bach Island and Shepherds Hat, Maiden Island and Oban Bay give good mackerel fishing in July and August. These places are very exposed and should only be attempted in good settled weather.

Types of fish: Boat – mackerel, dogfish, rays, pollack and occasionally cod and haddock. Heavy catches (mainly dogfish) have been taken in the entry to Loch Feochan during the past two seasons.

Tackle: The Tackle Shop, 6 Airds Place, Oban; David Graham, 9 Combie Street, Oban.

Bait: Mussels and lugworm, etc. can be dug from the Kerrera beaches.

Season for fishing: May-November. Contact: J. Williams, Oban (0631) 63662.

Sea Life Centre
11 miles north of Oban on A828. Underwater observatory for seals and other fascinating sea creatures and fish. Ideal viewing conditions. Restaurant.

Isle of Islay
This is the southernmost of the islands. Several of the larger communities like Port Ellen and Port Askaig have good harbours. With the exception of a small area much remains unexplored.

Types of fish: Boat – cod, haddock, whiting, coalfish, pollack, mackerel, gurnard, dogfish, spurdog, plaice, flounder, tope, ling, conger, skate and rays.

Boats: A 20 ft. motor boat from Port Charlotte Hotel, organised fishing parties catered for. Also available from Mr Alan Jenkins, Church Street, Portnahaven, Tel: Portnahaven 212

Tackle: available from Mr. Hodkinson, The Square, Bowmore; Mini-market, Bruichladdich; J. Campbell, sub-Post Office, Bridgend.

Bait: Lugworm plentiful on most beaches. Clam skirts from fish factory waste. Bait can be purchased from fishing boats at the piers.

Season for fishing: July, August and September. Trout and salmon are available from all estates, details from Tourist office or Estate Offices.

Further information from: Tourist Information Centre, The Square, Bowmore, Isle of Islay, Argyll.

Isle of Mull (Salen)
Salen is situated on the east coast of Mull facing the Sound of Mull in a central position, 11 miles from Craignure and 10 miles from Tobermory. The village is sited between Aros River and a headland forming Salen Bay. The Sound of Mull is on the main skate marks in the Argyll area. Over twenty 100 lbs., plus skate have now been taken. One of the contributing factors is the sheltered nature of the Sound, which can allow practically uninterrupted angling. This area has also yielded a number of fine tope, the largest of which was a specimen of 50 lbs. It is worth noting that cod and haddock seldom frequent the sound and should not be expected. This is an area recommended for dinghy owners.

Types of fish: Coalfish, pollack, cod, wrasse, flounder, mullet sea trout, and mackerel from the shore. Ray, skate, ling, pollack,

coalfish, cod, spurdog, tope, conger and gurnard from boats.
Tackle: Available from the Tackle and Books, Main Street, Tobermory, 10 miles away.
Bait: Easily obtainable from shoreline. Mackerel bait from Tackle and Books.
Season for fishing: March-November.
Further information from: Mr. Duncan Swinbanks, Tackle and Books, 10 Main Street, Tobermory. Tel: Tobermory 2336.

Isle of Mull (Tobermory)

The principal town on Mull, it is situated on a very sheltered bay at the north eastern tip of the island. Apart from hitting the headlines in the national press with its treasure, Tobermory has been extensively covered in the angling press. It is the undisputed centre for skate fishing in 1985 and 86 claims for both British and World records were made. The largest fish captured was a giant of 227 lbs. Every year an average of 50 ton-up specimens are caught, tagged and returned alive. It is this thoughtful conservation that has maintained the quality of fishing in the area. Large tope of between 35 lbs., and 45 lbs., can be numerous. Nine Scottish records, red gurnard, grey gurnard, blonde ray, spotted ray, spurdogfish, angler fish, turbot and two wrasse, have come from these Mull waters. Every year dramatic catches of migratory fish can be made. Coalfish, whiting, haddock and cod may be encountered on a vast scale.
Types of fish: Tope, skate, rays, pollack, coalfish, ling, conger, gurnard, spurdog, cod, haddock, flatfish (plaice, dabs, and turbot) and whiting from boats. Coalfish, pollack, cod, wrasse, flounder, grey mullet, sea trout, conger, thornback and mackerel from the shore.
Boats: Mr. Brian Swinbanks, 8 Main Street, Tobermory, has a purpose built 38 ft. sea angling boat for fishing parties with boat rods and reel available. There are 14-16 ft. dinghies for hire for fishing in and around the bay.
Tackle: A tackle shop, with a complete range of stock is on the Main Street.
Bait: Herring and mackerel available from Tackle and Books, Tobermory. Mussels and lugworms are easily obtainable from the shoreline.
Season for fishing: May-November.

Further information from: Mr. Duncan Swinbanks, Tackle and Books, 10 Main Street, Tobermory. Tel: Tobermory 2336.

Isle of Coll

Coll is one of the smaller islands seaward of Mull. Fishing vessels concentrate on the Atlantic side, but good sport can be had on the Mull side and even at the mouth of Arinagour Bay where the village and hotel lie and the mail steamer calls. Fishing from rocks at several spots round the island can give good results.
Types of fish: Mackerel, coalfish, pollack, cod, conger, haddock, skate and flounder.
Boats: Dinghies with or without outboard engines can be hired from local lobster fishermen.
Tackle: Visitors are advised to bring their own.
Bait: Mussels, worms and small crabs can readily be obtained at low tide in Arinagour Bay.
Season for fishing: May to September and later depending on weather.
Further information from: Mr. & Mrs. Kevin & Julie Oliphant of Coll Hotel, Tel: Coll 334.

Constituent Area Tourist Organisations

City of Edinburgh District Council
Director,
Department of Public Relations & Tourism,
The City of Edinburgh District Council,
Waverley Market,
3 Princes Street,
Edinburgh EH2 2QP.
Tel: 031-557 2727/1700.

Forth Valley Tourist Board
Tourist Officer,
Forth Valley Tourist Board,
Burgh Hall, The Cross,
Linlithgow,
West Lothian EH49 7AH.
Tel: (0506) 84 3306.

**Loch Lomond, Stirling and Trossachs
Tourist Board**
Tourism Manager,
Loch Lomond, Stirling and Trossachs
Tourist Board,
41 Dumbarton Road,
Stirling FK8 2LQ.
Tel: Stirling (0786) 70945.

St. Andrews and North East Fife Tourist Board
Tourism Manager,
St. Andrews and North East Fife Tourist Board,
2 Queens Gardens, St. Andrews,
Fife KY16 9TE.
Tel: St. Andrews (0334) 74609.

Kirkcaldy District Council
Tourist Officer,
Kirkcaldy District Council,
Information Centre,
South Street, Leven,
Fife KY8 4PF.
Tel: Leven (0333) 29464.

East Lothian Tourist Board
Tourism Director,
East Lothian Tourist Board,
Brunton Hall,
Musselburgh, EH21 6AE.
Tel: 031-665 3711.

Other Tourist Organisations
MIDLOTHIAN

RIVER PURIFICATION BOARD
FORTH RIVER PURIFICATION BOARD
Colinton Dell House,
West Mill Road, Colinton,
Edinburgh EH11 0PH.
Tel: 031-441 4691.

RIVERS

Water	Location	Species	Season	Permit available from	Other information
Allan	Bridge of Allan	Salmon Sea Trout Brown Trout	15 Mar. to 31 Oct. 15 Mar. to 6 Oct.	D. Crockart & Son, King Street, Stirling. Allanbank Hotel, Greenloaning. McLaren Fishing Tackle & Sports Equipment, Bridge of Allan.	No Sat. or Sun. tickets after 31st July.
Almond	Cramond	Salmon Sea Trout Brown Trout	1 Feb. to 31 Oct. 15 Mar. to 6 Oct.	Cramond Angling Club. Post Office, Cramond, Edinburgh. Post Office, Davidsons Mains, Edinburgh. Shooting Lines, Roseburn Terr., Edinburgh.	Mouth to Old Cramond Brig. East bank only.
	West Lothian	Salmon Sea Trout Brown Trout	1 Feb. to 31 Oct. 15 Mar. to 6 Oct.	River Almond Angling Association, Secretary: Mr. Craig Campbell, 2 Canmore Street, South Queensferry. H. Meikle, 23 Glen Terr., Deans, Livingston. Livingston Sports, Almondvale Centre, Livingston. Country Life, Gorgie Road, Edinburgh. Shooting Lines, Roseburn Terr., Edinburgh.	20 miles of river.

Water	Location	Species	Season	Permit available from	Other Information
Devon	Dollar	Salmon Sea Trout Brown Trout	15 Mar. to 31 Oct. 15 Mar. to 6 Oct.	Devon Angling Association, R. Breingan, 33 Redwell Pl., Alloa. Tel: Alloa 215185. Scobbie Sports, 2/4 Primrose Street, Alloa. Tel: (0259) 722661. D.W. Black, Hobby Shop, 10 New Row, Dunfermline. J. Philp, High Street, Kinross. Leisure Centre, Mill Street, Alloa. D. Crockart & Son, 47 King Street, Stirling. Tel: (0786) 734433.	No Sunday fishing. Devonside Bridge upstream with excluded stretches. Fly fishing only from 15 Mar.-12 Apr. Permits to be obtained before fishing.
Eden (and Ceres Burn)	Cupar	Salmon Sea Trout Brown Trout	15 Mar. to 6 Oct.	Eden Angling Association, Secretary, 21 New Town, Cupar. Tel: Cupar 54842. J. Gow & Sons, Union Street, Dundee.	No Sunday fishing.
Endrick	Drymen	Salmon Sea Trout Brown Trout	11 Feb. to 31 Oct. 15 Mar. to 6 Oct.	Loch Lomond Angling Improvement Association. R.A. Clement & Co. C.A., 29 St. Vincent Place, Glasgow. Tel: 041-221-0068.	Members may fish all Association waters. No Sunday fishing. No worm fishing. Spinning restricted.
Esk	Musselburgh	Salmon Sea Trout Brown Trout	1 Feb. to 31 Oct. 15 Mar. to 6 Oct.	Givan Shop, 67 Eskside West, Musselburgh. Tel: 031-665 3371.	No Sunday fishing. Regulations on permit.
Esk (North and South)	Midlothian	Brown Trout	15 Mar to 6 Oct.	Esk Valley Angling Improvement Association. Kevin Burns, 53 Fernieside Crescent, Edinburgh. Tel: 031-664 4685. Local shops. Officials on water.	Fly rod and reel only to be used. Regulations on permit. Sunday fishing.
Forth	Stirling	Salmon Sea Trout Brown Trout	1 Feb.-31 Oct. 15 Mar. to 6 Oct.	D. Crockart & Son, 47 King Street, Stirling. Tel: (0786) 73443.	
Forth and Clyde Canal	Castlecary	Perch Pike Carp Roach Tench Bream	No close season	British Waterways Board, Canal House, Applecross St., Glasgow. Tel: 041-332-6936.	
Fruin	Helensburgh	Salmon Sea Trout Brown Trout	11 Feb. to 31 Oct. 1 Mar. to 6 Oct.	Loch Lomond Angling Improvement Association. R.A. Clement & Co. C.A., 29 St. Vincent Place, Glasgow. Tel: 041-221-0068.	Members only. Members may fish all Association Waters. Fly fishing only.
Water of Leith	Edinburgh	Brown Trout	1 Apr. to 30 Sept.	Lothian Regional Council, Reception, George IV Bridge, Edinburgh. Tel: 031-229 9292, ext. 2355. Post Office, Balerno. Post Office, Colinton. Post Office, Juniper Green.	Fly fishing above Slateford Road Bridge. No spinning at any time. Regulations on permit.
Leven	Dumbarton	Salmon Sea Trout Brown Trout	11 Feb. to 31 Oct. 15 Mar. to 6 Oct.	Loch Lomond Angling Improvement Association. R.A. Clement & Co. C.A., 29 St. Vincent Place, Glasgow. Tel: 041-221-0068. Various local tackle shops.	Members may fish all Association waters. No Sunday fishing.
Teith	Callander	Salmon	1 Feb. to 31 Oct.	J. Bayne, Main Street, Callander. Tel: (0877) 30218.	

Water	Location	Species	Season	Permit available from	Other Information
Teith contd.	Stirling (Blue Banks)	Salmon Sea Trout	1 Feb. to 31 Oct.	D. Crockart & Son, 47 King Street, Stirling, Tel: (0786) 73443.	
Tyne	Haddington	Brown Trout	15 Mar. to 6 Oct.	East Lothian Angling Association. J.S. Main, Saddlers, 87 High Street, Haddington. Major Edinburgh tackle shops.	Twenty miles of river. No Sunday fishing. No threadlines. No spinning.
Union Canal	Edinburgh to Falkirk	Pike Perch Roach Carp Tench	No close season	Lothian Regional Council, 12 St. Giles Street, Edinburgh. Tourist Office, Linlithgow.	Regulations on permit.

LOCHS AND RESERVOIRS

Water	Location	Species	Season	Permit available from	Other Information
Loch Achray	Callander	Brown Trout Perch Pike	15 Mar. to 6 Oct.	Forestry Commission, David Marshall Lodge, Aberfoyle. Loch Achray Hotel, Trossachs.	Bank fishing only.
Loch Ard	Aberfoyle	Brown Trout	15 Mar. to 6 Oct.	Alskeath Hotel, Kinlochard. Post Office, Kinlochard.	
Ballo Reservoir	Lomond Hills	Brown Trout	1 Apr. to 30 Sept.	Water Section, Fife Regional Council, Craig Mitchell House, Flemington Road, Glenrothes. Tel: (0592) 754411.	Fly fishing only. No Sunday fishing. No bank fishing.
Bonaly Reservoir	Edinburgh	Brown/ Rainbow Trout	1 April to 30 Sept.	None required.	
Beecraigs Loch	Linlithgow	Brown Trout Rainbow Trout Brook Trout	15 Mar. to 31 Oct.	Beecraigs Country Park. Tel: Linlithgow 844516.	Fly fishing only.
Bowden Springs	Linlithgow	Rainbow/ Brown Trout	10 Mar. to 12 Nov.	W. Martin, Bowden Springs Fishery, Linlithgow. Tel: Linlithgow 847269.	Bank and boat fishing. Fly fishing only. Minimum size 1 lb.
Cameron Reservoir	St. Andrews	Brown Trout	12 Apr. to 27 Sept.	St. Andrews Angling Club, Secretary, Mr. P. Malcolm, 54 St. Nicholas Street, St. Andrews. Tel: (0334) 76347. Fishing Hut, Tel: Peat Inn 236.	No Sunday fishing. Three rods per boat. Pre-season bookings to Secretary.
Carron Valley Reservoir	Denny	Brown Trout	17 Apr. to 23 Sept.	Director of Finance, Central Regional Council, Viewforth, Stirling. Tel: Stirling 73111.	Boat fishing only.
Loch Chon	Aberfoyle	Brown Trout Pike	15 Mar. to 6 Oct.	Mr. McNair, Frenich Farm, Aberfoyle.	Boats available.
Clatto Loch	Cupar	Brown Trout	1 Apr. to 30 Sept.	Crawford Priory Estate, Mr. Colombo, West Lodge, Crawford Priory Estate, Cupar. Tel: Cupar 2678.	No Sunday fishing.
Clubbiedean Reservoir	Edinburgh	Brown/ Rainbow Trout	1 Apr. to 30 Sept.	Lothian Regional Council, Dept. of Water & Drainage, Comiston Spring, Buckstone Terr., Edinburgh. Tel: 031-445 4141.	Three boats. Bag limit 6 trout. Fly fishing only. Sessions: May to Aug.

Water	Location	Species	Season	Permit available from	Other Information
Loch Coulter	Nr. Carronbridge	Brown/ Rainbow Trout	1 Apr. to 30 Sept.	Larbert & Stenhousemuir Angling Club, Mrs. Shaw, Sauchie Filters. Tel: (0786) 812434.	No Sunday fishing. Fly fishing only. Sessions: Day - 9 am-Dusk Evening - 6 pm-Dusk.
Crosswood Reservoir	West Calder	Brown Trout Brook Trout Rainbow Trout	1 Apr. to 30 Sept.	Lothian Regional Council, Dept. of Water & Drainage, Comiston Springs, Buckstone Terr., Edinburgh. Tel: 031-445 4141. Dept. of Water & Drainage, Lomond House, Livingston. Tel: Livingston 414004.	Three boats. Fly fishing only.
Danskine Loch	Gifford	Roach Perch Carp Crucian Carp	1 Mar. to 20 Oct.	Edinburgh Coarse Anglers, Sec., R. Woods, 23 Terregles, Penicuik. Tel: (0968) 74792.	Strictly members only.
Loch Doine	Balquhidder	Salmon Brown Trout	15 Mar. to 6 Oct.	Mrs. I.T. Ferguson, Muirlaggan Farm, Balquhidder. Tel: (087 74) 219.	Two caravans to let. Free fishing to occupants. Weekly bookings only.
Donolly Reservoir	Gifford	Brown Trout	1 Apr. to 30 Sept.	Lothian Regional Council, Dept. of Water & Drainage, Alderston House, Haddington. Tel: Haddington 4131.	One boat. Collect key from Goblin Ha' Hotel, Gifford. Fly fishing only.
Loch Drunkie	Aberfoyle	Brown Trout	15 Mar. to 6 Oct.	Forestry Commission David Marshall Lodge, Aberfoyle.	Bank fishing only.
Duddingston Loch	Edinburgh	Carp Perch Roach Tench	No close season	Historic Buildings & Monuments, 20 Brandon Street, Edinburgh. Tel: 031-244 3085.	Bird Sanctuary. Bank fishing. Restricted area. No lead weights.
Loch Fitty	Dunfermline	Brown/ Rainbow Trout	1 Mar. to Xmas	Mr. Mackenzie, The Lodge, Loch Fitty, Kingseat by Dunfermline, Fife. Tel: (0383) 723162.	Boat and bank fly fishing. Sessions: Day - 10 am-5 pm Evenings - 5.30 pm-dark. Reductions for single anglers, and 'Father & Schoolboy Son'. Boats, restaurant, tackle shop, fish farm, caravan park.
Free Loch	Ardlui	Pike		Ardlui Hotel, Ardlui by Arrochar. Tel: Inveruglas 243.	
Gladhouse Reservoir	Midlothian	Brown Trout	1 Apr. to 30 Sept.	Lothian Regional Council, Dept. of Water & Drainage, Comiston Springs, Buckstone Terr., Edinburgh. Tel: 031-445 4141.	Local Nature Reserve Double-sessions: May-Aug. Day - 8 am-4.30 pm Evening - 5 pm-sunset plus one hour. No Sunday fishing. Fly fishing only.
Glencorse Reservoir	Penicuik	Brown Trout Brook Trout Rainbow Trout	1 Apr. to 30 Sept.	Lothian Regional Council, Dept. of Water & Drainage, Comiston Springs, Buckstone Terr., Edinburgh. Tel: 031-445 4141.	Fly fishing only. 4 boats. Sessions: May to Aug.

Water	Location	Species	Season	Permit available from	Other Information
Harperrig Reservoir	West Calder	Brown Trout	1 Apr. to 30 Sept.	Boat fishing. Lothian Regional Council, Dept. of Water & Drainage, Comiston Springs, Buckstone Terr. Edinburgh. Tel: 031-445 4141. Dept. of Water & Drainage, Lomond House, Livingston, Tel: Livingston 414004. Bank fishing permits from machine at reservoir.	Correct coins required for machine, 50p, 10p, 5p denominations. Four boats and bank fishing. No Sunday fishing. Fly fishing only.
Harlaw Reservoir	Balerno	Brown/ Rainbow Trout	1 Apr. to 30 Sept.	Bank fishing Fleming Grocer, Balerno.	Fly fishing only. Bag limit 6 trout. Limited number of bank permits.
Holl Reservoir	Lomond Hills,	Brown Trout	1 Apr. to 30 Sept.	Water Section, Fife Regional Council, Craig Mitchell House, Flemington Road, Glenrothes. Tel: (0592) 754411.	Fly fishing only. No Sunday fishing.
Hopes Reservoir	Gifford	Brown/ Rainbow Trout	1 Apr. to 30 Sept.	Lothian Regional Council, Dept. of Water & Drainage, Alderston House, Haddington. Tel: Haddington 4131.	
Lindores Loch	Newburgh	Brown/ Rainbow Trout	15 Mar. to 30 Nov.	F.G.A. Hamilton, Kindrochet Fish Farm, St. Fillans PH6 2JZ. Tel: St. Fillans 337.	Two sessions.
Linlithgow Loch	Linlithgow	Brown/ Rainbow Trout	15 Mar. to 6 Oct.	Lothian Sports Regent Centre, Linlithgow. Tel: Linlithgow 845730. For Forth Area Federation of Anglers.	Fly fishing only. Sessions: (May to Aug.) Day: 9.00 - 4.30 Evening: 5.00 - dusk Sunday: 1.00 - dusk.
Lochore	Ballingry	Brown Trout	15 Mar. to 5 Oct.	Lochore Meadows Country Park, Crosshill, Lochgelly, Fife. Tel: (0592) 860086. Hobby & Model Shop, Dunfermline. Sports Shop, High Street, Cowdenbeath. West, 31 Main St., Kelty.	Reductions for clubs and groups. Sessions: Day - 9 am-5 pm. Evening - 5 pm-dusk. Fly fishing and spinning. Bait fishing from bank from 1 July.
Loch Lomond	Balloch to Ardlui	Salmon Sea Trout Brown Trout Pike Roach Perch	11 Feb. to 31 Oct. 15 Mar.-6 Oct. No close season	Loch Lomond Angling Improvement Association R.A. Clement & Co, C.A., 29 St. Vincent Place, Glasgow. Tel: 041-221-0068. Permits from many hotels, shops and tackle dealers in the area. Ardlui Hotel, Ardlui. Tel: (030 14) 243. Inversnaid Hotel, Inversnaid. Tel: Inversnaid 223.	Permits cover all Association waters. Boats for hire locally. No Sunday fishing.
Loch Lubnaig	Callander to Strathyre	Salmon Brown Trout	1 Feb.-31 Oct. 15 Mar.-6 Oct.	Forth Area Federation of Anglers, J. Bayne, Main Street, Callander. Tel: (0877) 30218.	
Lake of Menteith	Port of Menteith	Brown/ Rainbow Trout	April to Oct.	Lake Hotel, Port of Menteith. Tel: (08775) 664.	

Water	Location	Species	Season	Permit available from	Other Information
Morton Fishery	Mid Calder	Brown/ Rainbow Trout	15 Mar. to 31 Oct.	Morton Fishery, Waterkeepers Cottage, Morton Reservoir, Mid Calder, W. Lothian. Tel: (0506) 882293.	Fly fishing only. Advance bookings necessary Double sessions May-Aug, 9 am-5 pm, 5 pm-dusk. Bag limits 3-6 fish per rod.
North Third	Cambusbarron	Rainbow/ Brown Trout		North Third Fishery, "Greathill", Cambusbarron, Stirling. Tel: Stirling (0786) 71967.	
Lochan Reoidhe	Aberfoyle	Brown Trout	15 Mar. to 6 Oct.	Forestry Commission David Marshall Lodge, Aberfoyle.	Fly fishing only. Limited rods. Boat available. Advance bookings accepted.
Rosebery Reservoir	Gorebridge	Brown/ Rainbow Trout	1 Apr. to 30 Sept.	Waterkeepers Cottage, Rosebery Reservoir, Temple, Midlothian. Tel: (8300) 353.	Three boats & bank fishing. Fly fishing only.
Swans Water Fishery	Bannockburn Stirling	Rainbow Trout	All year	Swans Water Fishery, Cultonhove Fish Farm, Sauchieburn, Stirling. Tel: (0786) 814805.	
Threilpmuir Reservoir	Balerno	Brown/ Rainbow Trout	1 Apr. to 30 Sept.	Flemings, Grocer, Main Street, Balerno.	Limited number of permits covers Harlaw Reservoir as well.
Loch Venachar	Callander	Brown Trout	15 Mar. to 6 Oct.	J. Bayne, Main Street, Callander. Tel: (0877) 30218.	
Loch Voil	Balquhidder	Brown Trout Salmon	15 Mar. to 6 Oct.	Ledcreigh Hotel, Balquhidder. Tel: Strathyre 230.	
				Mrs. I.T. Ferguson, Muirlaggan Farm, Balquhidder. Tel: (087 74) 219.	Two caravans to let with free fishing. Weekly bookings only.
Whiteadder Reservoir	Gifford	Brown Trout	1 Apr. to 30 Sept.	Waterkeepers House, Hungry Snout, Whiteadder Reservoir, Cranshaws, by Duns. Tel: (036 17) 257.	Bank fishing from 1 June each year. Fly fishing only. 3 Boats.

FORTH AND LOMOND (CLYDE COAST)

Sea Angling
Helensburgh
Helensburgh is a small seaside town on the Firth of Clyde at the southern end of the Gareloch, easily reached by train or car.
Types of fish: Shore and boat – cod, flounder, coalfish, conger, rays, dogfish, whiting, dab, haddock, pollack and mackerel.
Boats: Modern Charters Ltd., Tel: Clynder (0436) 831312. J. Allison 0436 84 2569.

Self Drive Boats: T. Lambert, Tel: Helensburgh 2083; R. Clark, Tel: Rhu 820344.
Tackle: 'Carousel', West Clyde Street, Helensburgh.
Bait: Ragworm, lugworm, may be dug locally. Mussels and crabs can be gathered from the shore.
Season for fishing: All year, especially winter for large cod.

Garelochhead
Garelochhead is the village at the head of the Gareloch, with the whole shoreline within easy reach. Upper and lower Loch Long and Loch Goil are only a few miles away.

Types of fish: Cod, coalfish, pollack, dab, flounder, plaice, whiting, haddock, pouting, rays, mackerel, spurdog, lesser spotted dogfish.
Bait: Garelochhead – cockles and mussels. Roseneath – lugworm, ragworm and cockles. Rhu – ragworm. Kilcreggan – ragworm. Coulport – cockles.
Season for fishing:
December-March, migratory cod – June onwards.

Arrochar, Loch Long
The village lies at the northern end of the loch, and has waters sheltered by the high surrounding hills.

Types of fish: Shore – cod, conger, pollack, coalfish and rays. Boat – cod, haddock, whiting, conger, pollack, coalfish, mackerel, dogfish and rays.
Boats: Dinghies from Rossmay Boat Hire, (030 12) 250.
Tackle: Available from Mr. Findlater, Braeside Stores, Arrochar.
Bait: Fresh herring and mackerel, mussels and cockles usually available from the pier. Artificial baits, lures etc. available from shops in village.
Season for fishing: All year.

Clynder
Clynder is the fishing centre on the sheltered west side of the Gareloch and one mile north of the popular Rhu Narrows.
Types of fish: Shore: cod and mackerel. Boat: cod, conger, rays, plaice, flounders, dogfish, whiting, pouting and mackerel.
Boats: C. Moar (0436) 831336; Modern Charters (0436) 831312; Allisons Boat Hire (043684) 2237; Clynder Hotel (0436) 831248.
Tackle: The Modern Charters Ltd., Clynder,
Bait: Cockles, mussels, lug, ragworm, can be dug.
Season for fishing: All year, winter for large cod.
Further information from: Modern Charters Ltd., Victoria Place, Clynder. Tel: 0436 831312.

FORTH AND LOMOND (EAST COAST)

Anglers going afloat from Fife and Forth Harbours are advised to contact the coastguard at Fifeness for weather information. Tel: Crail (0333) 50666 (day or night).

Tayport
Tayport, on the Firth of Tay opposite Dundee, in the northern-most part of Fife, enjoys good shore fishing in sheltered waters. There are no hotels but there is a modern caravan and camping site with showers, laundry etc.
Types of fish: Cod, flounder and plaice from shore, with occasional sea trout (permit required).
Tackle: Available from W.

Sturrock, Mainland Street, Tayport.
Bait: Lugworm, ragworm, mussels, cockles and crabs available locally at low water.
Season for fishing: April- January.
Further information from: James O'Brien, Secretary, Cupar, St. Andrews and District S.A.C., 40 King Street, Kirkcaldy.

St. Andrews
St. Andrews is a leading holiday resort with sea angling as one of its attractions. Fishing is mainly from boats, but good sport can be had from the rocks between the bathing pool and the harbour.
Tackle: Messrs. J. Wilson & Sons (Ironmongers), 169-171 South Street, St. Andrews, KY16 9EE, Tel: 0334 72477.
Bait: Excellent supplies of Lugworm, ragworm and large mussels can be gathered on the beach.
Further information from: James O'Brien, Secretary, Cupar, St. Andrews and District S.A.C., 40 King Street, Kirkcaldy.

Boarhill and Kings Barns
Good beach fishing for cod and flatfish.

Anstruther
It is a fishing village with plenty of good boat and beach fishing. A very rocky coastline but can be very rewarding with good catches of cod, saithe, flounder, wrasse, and whiting. Be prepared to lose tackle.
Types of fish: Cod, saithe, wrasse, flounder, ling, conger and mackerel.
Boats: Plenty charter boats with local skippers who know all the hot spots.
Bait: Lug, rag, white rag, cockle, crab, mussel which can be dug locally.
Season: Boat – May-October. Beach – September-January.
Further information from: Mr. D. Williams, Secretary, Buckhaven & District SAC, 50 Lomond Gardens, Methil, Fife KY8 3JL.

Pittenweem
The nerve centre of the East Neuk with a large deep water harbour which boats can enter or leave at any stage of the tide. The European Cod Festival is now

held here each year and produces large catches of cod. The harbour wall is very popular with young and old alike, with some good catches.
Types of fish: Cod, saithe, flounder, wrasse, ling, conger, whiting, mackerel from boats. Cod, saithe, flounder, wrasse and whiting from beach.
Bait: Lug, rag, can be dug locally.
Season: Beach – September-January.

Leven
A holiday resort with about 2 miles of lovely sandy beaches. Beach fishing is very popular with some very good catches.
Types of fish: Flounder, cod, bass, mullet, saithe.
Boats: No charter boats.
Tackle: Dave's Sport, Bridge Street, Leven.
Bait: Lug available locally.
Season: July-January.

Buckhaven
A small town on the north side of the Firth of Forth, which is renowned for its boat and beach fishing. The Scottish Open Beach Competition is fished from Buckhaven to Dysart each year with large entries from all over Scotland.
Types of fish: Cod, saithe, flounder, whiting, mackerel from beach. Cod, saithe, flounder, whiting, ling, mackerel and wrasse from boat.
Bait: Lug available at Leven.
Tackle: The Sports Shop, Wellesley Road, Buckhaven.
Boats: No charter hire.
Season: Boat – June-November. Beach – October-January.
Further information from: D. Williams, Hon. Sec., Buckhaven & District Sea Angling Club, 50 Lomond Gardens, Methil, Fife KY8 3JL.

Kirkcaldy
Beach fishing at east and west end of town.
Types of fish: Cod, flatfish, saithe, mackerel.
Bait: Beach off bus station.

Pettycur and Kinghorn
Rock and beach fishing off Pettycur Harbour and Kinghorn Beach.
Types of fish: Saithe, flatfish.
Boats: Small boats can be

launched from beaches.
Bait: Plenty locally. Local caravan sites.

Burntisland
Permission required to fish the beach from harbour to swimming pool.
Types of fish: Saithe, flatfish, small cod.
Boats: None locally.
Bait: Lug available locally.
Further information from: J. O'Brien, Secretary, Cupar, St. Andrews and District SAC, 40 King Street, Kirkcaldy.

South Queensferry
A picturesque burgh overshadowed by the Forth Bridges.
Types of fish: Cod, whiting, coalfish, mackerel, flounder from boat and shore in season.
Tackle: Scott Lovat Stores, 6 High Street, South Queensferry, Tel: 031-331 1049
Bait: Lugworm, ragworm, mussel, cockle, clams and crabs at low water in the area.
Season for fishing: May to October.
Further information from: B. Plasting, 53 Somerville Gardens, South Queensferry. Tel: 031-331 1605. There are 3 launching slips in the area, but currents can be dangerous and local advice should be obtained before setting out in dinghies.

Edinburgh
Scotland's capital city, on the south of the Forth estuary, has several miles of shoreline. Most of this is sandy, and can produce good catches of flatfish, although codling, Ray's bream, whiting, eels and mackerel can be taken in season from the shore. Best marks are at Cramond, round the mouth of the River Almond, and the Seafield to Portobello area.
Tackle: Field and Stream, 61 Montrose Terrace. F. & D. Simpson, 28 West Preston Street, Tel: 031–667 3058. Shooting Lines Ltd., 23 Roseburn Terrace, Tel: 031-337 8616 or 18 Hope Park Terrace, Tel: 031-668 3746. John Dickson & Son, 21 Frederick Street. J. Robertson & Son, 17 North St. Andrew Street.
Bait: Worms and maggots sold at Shooting Lines. Lugworm, ragworm, mussels, cockles and clams from most beaches at low water.
Season for fishing: All year round.
Further information from: Mr G. A. Walker, 12/4 Murrayburn Park, Edinburgh. Tel: 031-442-3750

Musselburgh
This town stands on the estuary of the River Esk, 6 miles to the east of Edinburgh, overlooking the Firth of Forth. It has a small but busy harbour at Fisherrow, catering mainly for pleasure craft.
Boats: Enquiries should be made at the harbour. Best shore marks range from Fisherrow harbour to the mouth of the Esk.
Permits: J. Givan, Newsagent, 67 Eskside West, Musselburgh, Tel: 031–665 3371
Bait: Lugworm, ragworm, mussels, cockles and clams at low water.
Further information from: Brunton Hall, East Lothian. Tel: 031-665 3711.

Cockenzie
Mullet can be caught around the warm water outfall to the east of Cockenzie Power station and around the harbour. Other species include flatfish, codling and mackerel.

North Berwick
There is good boat fishing out of North Berwick and the coastline between the town and Dunbar is good for shore fishing.
Types of fish: Cod, haddock, plaice, mackerel and coalfish.
Boats: Launches occasionally run fishing trips from the harbour. Apply Fred Marr, Victoria Road, North Berwick.
Bait: Mussels, crabs and shellfish of various types available at low water.
Tackle: Tackle can be bought locally.
Further information from: Information Centre, Quality Street. Tel: North Berwick (0620) 2197 January-December.

Dunbar
The coastline from Dunbar to Eyemouth is very popular for rock and beach fishing.
Types of fish: Cod, haddock, flounder, coalfish, mackerel, wrasse and whiting.
Boats: Details can be obtained from The Tourist Information Centre, Dunbar.
Tackle: Available from Dunbar and Messrs Main, Saddlers, West Port, Dunbar.
Bait: Mussels, lug and ragworm available at low water, and also from tackle dealers.
Season for fishing: Best April to October.
Further information from: Information Centre, Town House, High Street. Tel: Dunbar (0368) 63353 January-December.

Constituent Area Tourist Boards

City of Dundee Tourist Board
Director,
City of Dundee Tourist Board,
City Chambers,
Dundee DD1 3BY.
Tel: Dundee (0382) 23141.

Perthshire Tourist Board
Director of Tourism,
Perthshire Tourist Board,
The Round House,
Marshall Place,
Perth PH2 8NU.
Tel: Perth (0738) 27958.

Angus Tourist Board
Tourist Manager,
Angus Tourist Board,
Market Place,
Arbroath, Angus DD11 1HR.
Tel: Arbroath (0241) 72609/76680.

RIVER PURIFICATION BOARD
TAY RIVER PURIFICATION BOARD
3 South Street,
Perth, PH2 8NJ.
Tel: Perth 27989.

RIVERS

Water	Location	Species	Season	Permit available from	Other information
Ardle	Kirkmichael	Salmon Trout	15 Jan.-15 Oct. 15 Mar.-6 Oct.	The Log Cabin Hotel, Glen Derby. Tel: Strathardle 288.	No Sunday fishing.
	Blairgowrie	Salmon Trout	15 Jan.-15 Oct. 15 Mar.-6 Oct.	Corriefodly Hotel, Bridge of Cally. Tel: (025 086) 236.	Sunday fishing for trout only.
Braan	Amulree	Brown Trout	15 Mar. to 6 Oct.	Amulree Hotel, Amulree, by Dunkeld. Tel: (035 05) 218.	Fly rods only.
Dean	Glamis	Brown Trout	15 Mar. to 6 Oct.	Canmore Angling Club, Forfar.	
	Strathmore	Brown Trout	15 Mar. to 6 Oct.	Strathmore Angling Improvement Association, Mrs. A.J. Henderson, 364 Blackness Road, Dundee. Tel: (0382) 68062.	
Dochart	Killin	Brown Trout	15 Mar. to 6 Oct.	D. & S. Allan, Tackle Dealer, Killin, Perthshire. Tel: (056 72) 362.	All legal lures permitted. Fly only on lower beat.
Earn	Crieff	Salmon Sea Trout Brown Trout	1 Feb. to 15 Oct. 15 Mar.-15 Sept.	Crieff Angling Club. W. Cook & Son, Tackle Dealer, High St., Crieff. Tel: (0764) 2081. Mr. A. Boyd, King Street, Crieff. Tel: (0764) 3871.	No prawn, diving, minnow or bubble floats.
	St. Fillans	Salmon Sea Trout Brown Trout	14 Feb. to 15 Oct. 15 Mar. to 6 Oct.	Mrs. A. Henry, St. Fillans & Lochearn Angling Association, Tullichettle Lodge, Comrie, Crieff PH6 2HU. Tel: (0764) 70323. Lochearn Post Office. St. Fillans Post Office.	Salmon and sea trout fishing for members only.
Ericht (and Ardle)	Bridge of Cally	Salmon Brown Trout	1 Jan.-15 Oct. 15 Mar. to 6 Oct.	Bridge of Cally Hotel, Blairgowrie, Perthshire. Tel: (025 086) 231.	Fly fishing only after 15 April.
	Craighall	Salmon Brown Trout	15 Jan.-15 Oct. 15 Mar to 6 Oct.	N.A. Rattray, Craighall-Rattray, Blairgowrie. Tel: (0250) 4749.	

Water	Location	Species	Season	Permit available from	Other Information
Gaur	Rannoch	Brown Trout	15 Mar. to 6 Oct.	Moor of Rannoch Hotel, Rannoch Station, Perthshire. Tel: (088 23) 238.	Free for guests.
Isla	Strathmore	Brown Trout	15 Mar. to 6 Oct.	Strathmore Angling Improvement Association, Mrs. A.J. Henderson, 364 Blackness Road, Dundee. Tel: (0382) 68062.	
Lochay	Killin	Brown Trout Pike Perch	15 Mar. to 6 Oct.	D. & S. Allan, Tackle Dealers, Main Street, Killin, Perthshire. Tel: (056 72) 362.	Fly only on upper beat.
Lunan	Arbroath	Sea/ Brown Trout	15 Mar. to 6 Oct.	Arbroath Angling Club. Arbroath Cycle and Tackle Centre, High Street, Arbroath. Tel: (0241) 73467.	Fly, bait or spinning.
Lyon	Aberfeldy	Salmon	15 Jan. to 15 Oct.	Fortingall Hotel, Fortingall, by Aberfeldy. Tel: (088 73) 367.	No Sunday fishing.
North Esk	Edzell	Salmon Sea Trout Brown Trout	16 Feb. to 31 Oct.	Matthew Ramage, Head Keepers House, Gannochy, Edzell. Tel: (035 64) 7331.	No Sunday fishing. Fly, bait or spinning.
South Esk	Kirriemuir	Salmon Sea Trout Brown Trout	16 Feb. to 31 Oct.	Kirriemuir Angling Club, 13 Clova Road, Kirriemuir. Tel: (0575) 3456. Permits issued only in advance.	No permits on Saturdays. No Sunday fishing.
Tay	Aberfeldy	Brown Trout Grayling	15 Mar. to 6 Oct.	Jamiesons Sports Shop, Dunkeld Street, Aberfeldy. Tel: (0887) 20385.	
		Salmon Brown Trout	15 Jan.-15 Oct. 15 Mar. to 6 Oct.	Weem Hotel, Aberfeldy. Tel: (0887) 20381.	
	Grandtully	Salmon Brown Trout Grayling	15 Jan.-15 Oct. 15 Mar. to 6 Oct.	Grandtully Hotel, Strathtay, Perthshire. Tel: (088 74) 207.	
	Ballinluig	Salmon Brown Trout Grayling Pike Perch Eels	15 Jan.-15 Oct. 15 Mar. to 6 Oct.	Logierait Hotel, Logierait, Perthshire. Tel: (079 682) 423.	
	Dunkeld	Salmon Trout	15 Jan.-15 Oct. 15 Mar.-6 Oct.	Manager, Burnside, Dalguise, by Dunkeld. Tel: (035 02) 593.	Best April to July, September to October.
		Salmon Brown Trout	15 Jan.-15 Oct. 15 Mar.-6 Oct.	Stakis plc. Dunkeld House Hotel, Dunkeld, Perthshire. Tel: (035 02) 771.	One boat with two rods. Ghillie available. Two bank rods. No salmon fishing on Sunday. Booking advisable.
		Brown Trout	15 Mar. to 6 Oct.	Kettles of Dunkeld, Atholl Street, Dunkeld. Tel: (035 02) 272.	Fly fishing only.
	Stanley	Salmon	15 Jan. to 15 Oct.	Ballathie Estate Office, Ballathie Farms, Nr. Stanley. Tel: (025 083) 250.	Advisable to book in advance. Spring and Summer salmon fishing only.

Water	Location	Species	Season	Permit available from	Other Information
Tay contd.	Stanley	Salmon Sea Trout Brown Trout	15 Jan.- 13 Oct. 12 Mar.- 6 Oct.	Tayside Hotel, Stanley, Nr. Perth. Tel: (0738) 828249.	Inclusive hotel and fishing breaks and holidays. Ghillies by arrangement.
	Perth	Salmon Sea Trout Flounders Roach	15 Jan. to 15 Oct. •	Director of Leisure & Recreation, Perth & Kinross District Council, 3 High Street, Perth. Tel: (0738) 39911, (Monday to Friday). Tourist Information Centre, Round House, Marshall Place, Perth.	Advisable to book in advance. Only 20 permits per day. Only 2 permits may be booked in advance by any one person. No weekly permits. Proof of identification is required.
Tummel	Pitlochry	Salmon Sea Trout	15 Jan. to 15 Oct.	Pitlochry Angling Club c/o Tourist Office, Pitlochry. Tel: Mr. Gardiner (0796) 2157 (evenings).	Permits available Monday to Saturday.
	Moulinearn to Ballinluig	Salmon Sea Trout	15 Jan. to 15 Oct.	Pitlochry Angling Club, c/o Tourist Office, Pitlochry. Tel: Mr. Gardiner, (0796) 2157 (evenings).	Only available July, August, September.
	Pitlochry to Ballinluig	Brown Trout Grayling	16 Mar. to 6 Oct.	Pitlochry Angling Club, Pitlochry Tourist Office. Milton of Fonab Caravan Site. Ballinluig Post Office. Malloch's Highland Gathering, Atholl Road, Pitlochry.	Five miles of river both banks. Map and rules on permit.

LOCHS AND RESERVOIRS

Water	Location	Species	Season	Permit available from	Other Information
Butterstone Loch	Dunkeld	Rainbow/ Brown Trout	1 Apr. to 31 Oct.	The Bailiff, Lochend Cottage, Butterstone, by Dunkeld. Tel: (035 04) 238.	Fly fishing only. 12 Boats. Day Session: 9 am-5 pm. Evening: 5.30 pm-dusk.
Castlehill Reservoir	Glendevon	Brown Trout	1 Apr. to 30 Sept.	Tormaukin Hotel, Glendevon. Tel: (025 981) 252.	Fly fishing only.
				The Boathouse, Tel: (025981) 239.	Fly fishing only
Crombie Reservoir	Crombie Country Park	Brown Trout	April to Sept.	Monikie Angling Club, Bailiff, Tel: (028 623) 300.	
Den of Ogil Reservoir		Brown Trout	1 Apr. to 6 Oct.	Canmore Angling Club, Forfar.	
Dunalastair Loch	Kinloch Rannoch	Brown Trout	15 Mar. to 6 Oct.	Lassintullich Fisheries, Kinloch Rannoch. Tel: (088 22) 238.	Five boats available. Half price for single rod.
Loch Earn	St. Fillans Lochearnhead	Brown/ Rainbow Trout	1 Apr. to 6 Oct.	St. Fillans & Lochearn Angling Association, Tullichettle Lodge, Comrie, Perthshire. Tel: (0764) 70323. Post Office, St. Fillans. Post Office, Lochearnhead.	
Loch Eigheach	Moor of Rannoch	Brown Trout	15 Mar. to 6 Oct.	Rannoch & District Angling Club, John Brown, The Square, Kinloch Rannoch. Tel: (088 22) 268.	Bank fishing only.

Water	Location	Species	Season	Permit available from	Other Information
Loch Faskally	Pitlochry	Salmon	Mar., May to Oct.	P. Williamson, Boathouse, Loch Faskally, Pitlochry. Tel: (0796) 2919/2612.	Any legal lure for salmon
		Brown Trout Pike Perch	Apr. to Sept.		
Glendevon (Upper Reservoir Lower Reservoir)	Glendevon	Brown Trout	1 Apr. to 30 Sept.	The Boathouse. Tel: (025981) 239.	Fly fishing only. No Sunday fishing.
Glenfarg Reservoir	Glenfarg	Brown Trout	1 Apr. to 30 Sept.	Water Section, Fife Regional Council, Craig Mitchell House, Flemington Road, Glenrothes. Tel: (0592) 754411.	Fly fishing only. No bank fishing. No Sunday fishing.
Glenquey	Glendevon	Brown Trout	1 Apr. to 30 Sept.	T.H. Sloan, Dollar. Muckhart Post Office.	Bank fishing only. Fly fishing only. No Sunday fishing. Regulations on permits.
Holl Reservoir	Leslie	Brown Trout	1 Apr. to 30 Sept.	Water Section, Fife Regional Council, Craig Mitchell House, Flemington Road, Glenrothes. Tel: (0592) 754411.	Fly fishing only. No Sunday fishing. No bank fishing.
Loch Kinardochy	Strathtummel	Brown Trout	15 Mar. to 6 Oct.	Pitlochry Angling Club, c/o Airdaniar Hotel, Atholl Road, Pitlochry. Tel: (0796) 2266.	No bank fishing. 10 am to dusk. Fly fishing only.
Loch Laidon	Rannoch Moor	Brown Trout	15 Mar. to 6 Oct.	Moor of Rannoch Hotel, Rannoch Station, Perthshire. Tel: (088 23) 238.	Boat available to guests and visitors.
Loch Leven	Kinross	Brown Trout (Loch Leven strain)	April to Oct.	The Pier, Kinross. Tel: (0577) 63407.	Fly and boat fishing only.
Lintrathen Reservoir	Kirriemuir	Brown Trout	1 Apr. to 6 Oct.	Lintrathen Angling Club Day permits: Tayside Regional Council, Water Services Dept., 10 Ward Road, Dundee. Tel: (0382) 21164. Club bookings: Dr. Parratt, 91 Strathearn Road, Broughty Ferry, Dundee. Tel: (0382) 77305. (Not after start of season). Lochside Tel: (057 56) 327.	Sixteen boats. Sunday fishing. Telephone for details of sessions.
Lassintullich Fisheries Dunalastair Loch	Kinloch Rannoch	Brown Trout	15 Mar. to 6 Oct.	Lassintullich Fisheries. Tel: (08822) 238.	Five boats. No bank fishing. Fly fishing only.
Loch Mharaich	Kirkmichael	Brown/ Rainbow Trout	15 Mar. to 6 Oct.	The Log Cabin, Hotel, Glen Derby. Tel: (025 081) 288.	
Monikie Reservoir	Monikie	Trout	April to Sept.	Monikie Country Park, Monikie Angling Club, Bailiff, Tel: (082 623) 300	Fly fishing. Boat fishing. Telephone Bookings 9.30 - 10.30 am 1.00 - 1.30 pm 4.30 - 6.30 pm.
Monzievaird	Crieff	Brown/ Rainbow Trout	April to Oct.	Loch Monzievaird Ltd., Ochtertyre House, by Crieff, Perthshire. Tel: (0764) 3963.	

Please mention this Pastime Publications Guide

Water	Location	Species	Season	Permit available from	Other Information
Lochan-na-Laraig	Killin	Trout	15 Mar. to 6 Oct.	D. & S. Allan, Tackle Dealers, Main Street, Killin. Tel: (056 72) 362.	All legal lures.
Loch Rannoch	Kinloch Rannoch	Brown Trout	15 Mar. to 6 Oct.	Loch Rannoch Conservation Association, Cuilmore Cottage, Kinloch Rannoch. Loch Rannoch Hotel, Bun Rannoch Hotel, Dunalastair Hotel.	Fly fishing only. 6 am - 10 pm.
Rescobie Loch	Forfar	Brown/ Rainbow Trout	15 Mar. to 31 Oct.	Bailiff, Rescobie Loch. Tel: (030781) 384.	Fly fishing only.
Sandy-knowes Fishery	Bridge of Earn	Rainbow Trout	1 Mar. to 30 Nov.	M.A. Brien, The Fishery Office, Sandyknowe Fishery, Bridge of Earn. Tel: (0738) 813033.	Bank fly fishing only. Session times 10 am-2 pm, 2 pm-6 pm, 6 pm-10 pm. Bag limit - 4 trout per session. Open 7 days per week. No Sunday evenings.
Loch Tay	Killin	Salmon	15 Jan. to 15 Oct.	Killin Hotel, Killin. Tel: (056 72) 296.	Ghillies available.
		Trout	15 Mar. to 6 Oct.	Claichaig Hotel, Killin. Tel: (056 72) 270/565.	
				D. & S. Allan, Tackle Dealers, Main Street, Killin. Tel: (056 72) 362.	All legal lures permitted.
	Milton Morenish	Salmon Trout	15 Jan.-15 Oct. 15 Mar.-6 Oct.	Loch Tay Highland Lodges, Milton Morenish, by Killin. Tel: (056 72) 323.	Sixteen boats available. Special offers for mid-week fishing, 'phone for details.
	Ardeonaig	Salmon Trout Char	15 Jan.-15 Oct. 15 Mar. to 6 Oct.	Ardeonaig Hotel, South Loch Tay, by Killin. Tel: (056 72) 400.	Own harbour with 7 boats available, both wooden and fibre glass, for trolling and drifting.
	Kenmore	Salmon Trout	15 Jan.-15 Oct. 15 Mar. to 6 Oct.	Kenmore Hotel, Kenmore, by Aberfeldy. Tel: (08873) 205.	Boats available on Loch Tay. Ghillie service, rod hire to residents. Fishing for two miles on River Tay.
	Lawers	Salmon Brown Trout	15 Jan.-15 Oct. 15 Mar. to 6 Oct.	Ben Lawers Hotel, Lawers, Aberfeldy. Tel: (056 72) 436.	Boats and ghillies available.
Loch Turret	Crieff	Brown Trout	1 Apr. to 30 Sept.	Director of Finance, Central Scotland Water Development Board, 30 George Square, Glasgow. Tel: 041-248 5855. W. Cook & Son, 19 High Street, Crieff. Tel: (0764) 2081.	Four boats available with outboards.

TAYSIDE
Sea Angling

Arbroath
Situated on the east coast of Angus, 17 miles north-east of Dundee, Arbroath is easily accessible by road and rail. It is the centre for commercial fishing, and famous for its smokies. Pleasure boats ply for short cruises to local sea cliffs and caves, from the harbour. There are about 10 boats between 15ft and 35ft used for lobster and crab fishing, taking out parties for sea angling.
Types of fish: Cod, coalfish, mackerel, flounder, conger, plaice, haddock and pollack.
Boats: Available through local fishermen and part time lobster and crab fishermen at reasonable prices.

Tackle: Available from Arbroath Cycle & Tackle Centre, 274 High Street, Arbroath DD11 1JE. Tel: Arbroath 73467.

Dundee
Dundee is situated on the estuary of the River Tay and has sea fishing in the city centre, while Broughty Ferry, a suburb of Dundee, Easthaven and Carnoustie, all within easy reach

by road and rail, have sea fishing from rocks, piers or from boats. There are good marks around the Bell Rock about 12 miles offshore.

Types of fish: Cod, flatfish from shore plus cod, haddock, coalfish, ling, pouting and plaice from boats.

Tackle: All types of tackle available from Messrs John R. Gow and Sons, 12 Union Street, Dundee. Shortcast Ltd., 8 Whitehall Crescent, Dundee.

McGill Bros Ltd., 18 Victoria Road, Dundee.

Bait: Available locally.

Season for fishing: All year.

Further information from: Messrs John R. Gow and Sons, 12 Union Street, Dundee.

Codling, the mainstay of sea angling sport ashore and afloat around Scotland.

Constituent Area Tourist Organisations

Aviemore and Spey Valley Tourist Organisation
Area Tourist Officer,
Aviemore and Spey Valley Tourist Organisation,
Grampian Road, Aviemore,
Inverness-shire PH22 1PP.
Tel: Aviemore (0479) 810545.

Banff and Buchan Tourist Board
Tourism Manager,
Banff and Buchan Tourist Board,
Collie Lodge,
Banff AB4 1AU.
Tel: Banff (026 12) 2789.

Kincardine and Deeside Tourist Board
Tourist Officer,
Kincardine and Deeside Tourist Board,
45 Station Road, Banchory,
Kincardineshire AB3 3XX.
Tel: Banchory (033 02) 2066.

City of Aberdeen Tourist Board
Director,
City of Aberdeen Tourist Board,
St. Nicholas House, Broad Street,
Aberdeen AB9 1DE.
Tel: Aberdeen (0224) 632727.

Gordon District Tourist Board
Director,
Gordon District Tourist Board,
St. Nicholas House, Broad Street,
Aberdeen AB9 1DE.
Tel: Aberdeen (0224) 632727.

Moray District Council
Chief Tourist Officer,
Moray District Council,
17 High Street, Elgin,
Morayshire IV30 1EG.
Tel: Elgin (0343) 2666.

RIVER PURIFICATION BOARD
NORTH EAST RIVER PURIFICATION BOARD
Greyhope House,
Greyhope Road, Torry,
Aberdeen AB1 3RD.
Tel: Aberdeen (0224) 248338.

RIVERS

Water	Location	Species	Season	Permit available from	Other information
Avon	Ballindalloch	Salmon Sea Trout	11 Feb. to 30 Sept.	Delnashaugh Hotel, Ballindalloch, Banffshire. Tel: Ballindalloch 210.	No prawn. Fly fishing during September. No lead attached to fly.
	Tomintoul	Salmon Sea Trout	Feb. to end Sept.	Gordon Arms Hotel, Tomintoul, Banffshire. Tel: Tomintoul 206.	No prawn. Fly fishing during Sept. Max. breaking strain 10 lb. No lead attached to fly.
		Salmon Sea Trout	May to 30 Sept.	Richmond Arms Hotel, Tomintoul, Ballindalloch AB3 9ET. Tel: (08074) 209.	No prawn. Fly fishing only in September. Permits given to hotel guests only.
Bervie	Laurence-kirk Fordoun	Salmon Sea Trout Brown Trout		W. Davidson, 26 Provost, Robson Drive, Laurencekirk. Tel: Laurencekirk 8140	
Carron	Stonehaven	Brown Trout	1 May to 31 Aug.	Davids Sports Shop, 31 Market Square, Stonehaven. Tel: Stonehaven 62239. Stonehaven Angling Assoc. Sec. C.M. MacDonald, 'Clachaig', 92 Forest Park, Stonehaven AB3 2GF.	Visitors permits. Sea pool to railway viaduct.
Cowie	Stonehaven	Salmon Sea Trout Brown Trout	1 May to 31 Aug.	Davids Sports Shop, 31 Market Square, Stonehaven. Tel: Stonehaven 62239. Stonehaven Angling Assoc. Sec. C.M. MacDonald, 'Clachaig', 93 Forest Park, Stonehaven AB3 2GF.	Visitors permits. Sea pool to railway viaduct.

Water	Location	Species	Season	Permit available from	Other Information
Bogie	Huntly	Salmon Sea Trout Brown Trout	11 Feb. to 31 Oct. 1 Apr. to 6 Oct.	Clerk of Fishings, Huntly Fishings Committee, P.O. Box 2, Royal Bank Buildings, 27/29 Duke Street, Huntly. Tel: (0466) 2291/2292.	Permit covers Bogie, Deveron and Isla.
Dee	Aboyne	Salmon Sea Trout Brown Trout	1 Feb. to 30 Sept.	Estate Office, Glen Tanar. Tel: (0339) 2451.	No Sunday fishing. Fly fishing only.
	Braemar	Salmon	1 Feb. to 30 Sept.	Invercauld Arms Hotel, Braemar. Tel: Braemar 605.	Fishing on adjacent beats can be arranged on request.
	Banchory	Salmon Sea Trout	1 Feb. to 30 Sept.	Banchory Lodge Hotel, Banchory. Tel: Banchory 2625.	Rods available by booking in advance.
	Blairs	Salmon Sea Trout	1 Feb. to 30 Sept.	Ardoe House Hotel, North Lodge, Banchory, Derenick. Tel: Aberdeen 867752/867355.	
Deveron	Banff	Salmon Sea Trout Brown Trout	11 Feb. to 31 Oct.	Jay-Tee Sports Shop, Low Street, Banff. Tel: Banff 5821.	
	Huntly	Salmon Sea Trout Brown Trout	11 Feb. to 31 Oct. 1 Apr. to 6 Oct.	Clerk of Fishings, Huntly Fishings Committee, P.O. Box 2, Royal Bank Buildings, 27/29 Duke Street, Huntly. Tel: (0466) 2291/2292.	Permit covers Deveron, Bogie and Isla.
		Salmon Sea Trout Brown Trout	Feb. to Oct.	Castle Hotel, Huntly. Tel: Huntly 2696.	
	Rothiemay	Salmon Sea Trout Brown Trout	11 Feb. to 31 Oct.	Forbes Arms Hotel, Rotheimay, Huntly. Tel: Rothiemay 248.	Fly fishing and spinning. Worm in spate only.
	Turriff	Salmon Sea Trout Brown Trout	11 Feb. to 31 Oct.	Turriff Angling Assoc., I. Masson, The Cross, 6 Castle Street, Turriff. Tel: Turriff 62428.	No day tickets. Six weekly tickets available to visitors. Restrictions on spinning.
Don	Glenkindie	Salmon Brown Trout	11 Feb.-31 Oct. 15 Mar.-1 Oct.	Glenkindie Arms Hotel, Glenkindie, by Alford. Tel: Glenkindie 288.	
	Grandhome	Salmon Sea Trout	11 Feb. to 31 Oct.	D. Hunter, Mains of Grandhome, Woodside, Aberdeenshire. Tel: (0224) 723408.	
	Manar Fishings	Salmon Sea Trout Brown Trout	11 Feb. to 31 Oct. 1 Apr.-30 Sept.	J.J. Watson 44 Market Place, Inverurie. Tel: (0467) 20321.	No worm, shrimp or prawn. Limit of 8 rods per day.
	Monymusk	Salmon Brown Trout	11 Feb. to 31 Oct.	Grant Arms Hotel, Monymusk, Aberdeenshire. Tel: Monymusk 226.	Fly or spinning only.
	Kemnay	Salmon Brown Trout	11 Feb. to 31 Oct.	F.J. & S.L. Milton, Kemnay House, Kemnay, Aberdeenshire AB5 9LH. Tel: Kemnay 42220	Advance booking essential.
	Kildrummy Fishings	Salmon Brown Trout	11 Feb.-31 Oct. 15 Mar.-6 Oct.	T. Hillary, Achnavenie, Kildrummy, Alford. Tel: Kildrummy 208.	Best April, May, June. Approx. 4 mile north bank.
	Strathdon	Salmon Brown Trout	11 Feb. to 31 Oct.	Colquhonnie Hotel, Strathdon, Aberdeenshire. Tel: Strathdon 210.	

Water	Location	Species	Season	Permit available from	Other Information
Don contd.	Kintore	Salmon Brown Trout	11 Feb. to 31 Oct.	Kintore Arms Inn, Kintore. Tel: Kintore 32216. J.A. Copland, Newsagent, 2 Northern Road, Kintore. Tel: Kintore 32210. S.P. Amin, Post Office, The Square, Kintore. Tel: Kintore 32201.	
	Alford	Salmon Brown Trout	11 Feb. to 31 Oct.	Forbes Arms Hotel, Bridge of Alford. Tel: Alford 2108.	
	Inverurie	Salmon Sea Trout Brown Trout	11 Feb. to 31 Oct. 1 Apr.-30 Sept.	J.J. Watson, 44 Market Place, Inverurie. Tel: (0467) 20321.	No worm till 1 Apr. No natural minnow. No shrimp or prawn. Reductions for school children and OAP's.
Dulnain	Grantown-on-Spey	Salmon Sea Trout Brown Trout	11 Feb. to 30 Sept. 15 Mar.-30 Sept.	Strathspey Angling Assoc., Mortimer's, 61 High Street, Grantown-on-Spey. Tel: Grantown-on-Spey 2684.	Visitors resident in Grantown, Cromdale, Duthill, Carrbridge, Dulnain Bridge and Nethy Bridge areas. 12 miles of river.
Feugh	Feughside	Salmon Brown Trout		Feughside Hotel, Tel: (033045) 225.	
Fiddich	Dufftown	Salmon Sea Trout Brown Trout	May to Sept.	E. & D. Smith, The Square, Dufftown.	Fly or worm.
Findhorn	Findhorn (Estuary)	Sea Trout	11 Feb. to 6 Oct.	Moray Water Sports, Findhorn.	Bait, fly, lures. Fly only 1 May-15 June.
	Forres	Salmon Sea Trout	11 Feb. to 30 Sept.	J. Mitchell, Tackle Shop, 97D High Street, Forres. Tel: Forres 72936.	All visiting anglers must reside in parishes of Forres and Rafford.
Isla	Huntly	Salmon Sea Trout Brown Trout	11 Feb. to 31 Oct. 1 Apr. to 6 Oct.	Clerk of Fishings, Huntly Fishings Committee, P.O. Box 2, Royal Bank Buildings, 27/29 Duke Street, Huntly. Tel: (0466) 2291/2292.	Permit covers Isla, Deveron and Bogie.
Livet	Tomintoul	Salmon Sea Trout		Richmond Arms Hotel, Tomintoul, Ballindalloch AB3 9ET. Tel: (08074) 209.	No prawn. Fly fishing only in September. Permits given to hotel guests only.
Lossie	Elgin	Salmon Sea Trout Brown Trout	11 Feb. to 15 Oct. 15 Mar.-6 Oct.	Elgin & District Angling Association, The Tackle Shop, High Street, Elgin.	
Muckle burn	Forres	almon Sea Trout	1 Apr. to 30 Sept.	J. Mitchell, Tackle Shop, 97D High Street, Forres. Tel: Forres 72923.	Reductions for juveniles
Spey	Aberlour	Salmon Sea Trout Brown Trout	11 Feb. to 30 Sept.	J.A.J. Munro, 93-95 High Street, Aberlour. Tel: Aberlour 428. Lour Hotel, Aberlour, Tel: Aberlour 224. Aberlour Hotel, Aberlour, Tel: Aberlour 287. Dowans Hotel, Aberlour. Tel: Aberlour 488.	Visitors tickets available from J.A.J. Munro. 3 tickets per hotel, overnight accommodation in village hotel necessary prior to fishing. One fish above bridge (9 am-5 pm), one fish below bridge (9 am-midnight), other fish sold for club funds. No day tickets on Saturday or local holidays.

Water	Location	Species	Season	Permit available from	Other Information
Spey contd.	Fochabers	Salmon	11 Feb. to 30 Sept.	Gordon Arms Hotel, Fochabers. Tel: (0343) 820508/9.	
	Grantown on-Spey	Salmon Sea Trout Brown Trout	11 Feb. to 30 Sept. 15 Mar.-30 Sept.	Strathspey Angling Assoc., Mortimer's 61 High Street, Grantown-on-Spey. Tel: Grantown-on-Spey 2684.	7 miles both banks. No prawn. No Sunday fishing.
		Salmon Sea Trout Brown Trout	11 Feb 30 Sept	Seafield Lodge Hotel Grantown-on-Spey Tel: (0479) 2152	Fly fishing courses include full board, permit and instruction.
	Boat of Garten	Salmon Sea Trout Brown Trout	11 Feb. to 30 Sept. 15 Mar.-30 Sept.	Craigard Hotel, Boat of Garten. Tel: Boat of Garten 206. The Boat Hotel, Boat of Garten. Tel: Boat of Garten 258. Ben-o-Gar, Deisher Road, Boat of Garten. Tel: Boat of Garten 372. River Spey and several trout lochs.	
	Nethy Bridge Boat of Garten	Salmon Sea Trout Brown Trout	11 Feb. to 30 Sept.	Abernethy Angling Assoc. Boat of Garten. Ben-o-Gar Stores, Deisher Road, Boat of Garten. Tel: 372.	
	Aviemore	Salmon Sea Trout Brown Trout	11 Feb. to 30 Sept.	Rothiemurchus Estate, Inverdruie, Aviemore. Tel: 810858. Kinrara Estate Office, Aviemore. Tel: (0479) 810240.	Four beats available on River Spey. Stocked rainbow trout loch.
	Aviemore	Salmon Sea Trout Rainbow Trout Brown Trout Salmon Sea Trout	11 Feb.-30 Sept. 15 Mar.-6 Oct. 11 Feb. to 30 Sept.	Osprey Fishing School, The Fishing Centre, Aviemore. Tel: Aviemore 810767/810911. Alvie Estate Office, Kincraig, by Kingussie. Tel: Kincraig 255. Dalraddy Caravan Park, Aviemore. Tel: Aviemore 810330.	Fly fishing or spinning. River Spey, River Feshie and Lochs arranged. Fly fishing or spinning. Permit also covers River Feshie and lochs Alvie and Insh.
	Kingussie	Salmon Brown Trout	15 Mar. to 30 Sept.	Badenoch Angling Assoc., Secretary, J. Dallas, The Mills, Kingussie. Local tackle shops in Kingussie and Newtonmore.	Spinning allowed when fly fishing applicable.
Ugie	Peter-head	Salmon Sea Trout Brown Trout	11 Feb. to 31 Oct.	Spar, Eight till Late, 3 Ugie Road, Peterhead. Dicks Sports, 54 Broad Street, Fraserburgh. Robertson Sports, 1-3 Kirk Street, Peterhead. Tel: Peterhead 72584.	Bag limit - 8 fish per day. Worming only in spates. No spinning (Apr-Aug inc.).
Urie	Inverurie	Salmon Sea Trout Brown Trout	11 Feb. to 31 Oct. 1 Apr.-30 Sept.	J.J. Watson, 44 Market Place, Inverurie. Tel: (0467) 20321.	No worm till 1 Apr. No natural minnow. No shrimp or prawn. Reductions for school children and OAP's.
Ythan	Ellon	Salmon Sea Trout Brown Trout	11 Feb. to 31 Oct.	Buchan Hotel, Ellon, Aberdeenshire. Tel: Ellon 20208.	Machar Pool for hotel guests only £7 per day.
	(Estuary) Newburgh	Salmon Sea Trout	11 Feb. to 31 Oct.	Mrs. Forbes, 3 Lea Cottages, Newburgh. Tel: (03586) 89297. boats available.	No lead core lines. No more than 2 lures or flies at one time. No live bait.

Please mention this Pastime Publications Guide

Water	Location	Species	Season	Permit available from	Other Information
Ythan contd.	Fyvie	Salmon Sea Trout	11 Feb. to 31 Oct.	Fyvie Angling Assoc., G.A. Joss, Clydesdale Bank plc, Fyvie, Turriff. Tel: (06516) 233.	
	Methlick	Salmon Sea Trout	11 Feb. to 31 Oct.	Haddo House Angling Assoc., Secretary, Kirton, Methlick, Ellon, Aberdeenshire.	

LOCHS AND RESERVOIRS

Water	Location	Species	Season	Permit available from	Other Information
Aboyne Loch	Aboyne	Pike Perch		The Warden, Aboyne Loch, Holiday Park. Tel: Aboyne 86244.	Fishing parties restricted on Sat. and Sun. afternoons.
Loch Alvie	Aviemore	Brown Trout	15 Mar. to 6 Oct.	Kinrara Estate Office, Tel: (0479) 810240.	Three Boats.
		Brown Trout Pike		Alvie Estate Office, Kincraig, by Kingussie. Tel: Kincraig 255. Dalraddy Caravan Park, Aviemore. Tel: Aviemore 810330.	2 Boats. Fly fishing or spinning. Permit also covers Rivers Feshi, and Spey and Loch Insh.
Avielochan	Aviemore	Rainbow/ Brown Trout	Apr. to Sept.	Mrs.M. McCook, Avielochan, Aviemore. Tel: Aviemore 810450. Mortimer's, 61 High St., Grantown-on-Spey. Tel: Grantown on Spey 2684.	Bank fishing only. Spinning area designated.
Loch of Blairs	Forres	Brown/ Rainbow Trout	Easter to Mid-Oct.	Moray District Council, Dept. of Recreation, 30-32 High Street, Elgin. Tel: Elgin 45121. J. Mitchell, 97D High St., Forres. Tel: Forres 72936.	Two sessions. Boat fishing. Fly only. Sunday fishing. Four boats available.
Loch Dallas	Boat of Garten	Brown/ Rainbow Trout	Apr. to Sept.	Mortimer's 61 High Street, Grantown-on-Spey. Tel: Grantown on Spey 2684.	Fly fishing only.
Loch Ericht	Dalwhinnie	Brown Trout	15 Mar. to 6 Oct.	Badenoch Angling Association, Loch Ericht Hotel, Dalwhinnie.	
Glen Latterach Reservoir	Elgin	Brown Trout	1 Apr. to 30 Sept.	Dept. of Water Services, Grampian Road, Elgin. Tel: Elgin 41144.	
Loch Insh	Kincraig	Brown Trout Char Salmon Salmon Sea Trout Brown Trout	15 Mar. to 6 Oct. 11 Feb. to 30 Sept.	Kinrara Estate Office, Aviemore, Tel: (02479) 810240. Alvie Estate Office, Kincraig, by Kingussie. Tel: Kincraig 255. Dalraddy Caravan Park, Aviemore. Tel: Aviemore 810330.	One boat. Boat fishing only. Fly fishing or spinning. Permit also covers Rivers Feshie and Spey and Lochs Insh and Alvie.
Loch Laggan	Dalwhinnie	Brown Trout	15 Mar. to 6 Oct.	Badenoch Angling Association. Local tackle shops in Kingussie and Newtonmore.	
Millbuies Loch	Elgin	Brown/ Rainbow Trout	Easter to Mid-Oct.	Moray District Council, Dept. of Recreation, 30-32 High Street, Elgin. Tel: Elgin 45121. Warden at Millbuies.	Boat fishing. Fly fishing only. Four boats available.
Loch Mor	Dulnain Bridge	Brown/ Rainbow Trout	Apr. to Sept.	Mortimer's 61 High Street, Grantown-on-Spey. Tel: (0479) 2684.	Fly fishing only.

Water	Location	Species	Season	Permit available from	Other Information
Loch Morlich	Aviemore	Brown Trout Pike	15 Mar. to 30 Sept.	The Warden, Campsite, Glenmore Forest Park, Aviemore. Tel: Cairngorm 271.	Reductions for children. Spinners and fly only.
Loch Na Bo	Lhanbryde	Brown Trout	1 Apr. to 30 Sept.	Keepers Cottage, Loch Na Bo. Tel: Lhanbryde 2214.	Fly fishing only.
Loch Saugh	Fettercairn	Brown/ Rainbow Trout	15 Mar. to 6 Oct.	Brechin Angling Club, D.E. Smith, 101 Market St., Brechin DD9 6BD. Tel: Brechin 4544. J. & J. Coghill, Newsagents, High Street, Brechin. Ramsay Arms Hotel, Fettercairn. Tel: Fettercairn 334. Drumtochty Arms Hotel, Auchenblae, Tel: Auchenblae 210. W. Phillips, Tackle, 180 High Street, Montrose, Tel: Montrose 72692.	£3.50 per day.
Rothiemurchus Estate (Lochs, Fish farm, Pityoulish, Lily & Morlich)	Aviemore	Sea Trout Rainbow Trout Brown Trout Pike	Check with manager, Aviemore.	Rothiemurchus Fish Farm, Aviemore. Tel: Aviemore 810858.	
Spey Dam	Laggan	Brown Trout	1 Apr. to 30 Sept.	Laggan Stores, Laggan Bridge, Inverness-shire. Tel: (05284) 257.	Boat available.
Loch Vaa	Aviemore	Brown/ Rainbow Trout	Apr. to Sept.	Mortimer's 61 High Street, Grantown-on-Spey. Tel: Grantown-on-Spey 2684.	Boat fishing only.

NORTH EAST AND SPEY VALLEY

Sea Angling

Moray Firth
The Moray Firth has always been famous for its fishing grounds and most of the towns along the south coastline depend largely on commercial fishing for their prosperity; cod, haddock, flatfish of many kings, pollack, coalfish and mackerel being landed.

Nairn
Nairn is set on the pleasant coastal plain bordering the southern shore of the Moray Firth. There is a beautiful stretch of sands to the east. Most fishing is done from two small piers at the entrance to the tidal harbour.
Types of fish: Mackerel, small coalfish, pollack, dab and cod.
Boats: One or two, privately owned, will often take a passenger out. Enquiries should be made at the harbour.

Tackle: P. Fraser, 41 High Street, Nairn. Harbour Street General Store, Harbour Street.
Bait: Lugworm available on the beach at low water. Mackerel etc. mostly taken on flies.
Further information from: The Harbour Master, Nairn.

Lossiemouth and Garmouth
Lossiemouth, a small, prosperous town, is a unique combination of white fish centre, seaside, shops and hotels. The angler will find unlimited sport of a kind probably new to him, for off the east and west beaches sea trout and finnock abound, and spinning for these into the sea, especially into the breakers, is a magnificent sport.
Types of fish: Sea trout, conger from the pier, coalfish, flatfish, 6½ miles of shore fishing. Haddock, cod, plaice and coalfish from boats. Shore fishing – sea trout between harbour and Boar's Head Rock and at the old cement works Garmouth.

Tackle: Angling Centre, Moss Street, Elgin; The Tackle Shop, High Street, Elgin.
Bait: Lugworm on the west beach and the harbour at low water. Also plenty of mussels to be collected. Spinners, Pirks.
Permits: Angling Centre, Moss Street, Elgin; The Tackle Shop, 188 High Street, Elgin, Tel: 3129.
Season for fishing: Migratory fish season, October. Best months – late July, early August.

Buckie
Buckie is a major commercial fishing port on the eastern side of Spey Bay. It has become increasingly popular over the last few years as a tourist area and is well supplied with hotels, golf courses and caravan sites. It offers a varied coastline in the form of sandy beaches and quite spectacular rugged cliff formations.
Types of fish: Cod, coalfish, conger, pollack, mackerel, haddock, whiting, flatfish.

Tackle: Slater Sports, 5 High Street, Buckie.
Bait: Lugworm, ragworm, mussels, cockles and crabs freely available along the shoreline eastwards.
Season for fishing: April-October. Winter months best for cod.

Portknockie

Portknockie is a quaint little fishing village to the west of Cullen Bay. The small harbour is used by two small mackerel boats.
Types of fish: Excellent rock fishing here for cod, coalfish, and some mackerel from the piers. Good boat fishing for haddock, ling and gurnard.
Boats: There are no boats for hire as such, although it is possible to get out in two small (18ft) mackerel boats.
Tackle: Wood, General Dealer, has a small supply.
Bait: Lugworm and mussels in the harbour at low water.
Further information from: Moray District Council, Tourist Information Centre, 17 High Street, Elgin, IV30 1EG. Tel: Elgin (0343) 2666/3388 will provide information for sea anglers.

Portsoy

One of the numerous small towns that line the Banffshire coast. It is a former seaport but the harbour is silting up.
Types of fish: Coalfish and mackerel from the small pier and some good rock fishing east and west for cod. From boats, mackerel, cod, haddock, plaice, coalfish and dab.
Tackle: Peter Lyon, 36 Low Street, Banff.
Bait: Some lugworm at low water mark.

Gardenstown and Crovie

These are traditional fishing villages. Mackerel are plentiful, June-September. Anglers would be well advised to follow local

boats which are fishing commercially.
Types of fish: From shore – coalfish, pollack, flatfish, conger. From boats – mackerel, cod, haddock, flounder, plaice, conger, dab, catfish, gurnard and ling.
Bait: Available on beach, but local people prefer to use flies.

Fraserburgh

Situated on the north-east shoulder of Scotland, Fraserburgh has the Moray Firth to the west and north and the North Sea to the east. The Burgh was primarily given over to the herring and white fish industry, but has developed as a holiday resort with the decline of commercial fishing in the North Sea. Tickets and permits for game fishing from the beaches can be had at Weelies, Grocer, College Bounds.
Types of fish: Shore – cod, coalfish and mackerel. Boat – as shore.
Tackle: Available from Caledonian Fish Co., Shore Street. P. & J. Johnstone, Balclava Sports Shop, Charlotte Street, Fraserburgh.
Bait: Mussels and lugworm can be dug from the beach.
Season for fishing: May- October.

Peterhead

Peterhead is an important fishing port situated north of Buchan Ness, the most easterly point of Scotland. Excellent breakwaters, 1900ft and 2800ft long, are the main shore marks for holiday anglers. Access to the breakwaters is dependent on weather conditions and can be restricted when vessels are being worked. A safety access procedure has been agreed with the North Breakwater Sea Angling Society to whom further queries should be directed. However passengers are at times taken out by private boats.
Types of fish: From the pier –

mackerel, coalfish, dab and cod. From boats – cod, haddock, dabs, ling, coalfish and mackerel.
Boats: There are a number of privately owned boats which will sometimes take out passengers. Enquiries should be made at the harbour.
Tackle: Available from Insports, 71 Marischal Street, Peterhead, Tel: (0779) 72749; Robertsons Sports, 1 Kirk Street, Peterhead.
Bait: Lugworm can be dug from shore at low water while mussels can be gathered from the rocks.
Further information from: Aberdeen Service Co (Nr. Sea) Ltd.

Stonehaven

Stonehaven is a holiday resort 15 miles south of Aberdeen on main road and rail routes. Magnificent catches of cod and haddock are taken regularly by boat. Anglers obtain great co-operation from angling boat skippers and local professional fishermen. On either side of Stonehaven there are good rock fishing marks which should be approached with care especially during strong easterly winds.
Types of fish: Cod, haddock, pollack, coalfish, flounder, catfish and mackerel from the shore. Cod, haddock, coalfish, pollack, ling, catfish, plaice and other flatfish, ballan wrasse, cuckoo wrasse, whiting and Norway haddock from boats.
Boats: Boats are available from skippers: A. McKenzie, Tel: (0569) 63411; A. Troup, Tel: (0569) 62892; J. Loban, Tel: (0569) 65323; B. Lawson, Tel: (0569) 63565.
Tackle: Available from David's, Market Square, Stonehaven.
Bait: Mussels available if ordered from skippers of boats.
Season for fishing: All year.
Further information from: Information Centre, The Square. Tel: Stonehaven (0569) 62806 Easter-September.

Constituent Area Tourist Boards

Fort William and Lochaber Tourist Board
Area Tourist Officer,
Fort William and Lochaber Tourist Board,
Cameron Centre, Cameron Square,
Fort William,
Inverness-shire PH33 6AJ.
Tel: Fort William (0397) 3781.

Isle of Skye and South West Ross Tourist Board
Area Tourist Officer,
Isle of Skye and South West Ross Tourist Board,
Tourist Information Centre, Portree,
Isle of Skye IV51 9BZ.
Tel: Portree (0478) 2137.

Inverness, Loch Ness and Nairn Tourist Board
Area Tourist Officer,
Inverness, Loch Ness and Nairn
Tourist Board,
23 Church Street,
Inverness IV1 1EZ.
Tel: Inverness (0463) 234353.

RIVER PURIFICATION BOARD
HIGHLAND RIVER PURIFICATION BOARD
Strathpeffer Road,
Dingwall IV15 9QY.
Tel: Dingwall 62021.

RIVERS

Water	Location	Species	Season	Permit available from	Other information
Ailort	Arisaig	Salmon Sea Trout	11 Feb. to 31 Oct.	Lochailort Inn, Lochailort, Inverness-shire.	
Broadford	Skye	Salmon Sea Trout	11 Feb. to 31 Oct.	Broadford Hotel, Broadford, Isle of Skye.	
Coe	Glencoe	Salmon Sea Trout	11 Feb. to 31 Oct.	National Trust for Scotland, Achnambeithach Farm, Glencoe.	
Croe		Salmon Sea Trout	11 Feb. to 31 Oct.	National Trust for Scotland, Morvich Farm, Inverinate, By Kyle. Tel: Glenshiel (05998) 219.	
Enrick	Drumna-drochit	Salmon Brown Trout	15 Jan.-15 Oct. 15 Mar.-6 Oct.	Kilmartin Hall, Glenurquhart, Inverness-shire. Tel: Glenurquhart 269.	
Farrar	Struy	Salmon	11 Feb. to 15 Oct.	Glen Affric Hotel, Cannich. Tel: Cannich 214.	
Garry	Invergarry	Salmon Brown Trout	15 Mar. to 6 Oct.	Garry Gualach, Invergarry. Tel: Tomdoun 230.	Fly only.
Glass	Cannich	Salmon	11 Feb. to 15 Oct.	Glen Affric Hotel, Cannich. Tel: Cannich 214.	
Lealt		Salmon	14 Feb. to 31 Oct.	Portree Radio & Electrical Stores, Wentworth Street, Portree. Tel: (0478) 2854. Co-Chomunn Stafainn.	£5 per session.
Lochy	Fort William	Salmon Sea Trout	May to Sept.	Rod & Gun Shop, Station Square, Fort William. Tel:(0397) 2656.	
Moriston	Glen-moriston Estuary beat Dundreggan	Salmon	15 Jan. to 15 Oct. Spring June onwards	Head Gamekeeper, A. Mackintosh, Tel: (0320) 51219.	
		Brown Trout	Mar. to Sept.		

Water	Location	Species	Season	Permit available from	Other Information
Nairn	Nairn	Salmon Sea Trout	11 Feb.-30 Sept.	Nairn Angling Association P. Fraser, High Street, Nairn. Clava Lodge Holiday Homes, Culloden Moor, Inverness. Tel: Culloden Moor (0463) 790228, Inverness (0463) 790405.	
Ness	Inverness	Salmon	15 Jan. to 15 Oct.	Inverness Angling Club, John Graham, 71 Castle St., Inverness. Tel: (0463) 233178.	No day permits on Saturdays.
Nevis	Fort William	Salmon Sea Trout		Rod & Gun Shop Station Square, Fort William. Tel: (0397) 2656.	
Ose	Skye	Salmon Sea Trout	11 Feb. to 31 Oct.	Ullinish Lodge Hotel, Struan, Isle of Skye. Tel: (047 072) 214.	
Scaddle	Ardgour	Salmon Sea Trout	2 June to 30 Sept.	Ardgour Hotel, Ardgour, by Fort William. Tel: (08555) 225.	
Sligachan	Skye	Salmon Sea Trout	End June Early Oct.	Sligachan Hotel, Sligachan, Isle of Skye. Tel: Sligachan 204.	
Snizort	Skye	Salmon Sea Trout Brown Trout Salmon Sea Trout Brown Trout	15 Mar. to 31 Oct. 11 Feb. to 31 Oct.	Skeabost House Hotel, Skeabost, Isle of Skye. Tel: Skeabost Bridge 202. Ullinish Lodge Hotel, Struan, Isle of Skye. Tel: (047072) 214.	Discounts for residents.
	Spean Bridge	Salmon Sea Trout	May to Sept.	Spean Bridge Hotel, Spean Bridge, Inverness-shire. Tel: Spean Bridge 250. Rod & Gun Shop, Station Square, Inverness-shire. Tel: (0397) 2656.	
Staffin		Salmon	14 Feb. to 31 Oct.	Portree Radio & Electrical Stores, Wentworth Street, Portree. Tel: (0478) 2854. Co-Chomunn Staffainn.	£2 per day.

LOCHS

Water	Location	Species	Season	Permit available from	Other Information
Loch Arkaig	Fort William	Sea Trout Brown Trout Salmon (occasional) Pike	Mar.-Oct.	Locheil Estate Fishings, West Highland Estates Office, 33 High Street, Fort William. Tel: Fort William 2433. Tel: Spean Bridge 783.	
Ardtornish Estate Waters	Morvern	Salmon Sea Trout Brown Trout	Apr.-Oct.	Ardtornish Estate Office, Morvern, by Oban, Argyll. Tel: (096 784) 288.	Six boats for hire.
Balmacara Estate Lochs	Kyle of Lochalsh	Brown Trout	Apr.-Oct.	Balmacara Hotel, by Kyle of Lochalsh, Wester Ross. Tel: (059 986) 283.	No Sunday fishing.
Loch Beannachran	Glen Strathfarrar	Brown Trout	15 Mar. to 6 Oct.	Glen Affric Hotel, Cannich. Tel: Cannich 214.	
Loch Benevean (Bheinn a' Mheadhoin)	Cannich	Brown Trout	15 Mar. to 6 Oct.	J. Graham & Co., 71 Castle Street, Inverness. Tel: (0463) 233178. Glen Affric Hotel, Cannich. Tel: Cannich 214.	Fly fishing only.

Water	Location	Species	Season	Permit available from	Other Information
Loch Cluanie	Glen-moriston	Brown Trout Pike	15 Mar. to 6 Oct.	Dochfour Estate Office, Dochgarroch, by Inverness. Tel: Dochgarroch 218.	One Boat. Two rods per boat.
Lochs Connan (Duagraich & Ravag)	Skye	Brown Trout	15 Mar. to 6 Oct.	Ullinish Lodge Hotel, Struan, Isle of Skye. Tel: (047 072) 214.	Sunday fishing permitted.
Loch Dochfour	Inverness	Brown Trout	15 Mar. to 6 Oct.	Dochfour Estate Office, Dochgarroch, by Inverness. Tel: Dochgarroch 218.	No Sunday fishing. Bank fishing only.
Loch Eilt (and hill lochs)	Glenfinnan	Salmon Sea Trout Brown Trout		Lochailort Inn, Lochailort, Inverness-shire. Tel: Lochailort 208.	
Loch Garry (and Loch Inchlaggan)	Invergarry	Brown Trout Arctic Char	May-Sept.	Garry Gualach, Invergarry, Inverness-shire. Tel: Tomdoun 230. Tomdoun Hotel, Invergarry. Tel: Tomdoun 218.	Boats available. Loch Inchlaggan fly only.
Glenmoriston hill lochs	Glen-moriston	Brown Trout	1 May to 11 Aug.	Glenmoriston Estate Office, Glenmoriston, Inverness-shire. Tel: Glenmoriston 51202.	Fly fishing only. Sunday fishing permitted.
Loch Lochy	Fort William	Brown Trout	15 Mar. to 6 Oct.	None required.	
Loch Loyne	Glen-moriston	Brown Trout Pike	15 Mar. to 6 Oct.	Cluanie Hotel, Glenmoriston, Inverness-shire. Tel: (0320) 40238. Tomdoun Hotel, Invergarry, Tel: Tomdoun 218.	Boats available.
Loch Monar	Inverness-shire	Brown Trout	15 Mar. to 6 Oct.	Glen Affric Hotel, Cannich. Tel: Cannich 214.	
Loch Morar (and hill lochs)	Morar	Salmon Sea Trout Brown Trout	11 Feb. to 1 Nov. 15 Mar. to 6 Oct.	Morar Fishings, Allt an Loin, Morar. Tel: Mallaig 2388. Morar Motors, Morar. The Mallaig Bookshop, Morar Hotel, Morar.	Eight boats available. Designated areas for fly fishing only. Spinning and trouting outwith fly area. Three boats available.
Loch Mullardoch	Cannich	Brown Trout	15 Mar. to 6 Oct.	Glen Affric Hotel, Cannich. Tel: Cannich 214.	
Loch Ness	Glen-moriston	Salmon Brown Trout	15 Jan. to Oct.	Glen Moriston Estate Office, Glenmoriston, by Inverness. Tel: (0320) 51202.	25% discount for holiday and hotel guests.
	Foyers	Salmon Brown Trout	15 Jan. to Oct.	Foyers Hotel, Foyers, Inverness-shire. Tel: Gorthleck 216.	
Loch Quoich	Tomdoun	Brown Trout	15 Mar. to 6 Oct.	Tomdoun Hotel, Invergarry. Tel: Tomdoun 218.	Boats available.
Loch Ruthven	Farr	Brown Trout	15 Mar. to 6 Oct.	Grouse and Trout Hotel, Flichity, Inverness-shire. Tel: (08083) 314.	Fly fishing only.
		Brown Trout	Apr.-Sept.	J. Graham & Co., 71 Castle Street, Inverness. Tel: Inverness 233178.	Fly fishing only.
Loch Shiel	Dalilea Acharacle	Salmon Sea Trout Brown Trout	May-Sept.	D. Macauley, Dalilea Farm, Acharacle. Tel: (096 785) 253.	Five boats available.

Water	Location	Species	Season	Permit available from	Other Information
Loch Shiel contd.	Glenfinnan	Salmon Sea Trout	Apr.-Oct.	Stage House Inn, Glenfinnan, Inverness-shire. Tel: (039 783) 246.	Seven boats available with outboards.
				Glenfinnan House Hotel, Glenfinnan. Tel: (039 783) 235.	Three boats available.
Storr Lochs (and other hill lochs)	North Skye	Brown Trout	15 Mar. to 30 Sept.	Portree Radio & Electrical, Stores, Wentworth Street, Portree. Tel: (0478) 2854. Co-Chomunn Stafainn.	
South Skye Fishings	South Skye	Sea Trout Brown Trout	Apr.-Oct.	Fearann Eilean Iarmain, Eilean Iarmain, An t-Eilean, Sgitheanach, Tel: (047 13) 266. Telex: 75252 iarman g.	No Sunday fishing.
Tomich Hill lochs	Tomich	Brown Trout	15 Mar. to 6 Oct.	Glen Affric Hotel, Cannich. Tel: Cannich 214.	
Whitebridge Lochs (Knockie & Bran)	White-bridge	Brown Trout	Mar.-Oct.	Whitebridge Hotel, Stratherrick, Gorthleck, Inverness-shire. Tel: Gorthleck 226.	Boats available. Fly fishing only.

GREAT GLEN AND ISLE OF SKYE

Sea Angling

Isle of Eigg
The Isle of Eigg lies 5m SW of Skye.
Types of fish: Pollack, conger, spurdog, skate, cod, mackerel.
Boats: Available from Eigg Estate, Estate Office, Isle of Eigg, Inverness-shire.
Tackle: As boats.
Bait: Lugworm, ragworm, shellfish, mackerel, available from Estate Office.
Season for fishing: Summer-Autumn.

Isle of Skye
The many lochs and bays around the beautiful Isle of Skye provide ideal facilities for sea angling. There is a great variety of fish, most of which can be caught from the shore because of the deep water found close inshore off rocky shores and headlands. Local residents are very knowledgeable about fishing in their own area. Loch Snizort has now been found to hold a number of large common skate and anglers could well contact these during a session there.

Isle of Skye (Portree)
Portree, the capital of Skye, is situated half way up the east coast of the island. There is a very good harbour and good fishing marks in and round it. Ample free anchorage and berthing available for visiting craft. Slipping, re-fuelling and watering facilities are easily accessible.
Types of fish: Cod, haddock, whiting, coalfish, pollack and mackerel.
Boats: Greshornish House Hotel, Edinbane, by Portree. Tel: (047082) 266, has one boat available.
Bait: Unlimited mussels and cockles available in tidal area of Portree Bay.
Tackle: Portree Electrical Stores, Wentworth Street, Portree. Skeabost House Hotel, Skeabost, by Portree. Tel: Skeabost Bridge (047032) 202.
Season for fishing: May-September.
Further information from: Isle of Skye & South West Ross Tourist Board, Tourist Information Centre, Portree (0478) 2137.

Isle of Skye (Camastianavaig by Portree)
To reach this sheltered bay which lies 4 miles south east of Portree,

turn off the A850 to Braes. Although local tactics are the use of feathers, bottom fishing with trace or paternoster has yielded heavy bags with skate of 62½lbs, cod 6lbs, whiting 3lbs, haddock 3lbs, spurdog 12lbs, gurnard 2lbs, pollacks 12lbs, coalfish 14lbs, all from boats.
Types of fish: Shore – coalfish, pollack, wrasse and mackerel. Boat – cod, haddock and spurdog.
Tackle: Obtainable at Portree.
Bait: Lugworm at Broadford Bay and Balmeanac Bay. Cockles and mussels at Portree Loch.
Season for fishing: June- October.

Isle of Skye (Uig)
Uig, a picturesque village amidst some of the finest scenery in the north west, has excellent fishing on its doorstep. Loch Snizort and small islands at its entrance, together with the Ascrib Islands opposite, are well worth fishing. Fishing can be arranged as far round the coast as Score Bay, known to some ring net fishermen as the 'Golden Mile'.
Types of fish: Shore – coalfish, mackerel, pollack, conger and dogfish. Boat – coalfish, mackerel, pollack, conger, whiting, haddock, dogfish, flatfish, skate, cod and gurnard.

Boats: Available locally at Uig, Waternish and Kilmuir.
Season for fishing: May-September.

Isle of Skye (Skeabost Bridge)
Skeabost Bridge is situated 5 miles from Portree at the south east end of Loch Snizort.
Types of fish: There is no shore fishing but many types of sea fish can be caught from boats.
Boats: Available from Skeabost House Hotel. Tel: Skeabost Bridge (047 032) 202.

Tackle: Tackle available for hire or sale from the Skeabost House Hotel.
Bait: Available locally.
Season for fishing: July- October.

Kyle of Lochalsh
The village of Kyle, on the mainland opposite Kyleakin on the Isle of Skye, is a railhead and a car ferry link with Skye and the Hebrides.
Types of fish: Conger, coalfish, pollack and whiting from the harbour. Boat – pollack, cod,

coalfish, mackerel and whiting.
Tackle: Available from Marine Stores, Kyle of Lochalsh. IV40 8AE. Tel: (0599) 4208.
Bait: Mussels from Fishery Pier and clams and cockles at spring tides.

Season for fishing: June-September.

Further information from: Isle of Skye & South West Ross Tourist Board, Tourist Information Centre, Kyle of Lochalsh. Tel: (0599) 4276.

NORTH OF SCOTLAND

RIVERS AND LOCHS

Constituent Area Tourist Boards

Caithness Tourist Board
Area Tourist Officer,
Caithness Tourist Board,
Whitechapel Road, Wick,
Caithness KW1 4EA.
Tel: Wick (0955) 2596.

Sutherland Tourist Board
Area Tourist Officer,
Sutherland Tourist Board,
The Square, Dornoch,
Sutherland IV25 3SD.
Tel: Dornoch (0862) 810400

Ross and Cromarty Tourist Board
Area Tourist Officer,
Ross and Cromarty Tourist Board,
Information Centre, North Kessock,
Inverness IV1 1XB.
Tel: Kessock (0463 73) 505.

RIVER PURIFICATION BOARD
HIGHLAND RIVER PURIFICATION BOARD
Strathpeffer Road,
Dingwall IV15 9QY.
Tel: Dingwall 62021.

RIVERS

Water	Location	Species	Season	Permit available from	Other information
Alness	Alness	Salmon Sea Trout	11 Feb. to 31 Oct.	Coul House Hotel, Contin by Strathpeffer, Ross-shire. Tel: Strathpeffer 21487.	Six beats available on rotation. Four rods per beat. Fly fishing only.
Badachro	Gairloch	Salmon	1 Apr. to 31 Oct.	Shieldaig Lodge Hotel, Gairloch. Tel: Badachro 250.	
Blackwater (Ross-shire)	Strath-peffer	Salmon Sea Trout		Craigdarroch Lodge Hotel, Contin, by Strathpeffer, Ross-shire. Tel: Strathpeffer 21265.	
Upper Blackwater	Strathpeffer	Salmon Brown Trout	1 April to 30 Sept.	East Lodge Hotel, Strathconon, Ross-shire. Tel: (09977) 222. Loch Achonochie Angling Club.	
Brora	Brora	Sea Trout Finnock Brown Trout	1 June to 15 Oct.	Three-quarter mile of tidal water. No permit required.	Fly or worm fishing only. No spinning tackle.
Conon	Strathpeffer	Salmon Brown Trout	1 April to 30 Sept.	Craigdarroch Lodge Hotel, Contin, by Strathpeffer, Ross-shire. Tel: Strathpeffer 21265. East Lodge Hotel, Strathconon, Ross-shire. Tel: (09977) 222. Loch Achonochie Angling Club (under review)	

Water	Location	Species	Season	Permit available from	Other Information
Conon contd.	Contin	Salmon Sea Trout	26 Jan. to 30 Sept.	Coul House Hotel, Contin, by Strathpeffer, Ross-shire. Tel: Strathpeffer 21487.	Lower middle and upper Brahan. Coul water and lower Fairburn beats available at various times.
Lower Conon	Dingwall	Salmon Sea Trout	26 Jan. to 30 Sept.	Dingwall & District Angling Club, c/o Sports & Model Shop, Tulloch Street, Dingwall. Tel: (0349) 62346.	Fly only. Breast waders prohibited.
		Brown Trout		Seaforth Island Estate, Brahan, Dingwall.	
Damph	Torridon	Salmon Sea Trout Brown Trout		Loch Torridon Hotel, Torridon, by Achnasheen, Torridon. Tel: (044 587) 242.	Boats, motors & ghillie available.
Dionard	Durness	Salmon Sea Trout		Cape Wrath Hotel, Durness.	
Halladale	Forsinard (2 mile upper beat)	Salmon	1 Apr. to 30 Sept.	Forsinard Hotel, Forsinard, Sutherland. Tel: Halladale 221.	Fly fishing only (spate river).
Helmsdale	Helmsdale	Salmon	11 Jan. to 31 Oct.	A. Jappy, Dunrobin Street, Helmsdale. Tel: (04312) 654.	Association beat.
Kerry	Gairloch	Salmon Sea Trout		Creag Mor Hotel, Charleston, Gairloch, Ross-shire. Tel: (0445) 2068.	
Kirkaig	Lochinver	Salmon	1 May to 15 Oct.	Inver Lodge Hotel, Lochinver, Sutherland. Tel: Lochinver 496.	
Kyle of Sutherland	Bonar Bridge	Brown Trout Sea Trout Salmon		Bonar Bridge Angling Club, Secretary, W. Shannon, Tel: Edderton (086282) 288.	River boats are available.
	Sutherland	Salmon Sea Trout Brown Trout	1 June to 30 Sept.	Bill Knott, The Paper Shop, Ardgay. Tel: (08632) 682.	Any legal lure in most places. Fly only in 3 specific areas, Sea trout fishing below estuary at Bonar Bridge. Ask for prices.
Meig	Strathconon	Brown Trout	1 May to 30 Sept.	East Lodge Hotel & Inn, Strathconon. Tel: Strathconon 222.	River beats are available.
Migdale, Laggan, and Laro	Sutherland	Brown Trout	15 Mar. to 5 Oct.	Bill Knott, The Paper Shop, Ardgay. Tel: (08632) 682.	Boats available.
Naver	Bettyhill	Salmon	12 Jan. to 30 Sept.	Bettyhill Hotel, Bettyhill, Sutherland. Tel: Bettyhill 202.	
Oykel	Sutherland	Salmon Sea Trout	11 Jan. to 30 Sept.	Inver Lodge Hotel, Lochinver, Sutherland. Tel: Lochinver 496. Inveroykel Lodge Hotel, Strathoykel, by Ardgay, Sutherland. Tel: Rosehall 200.	
Polly	Ullapool	Salmon Sea Trout Brown Trout	May-Sept.	Mrs. A. MacLeod, Inverpolly, Ullapool, Ross-shire. Tel: Lochinver 482.	Fly fishing only. No Sunday fishing.
Thurso	Thurso	Salmon	11 Jan. to 5 Oct.	Thurso Fisheries Ltd., Thurso East, Thurso. Tel: (0847) 63134.	Fly fishing only.
Torridon	Torridon	Salmon Sea Trout	1 May to 31 Oct.	Loch Torridon Hotel, Torridon, by Achnasheen, Ross-shire. Tel: (044 587) 242.	Fly fishing angling instruction.

Water	Location	Species	Season	Permit available from	Other Information
Ullapool	Ullapool	Salmon Sea Trout Brown Trout	May to 30 Sept.	Loch Broom Hardware Shop, Ullapool. Tel: (0854) 2356.	
Wick	Wick	Salmon Sea Trout	11 Feb. to 31 Oct.	Wick Angling Association, 80 Wick Sports Shop, High Street, Wick.	

LOCHS

Water	Location	Species	Season	Permit available from	Other Information
Loch Achall	Ullapool	Salmon Sea Trout Brown Trout	1 April to 30 Sept.	Loch Broom Hardware Shop, Ullapool. Tel: (0854) 2356.	Boat and bank fishing.
Loch Achonochie	Strathpeffer	Salmon Brown Trout	1 Apr. to 30 Sept.	East Lodge Hotel, Strathconon, Ross-shire. Tel: (09977) 222. Loch Achonochie Angling Club.	
Loch Achility	Strathpeffer	Brown Trout	15 Mar. to 6 Oct.	Craigdarroch Lodge Hotel, Contin.	
Assynt Angling Club (numerous hill lochs)	Lochinver	Brown Trout	15 Mar. to 6 Oct.	Assynt Angling Club, Tourist Information Office, Lochinver. Tel: (05714) 330. Local hotels and shops.	No Sunday fishing. No dogs. Boats on some lochs. Spinning restricted to certain lochs.
Loch Assynt (and lochs Awe, Gillaroo, Grugach Borralam Cam Letteressie Loch)	Inchnadamph	Salmon Brown Trout	1 Apr.-15 Oct. 1 Apr.-6 Oct.	Inchnadamph Hotel, Inchnadamph, Sutherland. Tel: (05712) 202.	No Sunday fishing. Boats available.
Loch A'chroisg	Achnasheen	Pike Perch		Ledgowan Lodge Hotel, Achnasheen, Ross-shire. Tel: Achnasheen 252.	Free to residents.
Loch Badachro (and numerous other lochs)	Gairloch	Salmon Brown Trout	Apr.-Oct.	Shieldaig Lodge Hotel, Gairloch, Ross & Cromarty. Tel: Badachro 250.	No Sunday fishing. Fly only. Nine boats.
Loch Badanloch (and other hill lochs)	Kinbrace	Brown Trout	15 Mar. to 6 Oct.	Richard McNicol, Badanloch, Kinbrace, Sutherland. Tel: Kinbrace 232. Navidale House Hotel, Helmsdale, Sutherland. Tel: Helmsdale (04312) 258.	Nine boats. Fly only.
Balmacara hill lochs	Kyle of Lochalsh	Brown Trout	Apr.- Oct.	Balmacara Hotel, Kyle of Lochalsh. Tel: Kyle of Lochalsh 283.	
Loch Beannachairan	Strath-conon	Brown Trout	1 May to 30 Sept.	East Lodge Hotel & Inn, Strathconon, Ross-shire. Tel: (099 77) 222.	Restrictions on spinning. No Sunday fishing.
Loch Beannachan	Lairg	Brown Trout	1 May to 30 Sept.	Sutherland Arms Hotel, Lairg, Sutherland. Tel: Lairg 2291.	
Bettyhill hill lochs (Loch Meadie and others)	Bettyhill	Brown Trout	Mar.-July	Bettyhill Hotel, Bettyhill, Sutherland. Tel: Bettyhill 202.	
Loch Brora	Brora	Salmon Sea Trout Brown Trout	1 May. to 15 Oct.	Estate Office, Gordonbush, Brora, Sutherland. Tel: Brora 323. Rob Wilson, Fountain Square, Brora, Sutherland. Tel: Brora 373. See under 'Golspie Angling Club Waters'.	

Water	Location	Species	Season	Permit available from	Other Information
Loch Borralie	Durness	Brown Trout		Cape Wrath Hotel, Keoldale, by Lairg, Sutherland. Tel: (097181) 274.	
Loch Caladail	Durness	Brown Trout		Cape Wrath Hotel, Keoldale, by Lairg, Sutherland. Tel: (097181) 274.	
Cape Wrath hill lochs (30 plus)	Durness	Brown Trout		Cape Wrath Hotel, Keoldale, by Lairg, Sutherland. Tel: (097181) 274.	
Loch Calder	Thurso	Brown Trout	15 Mar. to 6 Oct.	None required	All legal methods.
Loch Craggie	Tongue	Brown Trout		Tongue Hotel, Tongue. Tel: Tongue 206.	
Loch Craggie (and Loch Ailsh)	Rosehall	Sea/ Brown/ Rainbow Trout		Tongue Hotel, Tongue. Tel: Tongue 206.	
Loch Culag (Fionn Loch and numerous others)	Lochinver	Brown/ Rainbow Trout	15 Mar. to 6 Oct.	Inver Lodge Hotel, Lochinver, Sutherland. Tel: Lochinver 496.	
Dornoch & District Angling Assoc. (7 lochs)	Dornoch	Brown Trout Sea Trout Salmon	15 Mar. to 6 Oct.	Dornoch & District Angling Association, William A. McDonald, Castle Street, Dornoch. Tel: Dornoch 810301.	No Sunday fishing. Fly fishing only. 7 boats available.
Drumbeg hill lochs (20 lochs)	Assynt	Brown Trout	Apr.-Sept.	Drumbeg Hotel, Assynt, by Lairg, Sutherland. Tel: Assynt 236.	Seven boats available. No Sunday fishing. Fly fishing only.
Loch Fannich	Achnasheen	Brown Trout	15 Mar. to 6 Oct.	Strathgarve Lodge Hotel, Garve, Ross-shire. Tel: Garve 204.	
Fionn Loch	Gairloch	Salmon Brown Trout		H. Davis, Creag Beag, Gairloch. Tel: (0445) 2322.	Fly only.
Forsinard Lochs (Loch Sletill and many others)	Forsinard	Brown Trout	1 May. to 30 Sept.	Forsinard Hotel, Forsinard, Sutherland. Tel: Halladale 221.	Fly fishing only. 5 Boats. Bank and boat fishing.
Loch Garve	Garve	Brown Trout		Strathgarve Lodge Hotel, Garve, Ross-shire. Tel: Garve 204.	
Loch Glasgarnock	Garve	Brown Trout		Aultguish Inn, Aultguish, Ross-shire. Tel: (09975) 254.	
Golspie Angling Club waters (Loch Brora Loch Lundie Loch Horn)		Salmon Sea Trout Brown Trout	15 Mar. to 15 Oct.	Golspie Angling Club, Lindsay & Co., Main Street, Golspie. Tel: (04083) 212.	Fly fishing only. Bank and boat fishing. No Sunday fishing.
Loch Kernsary (Tournaig Goose Ghiuragarstidh)	Gairloch	Brown Trout	15 Mar. to 6 Oct.	National Trust for Scotland, Inverewe Visitor Centre, Poolewe, Ross-shire. Tel: (044586) 229.	
Leckmelm Hill Lochs	Ullapool	Brown Trout	May to Sept.	Leckmelm Holiday Cottages, Leckmelm, Ullapool. Tel: (0854) 2471.	Bank fishing only. No Sunday fishing.
Loyal	Tongue	Brown Trout Salmon		Tongue Hotel, Tongue. Tel: Tongue 206.	

Water	Location	Species	Season	Permit available from	Other Information
Loch Maree	Ross-shire	Salmon Sea Trout Brown Trout	May-Oct.	Loch Maree Hotel, Achnasheen. Tel: Kinlochewe 288.	Several Boats
				Shieldaig Lodge Hotel, Gairloch. Tel: Badachro 250.	One boat.
				Kinlochewe Hotel, Kinlochewe. Tel: Kinlochewe 253.	Four boats.
Loch Meig	Strathpeffer	Brown Trout	1 Jun. to 30 Sept.	Loch Achonochie Angling Club, East Lodge Hotel, Strathconon. Tel: Strathconon 222.	
	Strathconon	Brown Trout	1 May to 30 Sept.	Loch Achonochie Angling Club, East Lodge Hotel, Strathconon. Tel: Strathconon 222.	
Melvich hill lochs (Loch Akran and others)	Melvich	Brown Trout	Jun-Sept.	Melvich Hotel, Melvich, by Thurso, Caithness. Tel: Melvich 206.	Eight boats available. Fly fishing only.
Loch Merkland	Lairg	Brown Trout		Overscaig Hotel, Overscaig, by Lairg, Sutherland. Tel: Merkland 203.	Boats and ghillies available.
Loch More	by Lairg	Salmon Sea Trout Brown Trout		Westminster Estate Office, Achfary, by Lairg, Sutherland. Tel: Lochmore 221.	Self catering accommodation available.
Loch Morie	Head of River Alness	Brown Trout Arctic Char	15 Mar. to 6 Oct.	Coul House Hotel, Contin, by Strathpeffer, Ross-shire. Tel: Strathpeffer 21487.	Boat available.
Scourie Lochs (over 200 available)	Scourie	Salmon Sea Trout Brown Trout	1 Jul.-15 Oct. 1May-30 Sept.	Scourie Hotel, Scourie, by Lairg, Sutherland. Tel: Scourie 2396.	Twelve boats available. No Sunday fishing. Fly fishing only.
Loch Shin	Lairg	Brown Trout	30 Apr. to 30 Sept.	Lairg Angling Club, J.M. Ross, Secretary, St. Murie, Church Hill Road, Lairg IV27 4BL. Tel: Lairg 2010. Local tackle shop. Club warden at boathouse.	Note: permits not issued at Post Office, nine boats available with outboards. No booking for half days. Advance bookings, Tel: Lairg 2010. Up to 3 rods per boat.
Loch Sionascaig (and other lochs)	Ullapool	Brown Trout		Inverpolly Estate Office, Inverpolly, Ullapool. Tel: Lochinver 252.	
Slaum	Tongue	Brown Trout Salmon		Tongue Hotel, Tongue. Tel: Tongue 206.	
Loch Stack	by Lairg	Salmon Sea Trout Brown Trout		Westminster Estate Office, Archfary, Lairg, Sutherland. Tel: (097 184) 221.	Self catering accommodation available.
Tongue Lochs (several hill lochs)	Tongue	Brown Trout	15 Mar. to 6 Oct.	Ben Loyal Hotel, Tongue. Tel: Tongue 216. Tongue Hotel, Tongue. Tel: Tongue 206.	
Loch St. Johns	Dunnet	Brown Trout	15 Mar. to 6 Oct.	Northern Sands Hotel, Dunnet, Caithness.	Two boats. Two sessions: 8.30 am to 6 pm, 6 pm to dusk. Fly fishing only.
Ulbster Estates Lochs (Ten hill lochs)	Halkirk	Brown Trout	15 Mar. to 6 Oct.	Ulbster Arms Hotel, Halkirk, Caithness. Tel: Halkirk 206.	No Sunday fishing. Fly fishing only. One boat on each of eight lochs.

Water	Location	Species	Season	Permit available from	Other Information
Loch Ussie	Dingwall	Pike		Seaforth Highland Estate, Brahan, Dingwall.	
Loch Watten	Caithness	Brown Trout	1 May to 30 Sept.	Loch Watten Hotel, Watten. Tel: Watten 232. D. Gunn, Watten Lodge, Watten. Tel: Watten 217.	Bank fishing. 32 boats. 7 am to half hour before dark. No Sunday fishing. Fly only.

NORTH SCOTLAND

Sea Angling

Gairloch

Gairloch Bay is very popular with sea anglers. There is good fishing in this lovely sea loch, especially around Longa Island which lies near the entrance to the Loch.
Tackle: Available from Wild Cat, Achtercairn. K. Gunn, Strath and Sand Holiday Centre. The Harbour Centre, Pier Road, Gairloch.
Boats: Mark Peter, Bains House, Strath, Gailoch, Wester Ross, Tel: (0445) 2472. Cruises from Gairloch Pier, sea fishing trips daily, rods and bait provided, fishing parties – day trips.

Poolewe and Aultbea

Situated amidst magnificent scenery, the sheltered waters of Loch Ewe offer the sea angler opportunities of fine catches. Suitable accommodation is available in surrounding villages and local advice is always available.
Types of fish: Shore – pollack, coalfish, dab, codling. Boat – haddock, cod, codling, gurnard, skate, whiting, mackerel, flatfish.
Boats: Several boats available locally.
Bait: Mussels, lugworm, cockles, etc. from shore. Artificial and preserved baits from D. Toop, Bridgend Stores, Aultbea.
Season for fishing: April- October incl.

Little Loch Broom

Ten miles north east Aultbea. Contact: Janoz Ertz (085 483) 262.

Ullapool & The Summer Isles

Loch Broom and the waters encircled by the Summer Isles offer excellent sea angling. The banks can be approached from Ullapool, which is an attractive holiday village sited on a peninsula projecting into Loch Broom. The numerous banks and islands offer superb fishing and beautiful scenery in sheltered waters. Many attractions on shore via local shops; hotels and sporting facilities available throughout the season. Morefield Motel, Ullapool. Tel: Ullapool (0854) 2161 offers day charters. Achiltibuie, a small village, also gives access to fishing grounds.
Types of fish: Shore – codling, coalfish, conger, pollack, mackerel, dabs, thornbacks, dogfish, flounders and plaice. Boat – as above plus haddock, whiting, wrasse, ling, megrim, gurnard, spurdog and turbot.
Tackle: Lochbroom Hardwear. Ullasport.
Boats: H. MacRae. Tel: Ullapool (0854) 2361. D. Maclean. Tel: Ullapool (0854) 2440. I. MacLeod, Achiltibuie. Tel: Achiltibuie (085 482) 200.
Season for fishing: June- October inclusive. Big skate best in autumn.

Lochinver

Lochinver is one of the major fishing ports in the north of Scotland. With a population of some 300 inhabitants it has a safe all - tides harbour with excellent shore services, including good moderately – priced accommodation and two fishing tackle shops. Excellent sea fishing within a short distance from the port, specialising in jumbo haddock, cod, skate and conger. It is one of the few areas where large halibut are caught. Boats available. A large fleet of fishing vessels operates from the harbour and bait is readily available.
Types of fish: Cod, haddock, whiting, saithe, gurnard, ling, pollack, mackerel, wrasse, conger, skate. Coalfish, pollack, cod and mackerel from the shore.
Boats: Norman Macaskill – *M.V. Stardust*, fast purpose built Aquastar 33. 10 rods. Weekdays and weekends. Jim Crooks – M.V. Opsrey. 4 rods, 4 hour trips. Rods for hire.
Tackle: Tackle is available from Newsagent, Lochinver and the Lochinver Fish Selling Co.
Season for fishing: April- October.
Further information from: N.A. MacAskill, 8 Cruamer, Lochinver, Sutherland. Tel: Lochinver (057 14) 291.

Drumbeg

Seven miles north of Lochinver. Contact: Lachie MacRae. Drumbeg (057 13) 243.

Caithness

With the prolific fishing grounds of the Pentland Firth, the north of Caithness has built up a reputation as being one of the premier sea angling areas in Scotland. It is now recognised that the chance of taking a halibut on rod and line is better in Pentland waters than anywhere else; more halibut have been taken here than in any other part of the British Isles. The presence of Porbeagle shark in these waters has been proved by the capture of two specimens, with many more hooked and lost. Among the notable fish caught were European halibut records of 194 lbs. in 1974, 215 lbs. in 1975, 224 lbs. in 1978 and 234 lbs. in 1979. This fish represented a world record catch for the species. The Scottish shore record ling of 12lbs 4oz was caught in these waters. With countless numbers of rocky coves and sandy beaches there is much for the shore angler to discover along the whole of the north coast of Scotland. Accommodation is available to suit everyone, from first class hotels, private B. & B. to caravan and camping sites with full facilities. It is also possible to have a full sea angling package holiday with full board at a hotel and all boat charges included.

The number of angling boats available increases each year, but it is still advisable to book boat places in advance.

Thurso and Scrabster
Thurso is the main town on the north side of Caithness and gives access through Scrabster to the waters of the Pentland Firth, where there are first class fishing grounds. Thurso Bay and the Dunnet Head area are sheltered from prevailing winds and it is reasonably easy for anglers to get afloat to the marks. Scrabster 1¼ miles from Thurso, is the main harbour in northern Caithness. Most of the angling boats are based here. There is also some excellent rock fishing, while conger may be caught from the harbour walls.
Types of fish: Cod, ling, haddock, conger, pollack, coalfish, dogfish, spurdog, plaice, wrasse, mackerel, dab, whiting, rays, halibut, porbeagle shark.
Boats: W. Kirk, 26 Traill Street, Castletown, Tel: Castletown (084 782) 662. G. Maynard, 23 Holborn Place, Scrabster, Tel: Thurso (0847) 64872. P.A. Mathieson, The Boatyard, Scarfskerry, by Thurso, Tel: Barrock (0847) 85332. J.W. Oag, Corbiegoe, Thrumster, Tel: Thrumster (0955) 85207. Mr. F. Johnson, 110 High Ormlie, Thurso. Tel: (0847) 63313/65406.
Tackle: Mrs. P. Brooks, The Drill Hall, Sinclair Street, Thurso. Pentland Sports Emporium, 14 Olrig Street, Thurso. A. & D. Mackay, Shore Street, Thurso. The Gun Shop, Dunnet.
Bait: Mussels, lugworm can be gathered at low water, mackerel and squid from fish shops and local fishermen. Most species take lures, feather and rubber eels, etc. and most fishing done with this type of artificial bait.
Season for fishing: April-November.
Further information from: Mr. Ian Myles, Secretary, Ormlie Lodge A.C., Thurso. (0847) 62000 and Caithness Tourist Board, Whitechapel Road, Wick KW1 4EA. Tel: Wick (0955) 2596 Jan-Dec.

Dunnet
Dunnet is situated 8 miles east of Thurso at the end of the famous Dunnet Sands, which are over 2½ miles long. Few anglers fish this beach, as there is excellent boat fishing nearby. There is plenty of lugworm and the beach is well worth trying. Information about boats can be obtained from the Northern Sands Hotel, Dunnet and the Seaforth Motel, Castletown, Caithness.
Types of fish: As for Thurso.
Boats and Tackle: As for Thurso.
Bait: Mussels from the rocks at low tide and lugworm all along Dunnet Sands.
Season for fishing: Shore – July and August. Boat – April-November.

Keiss
Good shore fishing is to be had around Keiss, a small fishing village between John o'Groats and Wick. It might be difficult to get out in a boat, but enquiries can be made at the Sinclair Bay Hotel (Tel: Keiss (0955 83) 233). The shore fishing is from the rocks around Keiss, and from the beach at Sinclair's Bay to the south of the village. Here some very good plaice have been taken and also anglers have caught sea trout while spinning for mackerel.
Tackle: Tackle shops at Wick.
Bait: Mussels and lugworm can be obtained at low tide.

Sutherland and Easter Ross Brora
Brora is a village situated on the A9, 12 miles south of Helmsdale. There is a small harbour and a few boats are available to sea anglers. There are rail links to Brora from the south and ample hotel accommodation and caravan facilities.
Types of fish: Cod, coalfish, cod, ling, haddock, rays and conger from boats.
Boats: B. Yates, 21 Johnson Place, Brora and some owners are willing to take visitors at nominal costs.
Tackle: Rob Wilson, Fountain Square, Brora.
Bait: Can be dug locally.
Season for fishing: July-September.

Grannies Heilan' Hame, Embo
This is a caravan holiday centre with extensive amenities 2 miles north of Dornoch. Manager is W. G. MacKay, Tel: Dornoch 810383.

Types of fish: Spinning for sea trout from the beach up to the mouth of Loch Fleet. Coalfish, mackerel and flatfish from the pier. The rocks provide good cod fishing. From boats, coalfish, mackerel, plaice, cod, haddock and whiting at times.
Boats: Contact the manager. Boat slip at harbour.
Bait: Lugworm can be dug at the ferry landing area and there are plenty of mussels and cockles near Loch Fleet.
Season for fishing: April-September.

Dornoch
Dornoch gives access to the fishing banks off the north coast of the Dornoch Firth. There is good shore fishing from the rocks at Embo, but to get afloat it is necessary to make arrangements in advance. Youngsters can enjoy good fishing from Embo Pier.
Types of fish: Sea trout from shore. Flat fish, haddock and cod from boats.
Boats: Boats are difficult to hire but there are one or two in Embo which is three miles from Dornoch.
Tackle: W.A. Macdonald, Castle Street, Dornoch.
Season for fishing: April-September.

Tain
Tain lies on the south side of the Dornoch Firth and gives access to excellent sea trout fishing, both shore and boat, in sheltered waters of the Firth.
Types of fish: Shore – wrasse, flatfish, pollack, mackerel. Boat – haddock, cod, skate, mackerel.
Boats: Available in Balintore, 6 miles from Tain.
Bait: Available from the shore.
Tackle: R. McLeod & Sons, 14 Lamington Street, Tain.
Further information from: G. McLeod, 14 Lamington Street, Tain.

Balintore
The village of Balintore, near Tain, has over the past 4 years increased in status and is now one of the recognised centres for big catches. Catches of up to 1,000lbs of cod and ling have been made (8 anglers) in a single morning's fishing.

Types of fish: Cod, ling, wrasse, pollack and mackerel.
Season from mid-April to beginning of November.
Boats: available from S.R. Coates, No. 4 Rannoch Place, Balintore, Nr. Tain, Ross-Shire, Tel: 086283 2863.
Further information from:
S.R.Coates, (Charter Angling Skipper) No. 4 Rannoch Place, Balintore, Nr. Tain, Ross-Shire. Tel 086283 2863.

Portmahomack
This fishing village is well situated in a small bay on the southern shore of the Dornoch Firth, 9 miles east of Tain and 17 miles from Invergordon to the south. There is a well-protected harbour and a good, safe sandy beach.
Types of fish: Cod from the shore. Haddock and cod from boats.
Tackle: Available at Tain.
Season for fishing: Spring to Autumn.

North Kessock, Avoch and Fortrose
These villages lie along the north-west side of the Moray Firth north of Inverness. This sheltered sea loch provides good fishing. Information regarding boats can be obtained from East Ross & Black Isle Tourist Office, Muir of Ord.

WESTERN ISLES
RIVERS AND LOCHS

Area Tourist Board
Outer Hebrides Tourist Board,
Area Tourist Officer,
Outer Hebrides Tourist Board,
4 South Beach Street,
Stornoway,
Isle of Lewis PA87 2XY.
Tel: Stornoway (0851) 3088.

RIVER PURIFICATION AUTHORITY
WESTERN ISLES ISLAND AREA
(No formal Board constituted)

RIVERS

Water	Location	Species	Season	Permit available from	Other information
LEWIS Creed	Stornoway	Sea Trout	June to 16 Oct.	Factor, Stornoway Trust Estate Office, Stornoway, Isle of Lewis. Tel: Stornoway 2002.	Four beats available. Day lets available.

LOCHS

Water	Location	Species	Season	Permit available from	Other information
An Ois	Stornoway	Salmon Sea Trout	June to 16 Oct.	Factor, Stornoway Trust Estate Office, Stornoway, Isle of Lewis. Tel: Stornoway 2002.	4 beats from the shore. Day lets available.
Breugach	Stornoway	Brown Trout	Mar. to 6 Oct.	The Sports Shop, 6 North Beach Street, Stornoway.	Two boats available.
Clachan	Stornoway	Sea Trout Salmon	June to 16 Oct.	Factor, Stornoway Trust Estate Office, Stornoway, Isle of Lewis. Tel: Stornoway 2002.	Two beats from shore. Day lets available. Two boats available.
Keose (and other lochs in Keose Glebe fishings	10 mls South of Stornoway	Brown Trout	15 Mar. to 30 Sept.	M. Morrison, 'Handa', 18 Keose Glebe, Lochs, Isle of Lewis. Tourist Information Centre, Stornoway, Isle of Lewis. Sports Shop, North Beach, Stornoway, Isle of Lewis.	Four boats, rods, tackle, life jackets, dinner, bed & breakfast at 'Handa', 18 Keose Glebe. No Sunday fishing.
HARRIS Drinisinader (and other lochs in Horsacleit Lodge Fishings)	Tarbert	Salmon Sea Trout Brown Trout	25 Feb.-31 Oct. 15 Mar. to 6 Oct.	The Manager, 7 Diraclete, Tarbert, Isle of Harris. Tel: Harris 2464.	
NORTH UIST Eashader (and other lochs)	Lochmaddy	Brown Trout	15 Mar. to 6 Oct.	The Factor, North Uist Estates, Estate Office, Lochmaddy, North Uist. Tel: Lochmaddy 329.	

Water	Location	Species	Season	Permit available from	Other Information
Fada, Loch an Duin and many other lochs	Newton Estate North Uist	Brown Trout		Senior Agricultural Officer, Dept. of Agriculture and Fisheries for Scotland, Balivanich, Benbecula. Tel: Benbecula 2346.	
Scadaway (and numerous lochs in southern part of island)	Lochmaddy	Brown Trout	15 Mar. to 6 Oct.	The Factor, North Uist Estates, Estate Office, Lochmaddy, North Uist. Tel: Lochmaddy 329.	
BENBECULA Langavat (Heorovay - Olavat) and numerous other lochs	Benbecula	Sea Trout Brown Trout	15 Mar. to 6 Oct.	Creagorry Hotel, Isle of Benbecula. Tel: Benbecula 2024. Creagorry Post Office, Benbecula. Tel: Benbecula 2080.	No Sunday fishing. No spinning.
Olavat (and other lochs)	Benbecula	Brown Trout	15 Mar. to 30 Sept.	Lands Officer, Dept. of Agriculture and Fisheries for Scotland, Balivanich, Isle of Benbecula. Tel: Benbecula 2346.	
SOUTH UIST All hill and Machair Lochs	South Uist	Salmon Sea Trout Brown Trout	Jul.-Oct. Apr.-Sept.	Resident Manager, Lochboisdale Hotel, Lochboisdale, South Uist. Tel: Lochboisdale (08784) 367.	Fourteen boats available on lochs. Fly fishing only.

WESTERN ISLES

Sea Angling

The Outer Hebrides
The Outer Hebrides form a north- south chain of islands off the west coast of Scotland. Separated from the mainland by the Minches, much of their rod and line fishing remains to be discovered, not only due to a lack of boats in the area, but also due to a lack of communications between and within the islands. Several of the islands, Barra, Lewis, Harris and Benbecula have regular air services and car ferries run from Oban and Ullapool on the mainland and Uig on Skye.

Isle of Harris (Tarbert)
The largest community on the southern part of the largest of the Hebridean islands, Tarbert stands on a very narrow neck of land where the Atlantic and the Minch are separated by only a few hundred yards of land. It is the terminal for the car ferry from Uig on Skye and Lochmaddy on North Uist.
Types of fish: Boat – mackerel, ling, coalfish, cod, rays, pollack and conger. Shore – plaice, haddock and flounder.

Boats: Check with Tourist Information Centre, Tarbert (0859) 2011.
Tackle: Available from J.S. Morrison, Tarbert.
Bait: Mussels available on the shore, lugworm, cockles.
Season for fishing: May- October.
Further information from: D.B. Deas, Hon. Sec. Harris Sea Angling Club, Invercarse, Kendebis, Isle of Harris.

Isle of Lewis (Stornoway)
Stornoway, the only town in the Outer Hebrides, is easily accessible by air from Glasgow Airport (1½ hours) and Inverness (25 mins.); there is also a drive-on car ferry service from Ullapool (3 hours crossing). Another car ferry service connects Uig (Skye) to Tarbert (Harris), which is only an hour's drive from Stornoway. Stornoway is now recognised as a mecca for sea angling in Scotland. There is an enthusiastic sea angling club with club boats and licensed premises which overlook the harbour. Each August the club runs the Western Isles (Open) Sea Angling Championships. Many skate over the 'ton' have been caught, the heaviest so far being 192 lbs. The Scottish blueshark record of 85½ lbs. was off Stornoway in August 1972. Visiting anglers may become temporary members of the Stornoway Club (one minute from the town hall) and can make arrangements for fishing trips with club members in the club boats. Accommodation can be arranged through the Outer Hebrides Tourist Board, Administration and Information Centre, 4 South Beach Street, Tel: Stornoway (0851) 3088.
Types of fish: Conger, cod, skate, rays, ling, pollack, whiting, dabs, bluemouth, flounder, dogfish, wrasse, haddock.
Tackle: Available from The Sports Shop, 6 North Beach Street, Stornoway, Isle of Lewis, Tel: 0851 5464 and C. Morrison & Sons, Point Street, Stornoway. C. Engebret & Co., Sandwick Road.
Bait: Mussels in harbour area; mackerel from local boats.
Further information from: The Secretary, Stornoway S.A.C., South Beach Quay, Stornoway, PA87 2BT. Tel: Stornoway (0851) 2021.

Isle of Barra
Sea angling boat hire and accommodation. Contact: George Macleod, Castlebay Hotel, Isle of Barra. Tel: Castlebay (08714) 223.

NORTHERN ISLES

Area Tourist Boards

Orkney Tourist Board,
Information Centre,
Broad Street, Kirkwall,
Orkney KW15 1DH.
Tel: Kirkwall (0856) 2856.

Shetland Tourist Organisation
Area Tourist Officer,
Shetland Tourist Organisation,
Information Centre,
Market Cross, Lerwick,
Sheltand ZE1 0LU.
Tel: Lerwick (0595) 3434.

PURIFICATION AUTHORITY
ORKNEY ISLANDS AREA
SHETLAND ISLANDS AREA
(No formal Boards constituted)

LOCHS

Water	Location	Species	Season	Permit available from	Other information
ORKNEY **Boardhouse**	Mainland	Brown Trout	15 Mar.-6 Oct.	None required	Boats available locally. All legal methods permitted. Anglers are recommended t join Orkney Trout Fishing Association, Kirkwall, who make facilities available to visitors.
Harray	Mainland	Brown Trout	15 Mar.-6 Oct.	Merkister Hotel, Tel: 77366.	
Hundland	Mainland	Brown Trout	15 Mar.-6 Oct.	None required	
Kirbister	Mainland	Brown Trout	15 Mar.-6 Oct.	None required	
Stenness	Mainland	Sea Trout	25 Feb.-31 Oct.	Bob & Linda Ross, Tel: Stromness 850 449.	
		Brown Trout	15 Mar.-6 Oct.	None required	
Swannay	Mainland	Brown Trout	15 Mar.-6 Oct.	None required	
SHETLAND **1000 lochs** **& voes**	Sheltand Islands	Sea Trout Brown Trout	25 Feb.-31 Oct. 15 Mar.-6 Oct.	Shetland Anglers Association, 3 Gladstone Terrace, Lerwick, Shetland.	

NORTHERN ISLES

Orkney

The waters around Orkney attract many sea anglers each year as big skate, halibut and ling are there for the taking. Ling of 36 lbs. skate of 214 lbs. taken by Jan Olsson of Sweden and the former British record halibut (161½ lbs.) taken by ex-Provost Knight of Stromness provide the bait which attracts anglers to these waters. The Old Man of Hoy, Scapa Flow and Marwick Head are well-known names to sea anglers. The Brough of Birsay, Costa Head and the Eday and Stronsay Firths are equally well known as marks for big halibut and skate. Fishing from Kirkwall or Stromness, there is easy access to Scapa Flow where wrecks of the German Fleet of the First World War provide homes for large ling and conger. In the fish rich sea surrounding Orkney the angler will find some excellent shore fishing, nearly all of which remains to be discovered. Furthermore, skate of over 100 lbs. are still common while specimens of 200 lbs. have been recorded. More halibut have been caught in the waters to the south separating Orkney from the mainland than elsewhere in the U.K. Shark have also been sighted and hooked but none so far have been landed. Around the islands, in bays and firths, there is excellent sport for the specimen fish hunter and the Orcadians are eager to help sea anglers share the sport they enjoy. There is a regular car ferry service from Scrabster (Thurso) to Orkney and daily air services from Edinburgh, Glasgow and other points of the U.K.

Types of fish: Sea trout, plaice, pollack and coalfish, mackerel, wrasse from the shore. Skate, halibut, ling, cod, pollack, haddock, coalfish, plaice and dogfish from the boats.

Boats: Booking for boats should be done via Barony Hotel, Tel: Birsay 327. Mr. Hay, Tel. Birsay 72270; Harray Loch - Merkister Hotel, Tel. 77366; Esslemont, Dalmahoy, Sandwick - "Spences Boat Hire", Bockan, Sandwick.

Tackle: Available from Stromnes and Kirkwall.
Bait: Available from most beaches and piers.
Season for fishing: June- October
Further information from:
Orkney Tourist Board
Information Centre, Broad

Street, Kirkwall. Tel: Kirkwall (0856) 2856.

Shetland
The Shetlands offer the best skate fishing to be had in Europe; during the years 1970-74 more than 250 skate over 100 lbs. were caught. These included a European record of 226½ lbs., and 12 other skate over 190 lbs. During the same period, Shetland held nine British records, ten Scottish records and six European records, giving some indication that the general fishing is of no mean standard. Halibut and porbeagle of over 300 lbs. have been taken commercially in the Sumburgh area with porbeagle shark now being landed by anglers from this area. The Scottish record porbeagle shark of 450 lbs. has been landed here and bigger fish have been taken by commercial boat. Shore- fishing remains for the most part to be discovered.

Types of fish: Shore – coalfish, pollack, dogfish, mackerel, dabs, conger and cod. Boat – skate, halibut, ling, cod, tusk, haddock, whiting, coalfish, pollack, dogfish, porbeagle shark, Norway haddock, gurnard, mackerel, cuckoo and ballan wrasse.

Boats: Many boats available for hire throughout the islands. Boats can also be arranged through the Shetland Tourist Organisation, Information Centre, Lerwick, Shetland.

Tackle: Available from J.A. Manson, 88 Commercial Street, Hay & Co., Commercial Road and Cee & Jays, Commercial Road, all Lerwick. 30 - 50 lb. tackle can normally be hired with the boat through the Shetland Tourist Organisation.

Bait: Fresh, frozen or salted fish bait available from fishmongers. Worm bait, crabs, etc. from beaches.

Season for fishing: Limited to May to October by weather conditions.

Further information from: Mr. M.S. Mullay, Shetland Association of Sea Anglers, Information Centre, Lerwick, Scotland, Tel: (0595) 3434.

SEA ANGLING INDEX

RIVERS INDEX

LOCHS INDEX